W9-BRY-518

Staying Well
—with the—
Gentle Art
of Verbal
Self-Defense

Suzette Haden Elgin, Ph.D.

MJF BOOKS

NEW YORK

Published by MJF Books
Fine Communications
Two Lincoln Square
60 West 66th Street
New York, NY 10023

Library of Congress Catalog Card Number 95-78753
ISBN 1-56731-081-0

This edition is reprinted by arrangement with Prentice-Hall,
Inc./Career & Personal Development.

Manufactured in the United States of America

MJF Books and the MJF colophon are trademarks of Fine Creative
Media, Inc.

10 9 8 7 6 5 4 3 2 1

PREFACE

The book you are about to read is the fifth in a series devoted to the *Gentle Art of Verbal Self-Defense*. If you know the *Gentle Art* system well, it will show you new ways to put your knowledge to practical use in your life. If you're new to the *Gentle Art*, you will find that no handicap; everything you need is included in the book.

Now, let me explain why I believe you should read *Staying Well with the Gentle Art of Verbal Self-Defense*.

IF YOU ARE IN A BUSINESS OR PROFESSION...

- The average cost of health care premiums to U.S. corporations in 1989 was more than $3,000 per employee, with *Fortune 500* companies spending nearly 25 percent of their after-tax profits on medical bills, health care premiums still going up 20 percent a year, and no end in sight.
- The cost of health care for employees in the U.S. in 1987 equaled 47 percent of corporate operating profits, up from only 9 percent in 1965.
- Stress-related health problems cost U.S. industry 150 billion dollars a year—more than the combined profits of all the *Fortune 500* companies. With three stress-related disorders—chronic pain, high blood pressure, and headache—accounting for more than half of all work absences. Chronic pain alone (especialy neck and back pain) accounted for a third of those absences.
- 81 percent of all business people and workers are estimated to feel work-related stress—nearly half report feeling it *every* working day!
- In 1982, work-related *accidents* cost more than 31 billion dollars in this country, and there has been no decline either in the rate of injuries or in associated expenses.
- 3 percent of American workers are absent every working day, with a cost in wages paid of 30 billion dollars a year; the total loss to our industry, including lost productivity, is estimated at 150 billion dollars a year.
- None of the above even begins to touch on the costs of decreased

productivity, poor performance, accidents, and the like from those who are sick or injured and *don't* take time off or seek care.

IF YOU ARE HOME-BASED...

- ☐ Total health care spending in the U.S. for 1989 was estimated at 600 billion dollars, approximately 12 percent of our gross national product—a higher percentage of GNP than for any other country in the world, up from about 9 percent in 1980 and still climbing.
- ☐ An estimated two-thirds of all deaths in the U.S. in 1988 were premature, and two-thirds of the years of life lost before age 65 were preventable losses.
- ☐ Health costs in the U.S. jumped 70 percent from 1980 to 1985, and the jump predicted from 1988 to 1989 is estimated at 20 percent to 40 percent.
- ☐ 60 percent to 90 percent of *all* visits to health care professionals are for stress-related problems.
- ☐ Injuries and associated trauma are fourth among the leading causes of death in the U.S., and they are the *leading* cause of death before age 45.
- ☐ All of the workplace statistics above affect you directly, because the cost of health care to business is passed on to the consumer. For example, *health care is the largest single item in setting the price of a General Motors car today.*
- ☐ The workplace statistics also affect you directly because you have to *deal* with all those stressed-out people. They are your doctor, dentist, lawyer, banker, mechanic, plumber, bus driver; your spouse, relative, adult child, friend, and neighbor. They are the clerks you face everywhere, and the salespeople, and the officials and bureaucrats at every level.
- ☐ Finally, chances are very good that you work at least part time, which means that you fall squarely into both groups.

Even a brief run through those facts makes it overpoweringly clear that we are all in a health care crisis—every last one of us.

How it happened and what can be done to make things better are matters for much passionate argument. The government and the patients think doctors and hospitals should charge less and business should spend more. Business thinks the doctors and hospitals should charge less and government and patients should assume more of the burden. The medical profession blames the costs on three factors: malpractice suits, new and expensive medical technology, and "third party payment"—that is, the fact that costs are paid not by the patients themselves but by insurance companies and government bureaucracies.

Businesses and institutions have been trying to reduce costs without reducing services by establishing "wellness" programs of all kinds— counseling, exercise classes, lifestyle classes, programs in relaxation and stress reduction. Governments have been trying to achieve the same goals with one drastic strategy after another—health maintenace organizations, caps on hospitals stays, limits on fees for Medicare and Medicaid, new (and unpopular) legislation. Insurance companies are slapping on higher deductibles, raising premiums, and adding ever more stringent restrictions. There's talk of a *national* health care and health insurance system, much of it from quarters that would have been screaming "socialized medicine!" at the suggestion of such a thing only a few years ago. Doctors queried in a recent nationwide survey see things differently: they insist that patients should be *charged* more. And recent increases in doctor's fees—several times as large as the rate of inflation—indicate thier intention to put that approach into practice.

Obviously, most of the population is caught in the middle of what looks like a long and bitter fight. While the various "providers" and officials are fighting...and we're waiting...it's clear that our best course is to (a) stay out of the medical system as much as possible and (b) be as well-informed as possible when, in spite of our best efforts, we *have* to get involved with it. That's what we want to achieve for ourselves, our families, our employees, and anyone else whose health care reflects directly on the state of our resources. That's what this book is all about—how to do that and do it well, with a minimum cost in time and money and energy.

Throwing money at the problem has been tried, and it has not helped. Let's try using something *free* for a change. Something that we already have and know how to use. Let's try using *language*.

My thanks are due to so long a list of scholars, researchers, students, colleagues, clients and readers that they cannot all be listed here. I am particularly grateful to Hal Davis, John Grinder, Thomas Gordon, Rebecca Haden, Edward T. Hall, Tia Johnson, Leonard Newmark, Michael P. O'Connor, and Virginia Satir. Special thanks are due to a host of physicians and other medical professionals who have asked to be anonymous; I am deeply in their debt. Any mistakes or omissions are my fault, and mine alone.

If you have questions about the contents of this book, or if I can help you in any way with the problems it addresses, please feel free to write directly to me at the address below.

Suzette Haden Elgin, Ph.D.
Ozark Center for Language Studies
PO Box 1137
Huntsville AR 72740

Contents

Preface

CHAPTER 1 □ INTRODUCTION: "WE NOW KNOW..." 1

So What? 3
The Three Rs 6
Technique #1—Applying Miller's Law 7
The Five Language Wellness Goals 9
Workout 10

CHAPTER 2 □ DEEP IN THE HEART OF YOU 15

Introduction—Why Hostility Is Dangerous to Your Health 15
The Four Types of Hostility 16
Technique #2—Avoiding the Hostility Modes 19

Blamer Mode (19) • Placater Mode (20) • Computer Mode (21) • Leveler Mode (21) • Distracter Mode (24)

Case Study 27
Technique #3—Using Three-Part Messages 29

For complaining (29) • For praising and evaluating (32) • To answer the questions "Why ME?" and "Why NOW?" (33) • For your Hostility Diary (35)

Workout 38

CHAPTER 3 □ WHAT'S IN IT FOR *YOU?* WHO *NEEDS* IT?   41

Introduction—The Problem of Blaming the Victim   41

Being—and Not Being—X-Prone   42

Technique #2, Continued—Using Satir Modes to Avoid X-Prone Behavior   44

Assuming the Sick Role   47

> *What your illness does for YOU (48)* • *What your illness does for OTHERS (50)*

Technique #4—Finding Your Real-Symptom Filter   53

Using Your Diary to Reduce the Stress of Change   56

Workout   57

CHAPTER 4 □ TAKING OUT THE TRASH   60

Introduction—Why Loneliness and Isolation Are Dangerous to Your Health   60

Feedback Loops and Self-Fulfilling Prophecies   61

Technique #5—Following the Language Traffic Rules   63

> *About turns (64)* • *About topics (66)*

Technique #6—Syntonic Listening   68

> *The language of music (70)*

Technique #7—Recognizing the Verbal Attack Patterns   72

> *The melody of verbal violence (72)* • *Performing the melody of verbal violence (74)* • *The All-Purpose Verbal Attack Response (75)*

Workout   77

CHAPTER 5 □ ACHES AND PAINS, MISERY AND DESPAIR   80

Introduction—Survivors and the Bodymind   80

The Interaction Between Pain and Language   83

Technique #8—Defining Pain with Semantic Features 86

Reality Statements (88)

Technique #9—Finding Your Personal Pain Metaphors 90

Putting It all Together 93

Workout 95

CHAPTER 6 □ KEEP THE HOME FIRES BURNING 99

Introduction—The Home as Toxic Waste Dump 99

Technique #10—Managing the Verbal Attack Patterns of English...Responding to Them and Getting Rid of Them 101

Verbal Attack Pattern #1 (101) • Verbal Attack Pattern #1A (101) • Verbal Attack Pattern #1B (105) • Verbal Attack Pattern #2 (107) • Verbal Attack Pattern #3 (108) • Vacuous VAPs (111) • Turning the Verbal Attack Patterns on yourself (112)

Verbal Violence Overview 113

Codependency—it takes two to tango (113) • Vicious cycles— training others to be verbal abusers and victims (114) • One small step—the connection between verbal violence and physical violence (115)

Workout 117

CHAPTER 7 □ THROUGH A GLASS DARKLY 121

Introduction—Is There Anything Out There? 121

The Sensory Modes 122

Technique #11—Percepting: "Visualization" and the Sensory Modes 124

The eyes have it: Sightism (126) • Constructing vivid perceptions (128) • Case study (133)

Technique #12—Setting Up Mindfiles 137

Demonstration: Setting up the "Small Pool of Water" mindfile (138)

Workout 141

CHAPTER 8 □ I'VE GOT YOU UNDER MY SKIN 145

Introduction—How Metaphors Can Be Dangerous to Your Health 145

Technique #13—Metaphor Math 148

Metaphor Algebra—Plain Vanilla (148) • Metaphor Algebra—Zigzag (149) • Metaphor Algebra—Stir-Fry (150) • Applied Metaphor Math (150)

Technique #14—Semantic Modulation 152

Demonstration (153)

Technique #15—working with the Language of Your Dreams: Dream-Mapping 157

Demonstration (160)

Workout 163

CHAPTER 9 □ AS YOU (AND OTHERS) SEE YOU 166

Introduction—The Inaccuracy of Perceptions 166

Self-perceptions...your internal image (168)

Technique #16—Simultaneous Modeling 171

To improve your voice quality (172) • To improve the rest of your body language (173)

Three Dread Words 174

The dread word FAT (174) • The dread word OLD (179) • The dread word DISABLED (183)

Technique #17—Using Twirks to Control Perceptions 184

Twirks and Perceptual Filters (187)

Workout 190

CHAPTER 10 □ YOUR HEAD BONE CONNECTED TO YOUR THIGH BONE 194

Introduction—Why "Partism" Is Dangerous to Your Health 194

Technique #18—Presupposing Holism 196

Factives (197) • Nominalizations (199) • Time-Word Presuppositions (200)

Technique #19—Translating Medical Regalian 203

Which part is being referred to? (204) • Where is it? • What's wrong with it? (208) • What are they proposing to do to it? (209)

CHAPTER 11 □ HOW TO COMMUNICATE WITH A MEDICAL PROFESSIONAL AND SURVIVE THE EXPERIENCE 212

Introduction—MDeityspeak and Malpractice of the Mouth 212

Technique #20—Using the Gentle Art Techniques in Response to the Medical Register 216

MDeityspeak lives, no question about it—but why? (222) • Language behavior modes, three-part messages, and Verbal Attack Patterns (225) • Why should you care? (226) • The peril of the subjective sign: What your doctor is reading (227)

Technique #21—Setting Up Trauma Mindfiles 228

Workout 231

CHAPTER 12 □ CONCLUSION: YOU'RE IN CHARGE HERE 235

Introduction—Why a Feeling of Helplessness Is Dangerous to Your Health 235

Sailing the Four Cs 238

Commitment (238) • Control (239) • Challenge (240) • Coherence (241)

Workout 242

APPENDIXES □ 244

Goals Directory 244
Problems Directory 245

RXtras: A set of Alternatives to Prescriptions   246
References and Bibliography   252
Index   268

1

INTRODUCTION

"WE NOW KNOW..."

- [ ] You're 45 years old. You smoke a pack of cigarettes a day, you're ten pounds overweight, and both of your grandfathers died after suffering strokes. This means you'll have a stroke, too, right? WRONG.

- [ ] In your business, you travel all the time, often in parts of the world where sanitation is anything but good. You have to eat the food and drink the water, whether they meet your sanitary standards or not. This means you're in for chronic stomach problems and—eventually—a case of serious food poisoning; you should also expect to get cholera from the water. Right? WRONG.

- [ ] You're a hard-driving, highly competitive workaholic, and you're not *about* to slow down. Half the time you forget to eat; and even when you remember, you usually just grab a hamburger or send out for pizza. You keep intending to fit some regular exercise into your schedule, but there's no place to put it. You don't smoke, and you're proud of that, but at the end of a day you need a couple of drinks to unwind. Your cholesterol is much too high. This means you're headed for a heart attack, right? WRONG.

- [ ] You have a large family to look after, and not a day goes by that you don't have to deal with somebody's crisis—your kids mean well, but their problems are endless and they don't seem to realize that you have problems of your *own*. Seeing all of them through college is going to be a financial horror story for you, but it has to be done—you want them to have the best possible chance in life. You just wish, once in a while, that you had somebody to take a little of the load off your shoulders. This means there's no way you can avoid an ulcer, right? WRONG.

- [ ] You have to work in a "sick building" where efforts to conserve energy have made the construction so airtight that every breath you take is full of at least formaldehyde and perhaps much worse. You have always been allergic to pollen and mold and various foods, and your mother has severe

1

asthma. This means that unless you change jobs you're in for serious respiratory problems and allergic reactions, right? WRONG.

☐ So many rotten things have happened to you in the past year or two that you can hardly believe it's possible. You've been through a divorce you never anticipated. You've lost two good friends to cancer. Your income has been cut back drastically. And now you've found out that the apartment building where you live is being converted to condominiums. This means a severe depression—maybe an oldfashioned "nervous breakdown"—is guaranteed for you. Right? WRONG.

☐ You've just had major surgery and you're in the hospital. Lying there in your bed, you know what's ahead of you: a week of severe pain and misery, if you're lucky, and months of weakness after you go home, while you try to get your strength back. Right? WRONG.

☐ Your doctor has diagnosed your recent health problems as cancer, cancer of the worst kind, and she tells you that you have perhaps five years to live. Sure, miracles happen, but expecting one is childish. You might as well give up, right? WRONG.

As recently as 1970, all of those "WRONGS" up there would have been assumed to be "RIGHTS." The public believed that was the way things were, and so did medical professionals. But today we know better. It's not a simple matter of Germ X plus Trauma Y equals Disease Z any more. Because—

☐ Most people who have the assorted "risk factors" for physical and emotional illnesses, like those described in the list above, *don't* get those illnesses.

☐ Many people who have few or none of the risk factors *do* get them.

And we are at last beginning to understand why. Finally we are beginning to have the answers to questions like this one: "Why did John, who smoked three packs of cigarettes a day for twenty-five years, die a peaceful death of old age at 83—while Tom, who *never* smoked, died at 50 of lung cancer?" Let's take a very brief look at the history behind this amazing change.

In the early 1900s, a Frenchman named Emile Coué traveled around the United States telling people they could make substantial improvements in their health and well-being by regularly reciting this sentence: "Every day, in every way, I am getting better and better!" The response he got was less than lukewarm, and he returned to his native land very discouraged.

Then came Dr. Norman Vincent Peale, proclaiming the power of positive thinking. Unlike Coué, he did well. His book on positive thinking, first published in 1952, was and still is a bestseller; and he has enjoyed a steady success over the years. But enthusiasm for his ideas has been confined primarily to devout Christians of the evangelical denominations—most of whom, in any health crisis, still turn without hesitation to their family doctor and the traditional medical system.

Throughout the 1960s, most of the scientific and academic communities, as well as the majority of the general population, still firmly believed in the traditional theory of medicine: If the wrong germ or toxin came your way, you would get sick; if the doctor gave you the right medicine, you would get well. The idea that the mind could have substantial effects upon the body was considered only charming claptrap at best.

Certainly people agreed that you could "make yourself sick" if you did nothing but dwell on your problems from morning till night; certainly they agreed that a cheerful attitude and a determination to get well are helpful when you're sick. Beyond that they would not go, and even the devout Christians looked upon Christian Science, with its near-total reliance on prayer for healing, as embarassingly *unscientific*.

But then things began to change. Scientific research began to provide results proving that the mind *does* directly affect the body, and not just in the vague ways indicated by common sense.

When such research is passed along to peers and public, those announcing it always begin by saying, "We now know...". Here are two dozen things that we now know:[1]

1. Athletes who rehearse a ski slope or a golf course or a tennis match in their minds, doing *mental* practice as well as physical, perform better than athletes who do only physical practice. And no amount of physical practice cancels this advantage.

2. In a person suffering from multiple personality disorder, one of the personalities can be allergic to substances while the others are not, one personality can be nearsighted while another has normal vision, and one personality's blood pressure can be dangerously high while another's is always normal—in spite of the fact that all the personalities share the same body.

3. In a study of women with advanced breast cancer who had survived substantially longer than the predicted five years, the strongest protective factor was not a medicine or diet or therapy, but JOY.

4. The single factor most likely to cause a heart attack in American adults is not high cholesterol, or smoking, or a history of heart disease in the family—it's chronic exposure to hostile interactions with other people.

---

1. The items on this list are discussed in more detail throughout the book, and references for the research studies are in the bibliography on pages 252-267. A key to the reference list, by item number and author name, appears on page 13.

5. After surgery, patients put in hospital rooms where they have a pleasant view go home sooner and have fewer complications than those who look out on a blank wall.

6. People with high blood pressure who can't tolerate standard medical treatment for the illness can keep their blood pressure down by learning to be good listeners. (And most people can reduce their blood pressure readings significantly just by taking them at home instead of in a doctor's office.)

7. Death rates are four to seven times higher in people who are *hostile, cynical,* and *suspicious* than in people who aren't.

8. Under hypnosis, people who are falsely told they will be touched with something dangerously hot develop blisters at the site of the "burn;" others, falsely told they will be stuck with a pin, bleed and then stop bleeding at the site of the nonexistent "puncture."

9. Patients given six weeks of training in relaxation techniques can reduce their physical symptoms by 22 percent; when they continue with the techniques for six months, they can cut their rate of symptoms by 50 percent.

10. Keeping a diary where important life events and feelings about those events are explored gives the body's immune system a dramatic boost—a boost that can still be verified by blood tests as long as six weeks after the diary-keeping has been discontinued.

11. People who learn a set of techniques for working *with* their dreams—sometimes called "dream-enhancement"—suffer less problem-related distress in their lives and are able to deal with their problems more successfully.

12. When men who do volunteer work at least once a week are compared with men who do none, those who don't volunteer show a death rate more than twice as high as those who do.

13. Intense attention given to the people-helping activities of *other people,* as in watching a film of such activities, can increase the level of immune response in the body.

14. Regardless of such other factors as race, income, and "lifestyle" matters, people who have few friends and who live isolated lives are twice as likely to die during a given period of time as those with strong social and family networks. Even relationships with pets provide substantial health benefits.

15. Patients who undergo surgery while carefully chosen music is played in the operating room, and who have access to such music after surgery, have less pain and fewer complications.

16. Migraine sufferers who learn to use biofeedback devices to monitor—and increase—the temperature in their hands have many fewer migraine headaches and suffer less pain from those they do have.

17. One of the most powerful painkillers available to human beings is not a drug—it's *laughter.*

18. Some people with asthma suffer full-blown attacks after looking at *artificial* flowers.

19. In a study of headache patients, the strongest predictor of a successful outcome after one year was the patients' perception that they had had an opportunity to talk the problem over fully with their doctor at their first visit.

20. Depression is a better predictor of heart attacks than existing artery damage, high cholesterol, or cigarette smoking.

21. People with high blood pressure who constantly talk about *themselves* are in more danger from heart disease than those who don't. And people *in general* whose conversation is made up largely of "I/me/my/mine" are twice as likely to have heart attacks.

22. In relaxation and meditation studies, *prayers* produced lower stress and blood pressure levels than non-prayer syllables.

23. Some of the natural painkillers produced by the human brain—the endorphins and enkephalins—are hundreds of times more powerful than morphine.

24. When people watch tropical fish in an aquarium with their full attention, they lower their blood pressure and their heart rate significantly.

The evidence for all these phenomena (and many more of the same kind) is now so compelling that it's no longer controversial, although there are arguments about details. So respectable has such knowledge become— so convinced are we that "we now know" all these things with certainty— that articles about them have begun appearing in even the stodgiest medical journals. Which brings us to the obvious question:

SO WHAT?

We Now Know that the human mind can directly and dramatically affect the body. We now know that under normal conditions our mental attitudes and the social situations associated with them have more influence on health than any other factors. That's interesting. No doubt it provides much entertainment for scientific researchers, medical professionals, professional athletes, and wealthy people with plenty of leisure. BUT WHAT GOOD DOES IT DO *EVERYBODY ELSE*?

People agree that they can change their diets or their exercise regimes voluntarily. They agree that they can convince their doctors to change their medications and other treatments—or failing that, they can change doctors. They agree that to some extent they can choose where they will live and where they will work, and that they can take deliberate action to keep their environment as free of dangerous elements as possible. But they ask me: "How am I supposed to change my mental attitude, for crying out loud? If I'm miserable, I'm miserable—how can I just decide *not* to be? How do I 'think positively'? I'm an ordinary busy person, not somebody lying around hooked up to fancy biofeedback gadgets—how am

I supposed to know what's going on inside me? And how—in this real world, surrounded by real people—am I supposed to be able to avoid hostile interactions? All this stuff 'we now know'—even when it tells me *what* to do, it doesn't tell me *how!*" And they are absolutely right.

Worse yet, once people are aware that such things as the emotions they feel and the attitudes they hold can actually make them sick or well, they face a cruel problem. Because it is bad enough to be sick or injured, bad enough to have to deal with the astronomical costs of health care in this country, without having to consider the possibility that IT'S THEIR OWN FAULT. People tell me, "I would rather *not* know all these things, since there's no way that I can put them to use—they just make me feel *worse!*" And, they say accurately, "It's not *fair*." What *makes* it unfair is the present distribution of information. Although the new knowledge about the health link between body and mind is readily available to almost everybody, the opportunity to put that knowledge to use is not. The only thing new about this situation is the specific "product" that the average person cannot have.

Physicians know which hospitals and clinics are the best ones and which medical professionals are the most skilled. When they or their loved ones need medical care, they don't settle for anything but the best. They can do this because their average *net* income is over one hundred thousand dollars a year and much of their medical care is free of charge as part of the system called "professional courtesy." Very wealthy people are able to shop around among medical professionals and facilities—traditional or nontraditional—until they are satisfied that the care they're getting is the care they want.

Average people, ordinary people—the vast majority of Americans— can't take these measures. It makes no real difference whether they feel confident about the care available to them or not. They take what they can get because they have neither the time nor the money to do anything else. This leaves them feeling angry about the potential care denied them, helpless to do anything about it, and angry yet one more time about their helplessness. The new bodymind medical "technology" looks to the average person like just another example of the same old familiar phenomenon: something new and terrific that they can't have. This book is designed to improve the situation, and to take some useful and substantial steps toward leveling the playing field.

THE THREE Rs

You can't do much to make life itself less dangerous, because the dangers are built in. Bacteria and viruses and fungi and parasites and allergens and chemicals and toxins and power tools and handguns and hurricanes and smog and ticks and obnoxious people are simply part of your internal and external universe. They make up the environment in which human beings live. But there *are* ways to take the new knowledge about health and put it to immediate practical use. Without fancy equipment. Without expensive experts. Without college degrees. And without disrupting the schedule of your daily life. You can in fact exert a significant degree of control in this situation through the Three Rs of personal health and well-being:

1. RECOGNITION: Knowing how to separate all the elements of life into those that are beneficial and those that are harmful, based not on myths and rumors but on facts.

2. RESISTANCE: Knowing how to create for yourself the kind of healthy and hardy immune system that can handle the vast majority of hazards with little or no difficulty.

3. REACTION: In those cases when something potentially harmful does get past your defenses, knowing how to cope with the problems so that the damage done is minimal.

The techniques you need already exist. They are already at your disposal. The single resource required in order to take advantage of them is one you already have and one with which you are superbly skilled— YOUR NATIVE LANGUAGE. I'm going to present to you a set of simple and practical techniques that you can begin using immediately. Techniques based on your already expert knowledge of your language—techniques that will put *you* in charge for a change.

Now I know the kinds of things you are expecting me to tell you about. Things so "far out" that you'd feel ridiculous doing them. Things that would make your family and friends suspect that you were going round the bend at last. Things requiring you to know a lot of fancy grammar and complicated academic or technical vocabulary. I want to clear this up right now. I want to prove to you that when I say "simple and practical" that is *exactly* what I mean. Let me give you one quick example, right now, so that you can go on to the rest of the book confident that I will not waste your time. Here it is.

TECHNIQUE #1—APPLYING MILLER'S LAW

Miller's Law is a statement made by psychologist George Miller. It goes like this:

IN ORDER TO UNDERSTAND WHAT ANOTHER PERSON IS SAYING, YOU MUST ASSUME THAT IT IS TRUE AND TRY TO IMAGINE WHAT IT COULD BE TRUE *OF*.

(Quoted in "Giving Away Psychology in the 1980s: George Miller Interviewed by Elizabeth Hall.": *Psychology Today* for January 1980, pp. 35-38 and 97-98, on page 46.)

This isn't what people usually do when they talk to one another. On the contrary, what they seem to do most is apply Miller's-Law-In-*Reverse*: They assume that what the other person is saying couldn't possibly be true, and then they try to imagine what's wrong with the person that might explain why anything so ridiculous is being said.

Let's suppose that Mary Jones has said something and Tom Smith has reacted with Miller's-Law-In-Reverse. One of two things will now happen.

1. Tom will say right up front, "Oh, that's *ridiculous*!" and go on to argue with Mary or ridicule her or ignore her words completely.

or

2. For the sake of politeness, or other personal reasons, Tom won't use any words that openly express his contempt for what Mary has said. But his tone of voice or other body language will leave her well aware of his feelings.

Either way, Mary will be resentful, and Tom will not be pleased.

If these two go on talking, the tension between them will grow and they'll both go away from the encounter in a state that guarantees trouble for the next person they talk to. If they don't talk further, they'll go away agitated all the same, and whoever they talk to next will reap the consequences. Like contaminated water that starts at one well and carries health problems from place to place all day long, this language pollution will spread from person to person in Tom and Mary's circle. Making ulcers worse, starting headaches, aggravating allergies, turning minor aches into major pains, causing distracted and irritated people to have careless accidents, and wreaking general havoc. At the end of the day Mary and Tom and everyone who has interacted with them will go home and announce that "people are really getting *weird*!"

Applying Miller's Law is like cleaning up the contaminated well. When Mary says something to you and you realize that you're about to say "Oh, that's *ridiculous*!" (either to Mary or to yourself), take *charge* of the situation. Use deliberate action, instead of kneejerk *reaction*. Say to yourself, "Let's assume that what she said is true. What could it be true *of*? What *else* would have to be true, to make her words true?"

The more difficult this is for you to do, the more carefully you will have to listen to what Mary says next, because you need that information to answer your own questions. And the more your mind is on the puzzle you've set yourself, the less it will be on your irritation with Mary. As a result, even if you go away from the encounter still thinking "Darned if *I* know what it could be true of!," the message you give Mary with your words and body language will not be "Oh, that's *ridiculous!*" It will be "I hear what you're saying and I'm interested in knowing what you mean."

This turns the most potentially maddening situations—a long ride on a Greyhound bus beside someone who claims to see your aura will do for an example—into the equivalent of a really good crossword puzzle.[2] And it puts *you* in control of your language behavior, with resulting significant benefits for both your own health and well-being and that of the people who interact with you.

Try it. Remember that Miller's Law says only that you will "assume" that what you're hearing is true. It does not say you will *accept* it as true. Try it for a week, and see what happens. Notice how the quality of people you're obliged to deal with improves. Notice how much better you *feel*. And notice how little it has cost you in time and money and energy.

We'll be coming back to Miller's Law and its varied applications to your language environment. And I give you my word: every technique presented in this book is equally practical, equally useful—and equally free of cumbersome investments of your limited resources. Each one is designed to help you achieve the five language wellness goals described below.

THE FIVE LANGUAGE WELLNESS GOALS

In order to make maximum use of the new information about the body/mind link for your health and safety and fitness, you need to aim toward five specific goals in your life:

GOAL ONE: Reduce hostility.

GOAL TWO: Reduce tension.

GOAL THREE: Replace negative thinking with positive thinking.

GOAL FOUR: Build strong social support networks.

GOAL FIVE: Build a perception of yourself as someone in *control*, rather than as a victim.

---

2. If you are someone who believes you do see auras, just reverse the example. Imagine a long bus ride sitting beside a person who believes auras are only figments of a disordered imagination.

These goals are interactive and synergistic. That is, movement toward any one of them guarantees movement toward all the others; improvement in any of the five areas guarantees improvement in all of them.

When you apply Miller's Law in response to someone's speech that you would ordinarily find annoying, you are using a deliberate language strategy for achieving the five goals.

1. Because you respond with interest instead of annoyance, you reduce hostility—you avoid the otherwise inevitable exchange of unpleasant messages.

2. Because that unpleasant confrontation would have caused you distress, you reduce tension for yourself when you avoid it.

3. The positive thought, "Okay, assuming that's true, what could it be true *of?*" replaces such negative ones as "Oh, no, don't tell me I'm going to have to listen to THIS kind of garbage again!"

4. People who are able to talk with you without finding themselves involved in hostilities will enjoy your company, and they will pass on their approving judgment about you to others—that's how strong social support networks are built.

5. Finally, the fact that you have (a) decided *not* to be part of a hostile interaction and (b) successfully avoided it with a positive language strategy demonstrates to you that you are *not* a helpless victim of circumstance, at the mercy of whatever comes along—*you are in charge.*

Welcome to *Staying Well with the Gentle Art of Verbal Self-Defense.*

WORKOUT SECTION

1. How high is your personal score for the *traditional* "risk factors"? Let's find out, to establish a baseline for your work with this book. The list below is a baker's dozen of the risk factors for the most common adult diseases in the United States. Circle those that apply to you and count them, for a total rough score.

1. Smoking or other tobacco use
2. Alcohol or other drug use
3. High cholesterol levels
4. High blood pressure
5. Not enough exercise
6. Overweight
7. Too much *stress*, at home or school or work

8. Allergies

9. Frequent exposure to dangerous substances (chemicals, toxic wastes, pesticides, etc.)

10. Frequent exposure to germs and viruses (as a teacher, day care worker, nurse, etc.)

11. Frequent exposure to dangerous situations (crowded freeways at rush hour, hazards associated with work or hobbies, etc.)

12. Family history of illness

13. Already existing personal illness

2. When people are asked if they know what "being sick" and "having symptoms" mean, they say yes readily enough. But when they are asked for definitions, they quickly realize that it's not as simple as they thought. Your dictionary will tell you that "sick" means "suffering from disease or illness," that "ill" means "not healthy," that "health" means "freedom from disease," that "disease" is "any departure from health" and that a "symptom" is "a condition accompanying or resulting from a disease." This tells you nothing at all—it's completely circular. Ernest Rossi defines sickness and symptoms as "problems in the natural flow of mind-body communication." How about you? What are your *personal* definitions for these words: *sickness* (or *illness*); *symptom; healthy; sick* or *ill*?

3. How do you *know* you are sick? Complete the following short exercise, in terms of your personal feelings about illness.

BEING SICK MEANS THAT...

	YES	NO	MAYBE
you hurt.	☐	☐	☐
you need a doctor.	☐	☐	☐
you have to go to bed.	☐	☐	☐
you can't work.	☐	☐	☐
you can't hide it.	☐	☐	☐
you can't play sports.	☐	☐	☐
you have to stay home.	☐	☐	☐
you don't want to eat.	☐	☐	☐
you're weak.	☐	☐	☐
you need some medicine.	☐	☐	☐
you're in danger.	☐	☐	☐
you're very tired.	☐	☐	☐
you're unhappy.	☐	☐	☐
you have symptoms.	☐	☐	☐

(You may find that you now want to make an adjustment in the definitions you proposed for #2.)

4. Substitute the word "injured" for "sick" and repeat the exercise in #3. How do you know when you are *really* hurt by accident and trauma?

5. For a quick overview of the new research discussed in this chapter, read the special report by Eric Olsen and others on pages 31–38 of the December issue of *Success*—titled "Beyond Positive Thinking."

6. To establish another baseline, fill in the exercise below as it applies to you, from 1 for "very low" to 10 for "very high."

DATE: _____

	1 2 3 4 5 6 7 8 9 10
Level of hostility in your life	☐☐☐☐☐☐☐☐☐☐
Level of tension in your life	☐☐☐☐☐☐☐☐☐☐
Level of negative thinking you maintain	☐☐☐☐☐☐☐☐☐☐
Strength of your social networks— your relationships with other people	☐☐☐☐☐☐☐☐☐☐
Strength of your feeling of control over what happens in your life	☐☐☐☐☐☐☐☐☐☐

7. The quotation below comes from psychologist Richard M. Suinn, talking of his experience with champion skiers (in Benedict Carey's "Sports: Playing Under Pressure," pages 110–112 of the November/December 1988 issue of *Hippocrates*.) Suinn says the champions ski a course one time to familiarize themselves with it, and then they...

"...imagine themselves doing it over and over, hitting every bump, every turn. When it's their turn to race, they feel like they've been there a hundred times..."

Think about it. What does this mean in terms of worrying about getting sick—imagining in detail the symptoms you will have, going to the doctor, feeling pain, perhaps going to the hospital?

SIGHT BITES

1. "The sages did not treat those who were already ill; they instructed those who were not yet ill. To administer medicine to diseases that have already developed is comparable to the behavior of those who begin to dig a well after they have become thirsty and of those who begin to cast weapons after they have already engaged in battle."

(An ancient Chinese emperor, quoted in "A Protocol for Periodic Health Examinations," by John E. Sutherland, M.D. and Richard M. Gebhart, M.D., *The Female Patient* for February 1986, pages 81–96; on page 81.)

2. "When...we say that a person is in touch with reality, the theologian immediately goes to work to evaluate the kind of reality with which he may be in touch."

(Wayne E. Oates, in *The Psychology of Religion*, Word Books, Waco, Texas; on page 86.)

3. "Years ago, a track coach gave me some advice about my event, the high jump. He told me, 'Throw your mind over the bar and your body will follow'."

(Louise Ritter, "Words To Grow On," in *Guideposts* for July 1989; on page 32.)

KEY TO REFERENCES

1. Williams 1988; Horn 1989; Carey 1988; Olsen 1988.
2. Goleman 1988.
3. Goleman 1987.
4. Green 1986; *Brain/Mind Bulletin* 3/88; Bagne 1988; Williams 1989; Dimsdale 1988; Blakeslee 1989; Guinard 1988; Fischman 1988; Barefoot et al. 1983; Diamond 1982; Williams et al. 1980.
5. Ulrich 1984; Baron 1986.
6. Pickering et al. 1988; *Emergency Medicine* June 1987; Elist 1987; Lynch 1985.
7. Bagne 1988; Williams 1988; Goleman 1987.
8. Rosenbaum 1978.
9. Squires 1987.
10. Elias 1987; Moss 1988.
11. Lamberg 1987.
12. Growald and Luks 1988.
13. Growald and Luks 1988; Lynch 1979; House et al. 1988.
14. Growald and Luks 1988.
15. Beuttler 1986; Wein 1987.
16. Langer 1989.
17. Cousins 1979.

18. Ader 1981.
19. *Modern Medicine* 1986.
20. Adessa 1988.
21. Fishman 1988; Harris 1989.
22. Harris 1989.
23. Ornstein and Sobel 1987.
24. Conniff 1989.

2

DEEP IN THE HEART OF YOU

INTRODUCTION—WHY HOSTILITY IS DANGEROUS TO YOUR HEALTH

Angry, cynical people are five times as likely to die under 50 as people who are calm and trusting....

(Redford B. Williams, quoted in "Cynicism and Mistrust Tied to Early Death," by Sandra Blakeslee; *New York Times* for January 17, 1989.)

In the 1950s researchers began reporting on a particular type of behavior—labeled "Type A"—which seemed to be strongly linked to heart disease. The set of traits that characterized Type A included fierce competitiveness, aggressiveness, strong ambition, a feeling of always being pressed for time, impatience and restlessness, abrupt speech and body language, hostility, a tendency to have multiple commitments, and an intense need to always be in charge. Type A people were described roughly as hard-working, hard-driving, and not about to take anything off anybody; they were contrasted to "Type B" people, who were relaxed, even-tempered, and in general more laid back. Over the next three decades studies of Type A behavior continued, but with confusing results: sometimes they bore out the hypothesis of increased risk for heart disease; sometimes they didn't. Fortunately, recent research appears to have solved this puzzle.

The real danger is not Type A behavior as it was originally described. It's not dangerous to be a hard worker and want to succeed. It's not dangerous to be determined to reach your goals in spite of all obstacles and willing to make a heavy investment in doing so. What's dangerous is the set of Type A characteristics associated with HOSTILITY. They are:

hostility itself; anger; cynicism; impatience; distrust; pessimism; self-centeredness; a drive to dominate others at all times; and frequent hostile interactions with other people.

Studies carried out with thousands of subjects show that this behavior pattern at least *doubles* the risk of heart disease. A study by Williams following 118 lawyers over twenty-five years found that those with high levels of hostility, cynicism, and anger were five times more likely to die before the age of 50 than those with low levels. In other studies he found death rates from four to seven times higher in people who were hostile. And other researchers have found abundant supporting evidence for his claims.

The reason for the original confusion is obvious—a very large percentage of people who are hard-working and ambitious and determined *also* have the dangerous hostility characteristics, and that muddied the waters. It's no wonder the evidence was hard to interpret for a while. In this book we will redefine the term "Type A behavior" to mean only behavior demonstrating the set of hostility characteristics.

It's important to understand that the idea of a "Type A personality"—a term used in many mass media accounts—is not accurate. The correct term is Type A *behavior*, and the difference is not trivial. The idea of changing an entire personality is intimidating; changing behavior is a far more manageable project.

THE FOUR TYPES OF HOSTILITY

Hostility—which we will be using as a cover word for the entire complex of hostility characteristics—is not just one big simple item. We need to break it down first into hostility coming *at* you and hostility coming *from* you, and then we need to break down each of those into two subtypes. As follows:

A. Hostility coming at you
1. Hostility coming at you—from other people
2. Hostility coming at you—from yourself
B. Hostility coming from you
3. *Active* hostility from you toward other people
4. *Passive* hostility from you toward other people

HOSTILITY COMING AT YOU—FROM OTHER PEOPLE

The first two basic principles of verbal self-defense are KNOW THAT YOU ARE UNDER ATTACK and KNOW WHAT KIND OF ATTACK YOU

ARE FACING. They are basic, but they are not necessarily as easy to apply as they might seem.

People tend to assume that verbal hostility will come at them in an obvious and open form. They expect utterances like these: "You NITWIT! WHY don't you LOOK where you're GOing?!!!" and "YOU'RE the STU-PIDEST PERSON I ever TALKED TO IN MY LIFE!" They expect curses and obscenities. They assume there will be epithets—racist and ageist and sexist and every other kind of "-ist." Such behavior exists, no question about it, but it's the most primitive kind of hostility and it's as rare as it's crude. Most verbal hostility is far less obvious. As a result, many people who are targets for hostility don't realize that that's what they're dealing with.

It's typical for verbal victims to be unaware that they *are* victims and convinced that they are the ones at fault. In this book we will carefully identify the other less obvious—but equally dangerous—forms that hostility coming at you can take. For the moment, we'll settle on a rough and ready definition, to be developed as we go along:

HOSTILE BEHAVIOR COMING AT YOU IS BEHAVIOR THAT HARMS YOU.

It's behavior that makes you feel hurt or angry, or that otherwise distresses you. Behavior that upsets you, in ways that interfere with your ability to function at your best.

Set aside for now all the questions about whether hostility can be accidental or "unconscious" behavior. Set aside the questions about whether you're making a mistake and perceiving hostility that isn't there. And set aside the question of the difference between physical hostility and verbal hostility. Hold on to that definition—HOSTILE BEHAVIOR IS BEHAVIOR THAT DOES HARM—and we'll come back to those questions as we go along.

HOSTILITY COMING AT YOU—FROM YOURSELF

We're accustomed to the idea that other people may be hostile toward us. But we are often unaware, or we simply forget, that a primary source of hostility is hostility we direct inward toward ourselves.

When we set up a negative endless-loop tape in our heads and play it over and over and over again, that's hostility. Here's a typical script: "It was so *stupid* of me to do that! I must have been out of my *mind*! I'll never get anywhere if I keep on making mistakes like that. I'm a born loser, that's all.

I do everything wrong. No *wonder* I'm a failure! No *wonder* nobody has any respect for me!! How could I have been SO STUPid????" For other people to talk to you that way they'd have to be able to find you and get your attention and keep you listening; there are limits on that. But you have unlimited access to yourself. You can keep that up all day and all night. You can even keep your abusive tapes running while you do other things, very efficiently and very dangerously. According to Dr. Edwin S. Shneidman of the UCLA Medical School, suicidal people share a single reason for wanting to kill themselves. They all, he says, "want to stop a steady stream of painful thoughts..." (quoted in *Family Practice News* for November 15–30, 1985, on page 34).

It's also hostility directed inward toward yourself when you interact with someone else and force yourself to hide your negative feelings toward that encounter. If you feel angry, but you force yourself to behave as though no anger existed, and if you have no other outlet for the emotion, you will inevitably turn that hostile energy on yourself. It has to go *somewhere*.

ACTIVE HOSTILITY FROM YOU TOWARD OTHER PEOPLE

This is easily identified. You feel anger or frustration or any of the dozens of related emotions (not all of which have convenient names in English) and you express it openly toward someone else. If this were the end of it...if it were just a matter of you expressing your negative feelings...it might not be so bad. For one thing, it would mean that you didn't turn that hostility inward with yourself as target.

Unfortunately, however, it's much more complicated. ALL LANGUAGE ENCOUNTERS ARE INTERACTIVE FEEDBACK LOOPS. When you express hostility toward people, they are likely to express hostility *back*. That will make you even more hostile and start you round the loop again, with each person's negativeness feeding the loop and provoking more of the same. You can't just get rid of it the way you'd get rid of a parcel by handing it to someone else. Hostility, passed on, comes right back at you and becomes still *more* hostility that has to have somewhere to go.

And let's not forget about that hostility turned inward on yourself, described in a previous section. Much of the time, after it has simmered along inside you long enough, you will pass it along to someone else—often someone who had nothing at all to do with it until you decided to use them as a hostility dump.

PASSIVE HOSTILITY FROM YOU TOWARD OTHER PEOPLE

When you express hostility actively, you say hostile things aloud and use hostile body language openly. But many people express their hostility passively. By sulking, for example. By behaving as if they don't understand when in fact they understand perfectly. By maintaining an elaborately well-mannered air of dignified contempt or dignified martyrdom. By pretending not to hear when they are spoken to. This can be *worse* than active hostility, because it's so much harder to object to. If you tell people you can't stand them, they can object to your words. If you behave with perfect correctness, while passively making certain that they know you can't stand them, it's very difficult for them to object effectively. Passive hostility, like active hostility, breeds yet more hostility. It may look more "polite," but it's no improvement.

All of this stuff—coming and going, active and passive—is DANGEROUS. It's not funny. It can put you in an early grave. The question is, then—what can you do about it? And that brings us to the next *Gentle Art* technique.

TECHNIQUE #2—AVOIDING THE HOSTILITY MODES

Virginia Satir was a world-famous family therapist. Over the course of her professional career she noticed that people who are tense and anxious tend to use one of five language behavior patterns that I call the "Satir Modes." Two of them—Blamer Mode and Placater Mode—are very common triggers for hostile interactions. I'm going to describe the Satir Modes for you here, so that you will recognize them when you hear them and when you use them yourself. And then I am going to begin showing you how you can use them systematically to head off all four types of hostility in your life.

BLAMER MODE

People who are Blaming come across as *openly* hostile and angry and threatening, in both their words and their body language. Everything about their language is rough and angular and choppy and unpleasant to be around. Some typical features of this mode are:

- constant use of "I, me, my, mine" and "you, your, yours" words and phrases
- very heavy use of strong emphasis on words and parts of words
- frequent use of words like "always, never, ever, nobody, nothing"
- frequent use of the verbal attack patterns of English (such as "EVen YOU should be able to understand THAT book!")
- threatening gestures and postures and facial expressions, such as jabbing fingers and shaking fists and *looming* over people

And here are some typical Blamer utterances, with the heavy emphatic stresses written all in capital letters...

- "WHY don't you EVER think about ANYbody but yourSELF?"
- "WHY do I ALways have to DO EVERYTHING FOR you? CAN'T you do ANYTHING RIGHT?"
- "IF you REALLY cared anything about your job, YOU'D get to work on TIME once in a while!"
- "WHAT'S THE MATTER with you, ANYway?"
- "It's ALL YOUR FAULT!!!"

PLACATER MODE

People who are Placating come across as pleading and whining and knocking themselves out to avoid any kind of argument or unpleasantness, no matter how trivial. Dr. Satir said that Placating people would remind you of a cocker spaniel puppy—desperate to please. Some typical features of this mode are:

- constant use of "I, me, my, mine" and "you, your, yours" words and phrases
- very frequent use of heavy emphatic stresses on words and parts of words
- frequent use of the verbal attack patterns—but with a whining intonation (the melody the words follow) rather than a bullying one
- frequent use of sequences such as "*I* don't care" and "*I* don't mind" and "I'm *sorry*..."
- body language filled with wiggling and writhing and leaning and fidgeting

Here are some typical Placater utterances...

- "Oh, YOU know me! WhatEVer YOU want to do is okay with ME!"
- "Of COURSE I don't mind if you leave me here with the kids— YOU know how I am! Just GO ON and HAVE A GOOD time..."
- "I KNOW you don't want to HEAR this, and I'm SO SORRY to have to TELL you, but..."
- "You KNOW I'd never try to tell you what to DO, but..."
- "It's all MY fault..."

(Notice that the first three characteristics of Blaming and Placating are the same, in spite of the very different communication styles involved.)

COMPUTER MODE

People who are Computing use a very neutral and seemingly emotionless style of language, with little body language to go along with their words. Some of the typical features of Computer Mode are:

- use of "I, me, my, mine" and "you, your, yours" words and phrases *only when they cannot be avoided*
- infrequent use of strong emphatic stresses on words and parts of words
- constant use of generalizations and abstractions instead of concrete or personal items, even in verbal attack patterns—for example, "A person who *really* wanted a loan would not be *rude*."
- an expressionless face and a nearly motionless body during speech, with a bland—sometimes monotonous—intonation

Here are some typical Computer utterances...

- "There is undoubtedly a good reason for this delay."
- "Trash has been left in the hallway."
- "It's possible that there has been some kind of accident."
- "People rarely understand the necessity for promptness."
- "Someone is responsible for this delay."

LEVELER MODE

The fourth Satir Mode is Leveler Mode. Leveling is most easily recognized by the *absence* of the typical features of Blaming, Placating, and

Computing. It is the "diagnosis of exclusion"—what's left over when you have eliminated the other possibilities. The person who is Leveling may use exactly the same *words* as would be used in any other Satir Mode—but the melody of the voice will be different, and so will the rest of the body language. Compare the following two examples:

"WHY do you eat SO MUCH JUNK food?"

Notice the intonation that goes with these words—the very strong stresses on "why" and "so much" and "junk." This is Blaming.

"Why do you eat so much junk food?"

This is Leveling. It doesn't have the strong stresses the Blaming speaker uses, although the word "junk" will have the normal emphasis required for at least one word in every English sentence. (This normal stress, usually near the end of the sentence, is never marked by punctuation.) It may be very rude, but it's not hostile—the Leveler is genuinely interested and wants an answer to the question. And since it *is* Leveling, you can Level right back with "That's a rude question, and it's none of your business." The Leveler will not react negatively to that answer. The Blamer, by contrast, would use it as a justification for further hostile language.

DISTRACTER MODE

Finally, there is Distracter Mode. The person who uses this mode cycles through the other modes, seemingly at random, with the body language cycling, too, instead of settling on one of the modes and maintaining it. The effect, like the name, is distracting.

In any situation of tension and stress, the potential for hostility (internal or external, active or passive) is always high. Because Blaming, Placating, and Distracting essentially *guarantee* hostility, we can call them the *hostility modes*. The other two—Computing and Leveling—can also lead to hostility, of course. But when they are used *with skill*, they offer the speaker an excellent chance to either avoid hostility altogether or reduce its level to a minimum. The hostility modes offer no such option.

When you hear Blaming utterances, you react with anger and feel that you have to defend yourself. When you hear Placating utterances, you are likely to react with annoyance and frustration and a feeling that you would far rather be somewhere else. Listening to Computer Mode can make you impatient, because so little information is being transmitted, and so slowly. Distracter speech is *always* maddening to listen to. And Leveler speech can bring you up against unpleasant truths that may be distressing or worse, depending on the situation. If you could just walk away from language when you don't like the sound of it, this might not matter—but most of the time, you can't. Most of the time you have to stay and deal with the language you are hearing. And this is where a deliberate and skillful use of the Satir Modes can be put into practice to reduce the level of hostility in your life. Here's the important metaprinciple on which you base your strategy:

ANYTHING YOU FEED WILL GROW.

Remember, language interactions are feedback loops. If you answer a Blamer by Blaming back, or answer a Placater by Placating back, you guarantee an escalation of the Blaming and the Placating. A Blaming loop always means a row, a scene, a confrontation of some kind; a Placating loop always means a frustrating and undignified delay. Both of these outcomes increase hostility not only at the time but later on, because you come out of them in a bad mood that you're likely to spread around for the rest of the day even if you make an honest effort to keep it to yourself.

The solution is to REFRAIN FROM FEEDING THE LOOP—to respond to Blaming or Placating with some other mode. Obviously you don't want to answer Blaming with Placating, or vice versa; that only substitutes one kind of hostile speech for another. And Distracting— which is the panicky language of someone who does not know *what* to say—is clearly never a desirable choice. That leaves Computing and Leveling to choose from. You base your choice on the circumstances in which you find yourself. Ask yourself: "Is this a situation in which I feel safe allowing the simple truth to be brought right out into the open?" If the answer is yes, choose Leveling; otherwise, choose Computing. And always use this rule:

IF YOU DON'T KNOW WHAT TO DO, GO TO
COMPUTER MODE.

Computing is the most neutral of the modes, the safest, the least likely to provoke unpleasantness, and the mode that can be relied on to gain you some time. It introduces delay, but it is *dignified* delay.

Compare these three brief dialogues. In the first one a Blaming utterance is answered with another Blaming utterance, in the second the Blaming is met with Computing, and finally there is an example of Blaming followed by a Leveler response.

BLAMING MET BY BLAMING...

PATIENT: "WHY IS it that EVERY TIME I COME here I have to wait FORTY-FIVE MINutes?! MY time is valuable TOO, you know!"

CLERK: "Mr. Jones, it's not MY fault that you have to wait! I only WORK here! And I RESENT being yelled at for something I can't HELP!"

PATIENT: "Oh, it's EASY for YOU to make excuses! YOU'RE not missing two hours of YOUR work!"

BLAMING MET BY COMPUTING...

PATIENT: "WHY IS it that EVERY TIME I COME here I have to wait FORTY-FIVE MINutes?! MY time is valuable TOO, you know!"

CLERK: "Busy people find it very hard to have to wait, especially when they already don't feel well."

PATIENT: "Yes, they do. I know *I* do. How much longer do you think it's going to be?"

BLAMING MET BY LEVELING...

PATIENT: "WHY IS it that EVERY TIME I COME here I have to wait FORTY-FIVE MINutes?! MY time is valuable TOO, you know!"

CLERK: "It's because the doctor tries to see twice as many patients as can reasonably be fit into only one day."

The example in Computer Mode does not feed the Blaming loop. It interrupts it and makes it difficult for the patient to continue with it. It's true that the clerk has not answered the patient's question—but this was not a real question, and an answer would only have made matters worse. Here is a valuable linguistic fact to remember:

> People who ask questions in Blamer Mode with multiple strong emphatic stresses on words or parts of words ARE NOT INTERESTED IN THE ANSWERS TO THOSE QUESTIONS.

If the patient above had really wanted to know the answer, he would have asked his question like this: "Why is it that every time I come here I have to wait forty-five *minutes*? My time is valuable *too*, you know." That's a very different melody accompanying those words, and is what someone would say who genuinely wanted an explanation for the delays.

And the third example, the one in Leveler Mode? It also interrupts the Blaming loop, and unlike the Computer response it does answer the question. But there are two problems with this strategy. One is that it's impossible to predict how the patient will react to hearing this sort of unvarnished truth. The other is that the doctor in question may disapprove of the clerk's statement in a way that has serious repercussions. Unless the clerk is confident of being able to deal with both problems, a Computer response is much safer.

When someone talks to you in a way that you recognize as Blaming or Placating (or Distracting), ask yourself: "Can I just respond to this by Leveling? Is that appropriate, and safe, in this situation?" If not, go through the following steps:

> STEP ONE: Run through the response that comes immediately to your mind, silently—don't say it aloud.
>
> STEP TWO: Translate that immediate response into Computer Mode, or substitute an equally appropriate Computer Mode sentence for it.
>
> STEP THREE: Answer with the Computer Mode response.

Here are two examples, to make this more clear.

BLAMING:	"WHERE did you put my socks THIS time?"
BLAMING RESPONSE:	"Look, I don't KNOW where your socks are! WHY can't you keep track of your OWN clothes?"
COMPUTING SUBSTITUTE:	"Not being able to find things when they're needed is a real nuisance."
PLACATING:	"I really WISH I could get to your CAR today, but there's just NO way I can DO it...you KNOW I'd do it today if I COULD!"
PLACATING RESPONSE:	"But I can't WAIT until tomorrow! COME on, you KNOW I wouldn't be pressuring you if I didn't HAVE to have the car—CAN'T you at least TRY?"
COMPUTING SUBSTITUTE:	"It's impossible to make sales calls without a car. Anything that could be done to speed up the work would be very much appreciated."

After you've used this technique for a while, you'll be able to go straight to Step Three. You'll find that Computer Mode sentences will come to your mind readily, without any need for the awkward and mechanical process of first deciding what you would have said and then substituting a Computer Mode response for that utterance. The length of the awkward stage when you have to go through the sequence of steps will be determined by your personal language behavior history. If you usually depend heavily on Blamer or Placater or Distracter Mode, you'll find it harder to give up your customary responses for Computer Mode substitutes. The stronger your hostility habit, the longer it will take before you feel comfortable with the technique—and the more important it is for you to master it.

Here are two practice techniques you can use to shorten the transition period.

PRACTICE TECHNIQUE #2–A

Make a list—in writing or on a tape recorder—of any set of infuriating things that you hear frequently in your daily life and know you are going to hear over and over again in the future. Then, either write or record a set of Computer Mode responses. This will give you practice in the technique in a situation of privacy and calm, when you have all the time you need to work out the best possible response and when you aren't actually in a stressful situation. If appropriate, repeat the practice exercise with Leveler Mode responses.

PRACTICE TECHNIQUE #2–B

This practice is done after the fact—*after* you've gone through an interaction that's left you upset. As soon as you can, write down or record what was said to you, and your responses. Then rewrite your responses in Computer Mode or write appropriate Computer Mode substitutions. If appropriate, repeat the exercise with Leveler Mode responses.

REVIEW

Now—let's review the ways in which avoiding the hostility modes helps you reduce the level and frequency of hostility in your life. Every time you use it to block a Blamer, Placater, or Distracter loop that someone else has tried to set up for you:

□ you reduce the hostility coming at you from external sources. It takes at least two people to maintain a hostile encounter, and the longer the row goes on, the harder it is to stop. By cutting it off at the very first speech made in the interaction, you make it difficult for the other person to go on being hostile.

☐ you reduce the hostility coming at you from internal sources—hostility directed by you at yourself. When you use language strategy with skill in this way you have nothing to reproach yourself with—no data for a tape in your head about how badly you handled the encounter. And putting an end to the hostility means that you have no hostile *reaction* to try to smother inside yourself.

☐ you reduce hostility on your part toward others, both active and passive. Not only hostility toward the person who would otherwise have been your opponent in a verbal struggle, but also the leftover effects that tend to leak into the rest of your interactions for a long time after the original row. If no row takes place—and if that positive outcome is due to your *skill*—you have nothing to be hostile about.

Notice that these are the same results you get from applying Miller's Law to language that strikes you as outrageous. In both cases, you defuse the potential fight before it can even begin, and you do so with no loss of face. An utterance that might cause you to use Miller's Law could appear in *any* of the Satir Modes.

CASE STUDY

Let's assume that you've invited a friend to visit you over the weekend and have been busy in another room while your guest puts away his coat and some personal belongings. Suppose he comes back and announces that he's just seen a ghost in the closet. Finally, we'll assume you're firmly convinced that ghosts do not exist. This sets the stage for a thoroughly unpleasant opening to your weekend that will spoil the rest of it as well—especially if, as so often the case, both you and your friend have a strong tendency to want to be *right*. Here's his announcement, in each of the Satir Modes.

> BLAMER: "*I* just saw a GHOST in your closet! And DON'T you try to tell me I'm IMAGINing things! I NEVER imagine things!"

> PLACATER: "I KNOW you'd rather I didn't TELL you this, and I KNOW you're going to say I'm iMAGining things...but I just saw a GHOST...in your CLOSet! No KIDDing, I really DID!"

COMPUTER: "Rational people don't believe in ghosts. Which makes it really wierd for one to turn up in your closet."

LEVELER: "Hey—there's a ghost in your closet!"

DISTRACTER: "I KNOW you're not going to beLIEVE me....That's natural, because rational people don't believe in ghosts, *do* they? But I KNOW what I SAW, and I swear to you—there's a ghost in your CLOSet, for crying out loud! I'm SOR-Ry, but I felt like you really ought to KNOW about it, okay?"

Resist the temptation to respond with any of the following:

1. "Oh, that's *riDICulous*! There's no such THING as a ghost!"
This carries as extra semantic baggage either "You're a liar" or "You're hallucinating" or "You're so stupid you can't tell the difference between a ghost and a raincoat."

2. "SURE you did! Why, when we bought this place we insisted on REFERENCES for the ghosts!"

This carries all the messages in #1, plus lots of provoking information about how witty you think you are.

3. "People who believe in ghosts are in big trouble, friend—time to call the guys in the white COATS with their BUTTERfly nets!"

Worse yet. This contains all of the anger-breeders in #1 and #2 plus an announcement of your own: "I have the power to decide whether you are sane or not, I have the right to tell you what I've decided, and how that might make you feel is of no interest to me at all."

You need a way to tell your friend you don't believe in ghosts and think he is mistaken, without provoking anger for either one of you. Instead of wasting your energy on useless hostilities that are dangerous to your health, use Technique #2 and construct substitute responses, backing it up with Technique #1 if you need more information. This does not require you to say anything you consider false, or contrary to your own beliefs or principles. It doesn't require you to give up any of your own dignity, or to challenge your friend's statement (or his sanity.) For example:

COMPUTING: "A person who could see ghosts would lead a very interesting life."

LEVELING: "I've never been able to believe in ghosts myself, but I bet seeing one would be an interesting experience."

AN IMPORTANT POINT TO KEEP IN MIND: When you substitute a Computer Mode response, always say something that you believe to be *true*. It doesn't have to be very significant, but it must not be a lie. Lies provoke just as much anger as hostile language does, and are sure to be spotted. Don't say, for example, that you've never believed in ghosts but you'd love to see one, unless that's *true*.

We will be coming back to the Satir Modes in later chapters. Right now we're going to move on to another technique for reducing hostility levels.

TECHNIQUE #3—USING THREE-PART MESSAGES

Psychologist Thomas Gordon is well known for his "Effectiveness Training" materials—Parent Effectiveness Training, Teacher Effectiveness Training, Leader Effectiveness Training, and more. A language pattern proposed by Gordon (which he called "the three-part assertiveness message") has proved extremely valuable in verbal self-defense, for a number of purposes. Since not all of those purposes involve "assertiveness," we won't be using that word here.

FOR COMPLAINING

We all have to make complaints, either on our own or because someone with authority has instructed us to make them. It's never pleasant. The metamessage of complaints is: "I am asking you to change something in your behavior that is unsatisfactory or unacceptable, or both, and I have the right to do that." A complaint is only a small semantic step away from a direct order—it's *requesting* change rather than commanding it—but the difference is very slight. Complaints provoke automatic knee-jerk negative reactions just because they *are* complaints; often the person complained to doesn't even hear the complaint's content. Since complaints can't be avoided, we need a way to make them that will bypass some of this automatic resistance. Gordon's pattern is ideal for the purpose. It looks like this:

When you (X)   I feel (Y)   because (Z).
    1   **2**   **3**

To use the pattern, you fill in (X) and (Z) with things that are concrete and directly verifiable in the real world. You fill in (Y) with an emotion, which is of course not concrete but is nevertheless directly verifiable from your body language and from the context. For example:

"When you don't water the tomato plants, I feel angry, because they die."

That the person spoken to has not watered the tomato plants, and that they have died for lack of water, can be directly verified; those are real-world events that can be observed by everyone involved. That you feel angry is verifiable because—if it's true—it will be demonstrated by your tone of voice, your facial expression, etc. And it's verifiable because it's appropriate in a context where people expect tomatoes as a result of the work of planting them and resent having their work wasted and their expectations foiled.

The pattern has to be followed exactly, or it won't work. It won't work if it's contaminated with things that are *not* verifiable, with moral judgments, with vague wanderings, with "you make me feel" instead of "I feel," or with any other extraneous material. It won't work if it has extra complaints that should each be in a separate three-part message. None of the examples below fits the pattern, and all would provoke automatic hostile reactions:

1. "When you don't water the tomatoes, you make me furious, because nobody with even a shred of decency would be so unreliable."

"You make me furious" is a separate charge, as well as an admission that the other person has the power to determine your emotions—this is a mistake. And the sentence that follows "because" cannot possibly be verified. It provides the other person with something that can be argued about—in the *Gentle Art* system, a proper three-part message never does that.

2. "When you don't do your fair share of the work with those tomatoes, I feel angry, because they die."

Here the problem is that there's no way to verify what a "fair share of the work" is—it can be argued about.

3. "When you don't water the tomatoes, I feel like you don't care anything at all about me, because if you did you wouldn't even *think* of letting them die after all the work that went into planting them."

I'm sure no comment is required for this one—and I'm sure the example sounds familiar to you even if you've never dealt with a tomato plant in your life. It's bad enough for someone to have to hear you make a complaint to them, with its annoying metamessage. If you add to that a wording that includes additional negative messages, you are *guaranteeing* hostility and resistance. A complaint should state exactly what has been done to provoke it, how that makes the complainer feel, and what real world result justifies the complaint—in terms that are immediately verifiable and allow little or no room for argument. The rule to use is this one.

IF A COMPLAINT CANNOT BE FIT INTO THE THREE-PART MESSAGE PATTERN, DON'T MAKE IT.

Whenever possible, write down your complaint in advance or record it on tape. This is good practice for the many times when you'll have to complain off the top of your head. It's also the best way to find out whether your complaint *will* fit the pattern. Furthermore, if the resulting message is one you'd rather not have said, far better to find that out before you say it.

Suppose you begin with "When you forget my birthday, I feel miserable"—both parts true and directly verifiable in the real world—but you can't think of anything to put after "because." That complaint isn't ready to be made yet, and should be delayed until you can finish it properly. Suppose you begin with "When you don't eat breakfast, I feel angry," and discover that what you are about to finish with is "because somebody always made *me* eat breakfast!" Presumably you would not care to hear yourself saying that. And the advance work will keep you from making complaints to which it would be literally impossible for anyone to apply Miller's Law—like those beginning with "when you do the things you do..." or "when you're the way you always are..."

One of the most common complaints I hear about materials on better communication is that they tell people what *not* to do but give them no information about what to do instead. Gordon's three-part messages don't have that flaw. They tell you *exactly* what you should substitute for the typical complaint, and that makes them very valuable indeed. They also create a need for this specific example:

> "When I want to complain to you about something and I can't do it properly, I feel frustrated, because it's hard for me to keep from thinking about it all the time."

The statement after "because" is not directly verifiable in the real world, but that's all right. Because in this case you're not complaining about the other person's behavior, you're complaining about your *own*. And you do have valid access to your own personal reality, in which "it's hard for me to keep from thinking about it all the time" is verifiable to you. This example accomplishes several very healthy things:

1. It allows you to say *something* about your discomfort, even if it's not adequate, instead of trying to smother your feelings completely.

2. It gives other people the information that if you seem to them to be distressed, their judgment is accurate, and that you'd like to talk about it if you could find a way to do so.

3. Sometimes it will prompt a response like "Can I help? Maybe if we talked about it we could straighten it out." And that's a beginning. You can then say either "Let's try" or "Let me think about it a little longer first—I'm not ready to talk about it yet."

FOR PRAISING AND EVALUATING

Logic would dictate that praising someone guarantees a *positive* reaction. After all, when you praise people you say something *good* about them. But logic, although necessary for doing formal math and theory, has little to do with language and even less to do with the way people behave. If logic were useful for persuading people to do things, everybody would buckle their seat belts and stop smoking.

Part of the problem with praise is that so often people assume there must be a *catch*. Another part of the problem is that behind a statement of praise is a metamessage similar to the one behind statements of complaint: "I have the right to judge you and tell you what my conclusions about you are, whether you like it or not." Praise is in fact only *positive criticism*. It's therefore useful to adapt the three-part message for any evaluation of another person, whether positive or negative. Compare these examples:

1–a. "You're such a terrific photographer—I'd give almost anything to be able to take great shots like you do!"

1–b. "When I look at the picture you took of your sister, I feel really impressed, because it looks just *like* her."

2–a. "I'm so proud of you for getting an A in algebra—that's wonderful! You're doing *great!*"

2–b. "When I see this A on your report card, I feel proud, because your algebra teacher says only the top three students in your class got A's this time."

Suspicious reactions to the *a* examples include "You want me to take some pictures for you, right?" and "You're going to expect me to get an A every time now, *aren't* you?" The *b* examples still allow suspicion, because anyone determined to be suspicious will find a reason to be—but they make it much harder to justify. As with complaints, the three-part messages say exactly what real-world behavior is being commented on, what your reaction to that behavior is, and what real-world information justifies the comment. And as with complaints, working out the messages in advance until they come naturally to you is strongly recommended whenever possible.

TO ANSWER THE QUESTIONS "WHY ME?" AND "WHY NOW?"

A primary characteristic of people who are cynical and hostile and suspicious (and useful as a way of identifying them) is a strong tendency to explain life events in negative ways. This doesn't mean that they are "paranoid" or irrational. These are not people who claim that their tv sets are giving them messages about traps being set for them round the world. It does mean that their *first* inclination when asked to explain things that happen to them—either positive or negative things—is to suspect and express the worst.

If someone leaves the room when they arrive, they will explain that the individual was trying to avoid them. If a payment does not arrive on time, it's because "they're trying to get out of paying the bill." If an item ordered by mail is the wrong size or color, it's because "mail order firms don't care anything about quality." If a client fails to keep an appointment, it's because "she's planning to sue." If one of their possessions isn't in its usual place, it's been stolen. If they get fired, it's because "personnel never liked me anyway, and they want to replace me with somebody younger." The attitude such people have toward others can be summarized as follows: "MOST PEOPLE ARE JUST NATURALLY BAD."

If you recognize yourself in this portrait, please stop and think about the consequences. It's time you realized that even if you're right—and I don't think you are—this attitude can put you in an early grave. Suppose you set up an appointment with John Smith for a business lunch and he not only doesn't show up, he doesn't call with an explanation and nobody answers when you try to call him. Here's the sort of tape that you create for yourself in such a situation and play over and over again in your head:

> "Smith obviously never intended to meet me in the first place. He was just blowing smoke when he set up the appointment, and he was too chicken to say no to my face. I'm not a bit surprised—I KNEW he was going to stand me up! I bet he's somewhere laughing at me RIGHT now for going to the restaurant and sitting there waiting for him for forty-five minutes...He could at LEAST have had the decency to save me all that wasted time! Well...that's the last time I try to work with HIM, or anybody LIKE him! And he's going to be damned SORry, because I'll see to it that everybody on my client list KNOWS how he treats people!" (And so on.)

You can do yourself a great deal of harm with this before you learn that Smith missed your appointment because his wife was in labor and he was driving her to the hospital, and that nobody answered his phone because his secretary was sick. Remember: your brain does not make any distinction between real insults and imagined ones. You get the same stress reactions either way. You get the same accelerated heartbeat, the same elevated blood pressure, the same unhealthy changes in the levels of essential chemicals throughout your body, either way. Every time you run that tape, your physical reaction is essentially the same one that would occur if you had evidence for your suspicions. You can't *afford* that, in health terms. It's hard enough for your body to handle the stress that goes with responding to real problems—don't run down your account by wasting your energy on imaginary ones.

When someone else says something to you that irritates or distresses you, you apply Miller's Law. I suggest that you do the same thing when *you* are the source of the hostility input. Take the incident with John Smith back there. Assume that it's true—he really did only pretend to make the appointment, intending all along to stand you up and laugh about it. What could that be true *of*? What else would have to be true, for that to be true? Ask yourself that question. Ask it *seriously*. And write down or tape record the resulting list. One of two things will happen:

1. You'll look at your list and realize that it's ridiculous. It could not possibly represent the facts.
2. You'll look at your list and realize that you have no desire to do business with anyone as rotten as John Smith and that he's done you a favor by standing you up and making that clear to you.

And then you redo your explanation of the event in the form of a three-part message. First, the negative one you started with. Next, a positive alternative.

ORIGINAL NEGATIVE VERSION:

"When Smith stands me up, I feel furious, because he does it deliberately in order to have an opportunity to sit and laugh at me about it."

POSITIVE ALTERNATIVES:'

"When Smith stands me up, I feel furious, because he wouldn't do that without a good reason and I want to know what the reason is."

---

1. Activites like this one are often called *reframing*.

"When Smith stands me up, I feel annoyed, because now I have to make another appointment to meet with him."

"When Smith stands me up, I feel frustrated, because I was looking forward to the meeting and didn't get to go through with it."

"When Smith stands me up, I feel concerned, because he is the kind of person who would not do that unless he was involved in a genuine emergency."

All right? You don't have to do anything in *Pollyanna* Mode. You don't go to "When Smith stands me up, I feel happy, because I get to spend forty-five minutes in a lovely restaurant." There are plenty of alternatives that are a legitimate—Leveling—expression of the inconvenience Smith has caused you, without being cynical or hostile or suspicious or pessimistic. If you need to do business with Smith and he misses your appointment, you *do* have to reschedule, and it *is* a nuisance. If you were looking forward to the meeting, it *is* a source of frustration for it to be delayed. But these messages are very different from one based on a conclusion that Smith has deliberately failed to keep the appointment for ulterior motives. The stress from "I'm annoyed" is very different from the stress caused by "Hey, somebody has deliberately MISTREATED me!"

Don't worry about whether the third part of the three-part message can be immediately verified in the outside world when it's used this way. You're not trying to get past someone else's automatic negative reaction in this case, just your own. That gives you a bit more slack. What matters is for you to break yourself of the habit of always explaining everything that happens in your life in negative terms automatically. You're using the three-part message technique as a strategy for becoming consciously aware of your behavior when you do that and deliberately substituting a positive explanation for the original negative one—for your health's sake.

FOR YOUR HOSTILITY DIARY

Redford Williams, one of the foremost researchers on hostility and Type A behavior, recommends that people with this trait keep a written record of situations in which they feel any of the set of hostile emotions. He suggests that you set up a sort of hostility log, stating exactly when and where you were when the situation occurred, who was involved, and precisely what happened—along with the thoughts you had at the time and your feelings about the incident.

There's substantial evidence that writing down your problems is good for you—so much evidence that I'll be coming back to the subject of diary and journal keeping throughout this book. (I'll be using the term "diary" to avoid the slightly formal feeling "journal" has for many people.)

One famous series of studies on diaries and health was done by psychologist James Pennebaker and his associates. In a Pennebaker study reported in the January/February 1987 issue of *American Health*, two groups of adults kept diaries, with one group recording "disturbing life events and how they felt about them" and the other group writing only about innocuous topics. The results: "People who bared all on paper showed strikingly improved immune function based on blood tests. Those who jotted down their trivial pursuits got no such boost." *Medical World News* for January 26, 1987 (page 39) reported of this study that "writing for 20 minutes a day for four days about deeply traumatic—but previously unshared—life events" caused a boost in immune system performance which "at follow-up six weeks later [was] as high as it was right after the writing exercise." Another study proved that writing down the feelings as well as the facts is critical, with the health benefits still demonstrable six months later. And of course the positive results of Ira Progoff's "Intensive Journal" workshops and materials have been well known for many years.

I agree with Redford Williams that a Hostility Diary is a good idea. Not only because it allows you to express your hostility without involving other people—making it less likely that you'll turn the negative emotions inward on yourself—but because it lets you see the patterns of hostility in your life more clearly. After keeping such a record for six months you will have a large database of information about the triggers for hostility in your life—where and when they are most likely to occur, how you typically deal with them, who else is frequently involved, how you feel about them weeks or months later, and so on. If you dislike the idea of spending twenty minutes on a detailed account, I suggest that you use the three-part message pattern, like this.

HOSTILITY DIARY ENTRY

DATE: _____

When _____ today,

I felt _____ , because _____

_____.

If you are a person who finds the whole idea of a diary intimidating, or frivolous, or if you feel that you can't take time to write one, this will get you started. You can always expand the process later if you decide it's appropriate. If you'd like to keep a detailed diary, but you're blocked by a conviction that you "can't write," see item number 4 on page 58 about writing with training wheels. A brief entry like the one above—which does include the information about your feelings—will give you the crucial data you need for tracking your own hostility patterns.

If you don't enjoy writing, you can keep a record like this on cassette tapes. If you like pictures with your records, add them—you can use drawings of your own, cartoons, photographs, pictures clipped from other sources, collages, or any other items that are appropriate for you. Keep in mind that *you* are the only critic for your diaries. Nobody is going to grade them on spelling, punctuation, grammar, elegance of style, artistic quality, or anything else.

Once you have your basic three-part message completed, I suggest two practice techniques for working with the message to make it even more valuable.

PRACTICE TECHNIQUE #3–A:

(1) Rewrite the message in the third person—as if it had happened to somebody else. Turn "When Mary insulted me this morning at breakfast, I felt..." into "When Mary insulted him (or her) this morning at breakfast, he/she felt...." This helps you step back a bit from the source of the hostility and works to counteract the constant "I/me/my/mine" language that has been proved to be so counterproductive and potentially dangerous.

PRACTICE TECHNIQUE #3–B:

(2) Rewrite the message from the point of view of the other person involved. Turn "When Mary insulted me this morning at breakfast, I felt...." into "When I insulted [YOUR NAME] this morning at breakfast, I felt..." If your first inclination is *always* to record something like "When I insulted [X] this morning at breakfast, I felt wonderful, because my favorite activity in the whole world is making other people feel terrible," you will recognize that as the typical—and unhealthful—reaction of someone with a low opinion of other people.

WORKOUT SECTION

1. In "Hostility Theory Rekindles Debate over Type A Behavior," (*Medical World News* for February 27, 1989, page 21), Linda C. Higgins reports that researcher R.H. Rosenman disagrees with the idea that hostility is the "toxic core" of Type A behavior. Rosenman insists that the critical element in Type A is *inappropriate competitiveness*. This is typical of the squabbling over the extent to which Type A behavior is relevant for heart disease, and why; the squabbles are of the kind usually called "only semantics." In my opinion, "inappropriate competitiveness"—a determination to be the winner, always, no matter what the circumstances, even when nobody else is interested in competing against you—is one of the major diagnostic components of hostility, making Dr. Rosenman's disagreement academic. How do you feel about this? Could *you* be "inappropriately competitive" without being hostile?

2. The following brief test is not intended for scientific purposes. But it will give you some idea how likely it is that you are someone who tends toward Type A behavior. For each question, fill in a number from 1 (strongly disagree) to 5 (strongly agree).

	1 2 3 4 5
a. I make sure I'm always on time, right to the minute, and I expect other people to do the same.	☐ ☐ ☐ ☐ ☐
b. Whatever I do, I do it as quickly as I can; I don't have any time to waste.	☐ ☐ ☐ ☐ ☐
c. Trusting other people is the surest way I know to fail in this world.	☐ ☐ ☐ ☐ ☐
d. There's no such thing as making too much money—money is how you keep *score*.	☐ ☐ ☐ ☐ ☐
e. Whenever I can, I do two things at once...like reading while I watch television.	☐ ☐ ☐ ☐ ☐
f. It's hard for me to pay close attention to what other people say, because I have a lot of things on my mind.	☐ ☐ ☐ ☐ ☐
g. I hate waiting in line more than almost anything else I can think of—I don't do it.	☐ ☐ ☐ ☐ ☐
h. I lose my temper easily—but I always have a good reason to do so.	☐ ☐ ☐ ☐ ☐
i. Half the people I know take so long to get to the point when they talk that I have to finish their sentences for them.	☐ ☐ ☐ ☐ ☐

j. I see no reason to waste my time talking about things that don't interest me and aren't important anyway—when people try that with me, I just change the subject. □ □ □ □ □

k. If I can't be the best at something, I'd rather not do it at all. □ □ □ □ □

l. This test is too long and it's probably not any good anyway. □ □ □ □ □

Add up the points... the higher your score, the more likely it is that you tend toward Type A behavior.

3. For a good brief discussion of the research on helping behavior, read "Beyond Selfishness," by Alfie Kohn, in *Psychology Today* for October 1988, pp. 34–38. Then take a look at "The Immunity of Samaritans: Beyond Self," by Eileen Rockefeller Growald and Allan Luks, in the March 1988 issue of *American Health*, pp. 51–53, for a report on the research demonstrating that helping other people is good for your health.

4. The sentences below are typical examples of remarks that—even if true— are almost guaranteed to provoke hostility. For each one, write a substitute sentence in Computer Mode that would serve the same linguistic purpose. (The first one has been done for you as a demonstration.)

a. "It's none of your *business* how much I smoke!"

IN COMPUTER MODE: "Very few people are interested in discussing their personal habits with others."

b. "The way you keep clicking that ballpoint pen in and out is driving me *nuts*."

c. "I can't *believe* you're going to wear those bluejeans to the Country Club brunch!"

d. "You obviously don't *care* if the whole neighborhood is laughing at you!"

e. "If you don't like the rules around here, you can go somewhere else."

f. "You have no right to take my blue shirt without asking me first!"

g. "Please... *please* don't make a scene like this in public! Everybody's *looking* at us!"

h. "Look, I'm entitled to take a break once in a while, you know! I'm not a *slave!*"

i. "I can tell just by *looking* at you—you're going to say it's *my* fault that it broke."

j. "There's nothing wrong with you that a little hard work wouldn't cure."

5. There are certain hostility-provoking situations that come up over and over in your life, almost routinely, that you can be sure you're going to have to deal with many more times. Make a list of at least ten of these and then work out two verbal self-defense measures against them: (a) some Computer Mode sentences you could use to keep them from heating up; and (b) a three-part message you could use to ask whoever is responsible to *stop*.

SIGHT BITES

1. "Type As see their lives as containers, good only to stuff full of as many possessions and events as possible."

   (Jeffrey Pepper Rodgers, in "Type A: Healing the Spirit," *Psychology Today* for April 1989; no pagination.)

2. "Dr. Friedman told APA members the interviewers should look for specific clinical signs that suggest the presence of type A, including fist clenching during ordinary conversation, jiggling knees, tense posture, a perspiring lip, eye blinking, and hurrying the conversation of others."

   (In "What Ails Type A Research?", *Medical World News* for October 14, 1985; page 57. Friedman is Dr. Meyer Friedman of the Harold Brunn Institute for Cardiovascular Research.)

3

WHAT'S IN IT FOR YOU? WHO NEEDS IT?

INTRODUCTION—THE PROBLEM OF BLAMING THE VICTIM

Being sick or injured is very unpleasant, even when the condition is a relatively minor one. In the United States, it's also extremely expensive and inconvenient. People in distress might well assume that putting up with unpleasantness and expense and inconvenience would be all that is expected of them. It can come as a considerable shock to find that instead of sympathy and tender loving care they are going to have to put up with being *blamed* for their condition. This was demonstrated not long ago in a fashion that dispels all doubt, when patients who died at a major hospital were described by the staff as having "failed to achieve their wellness potential..."!

One of the things doctors learn about in medical school that contributes to this victim-blaming is the concept known as The Sick Role. People who are healthy know what they have to do as part of The Healthy Role— they have to go to work and take care of the kids and look after the house and get the oil changed in the car and all the rest of the tasks that hold the social fabric together. Filling The Sick Role, on the other hand, is alleged to be like getting a hall pass from daily life. Sick people, doctors learn, expect to be *excused* from all those tasks and allowed to go to bed and rest while other people do the things that were previously their responsibility—this is called "assuming" The Sick Role.

It's possible that this idea once had some relevance for the average person of modest means. In the 1950s, when insurance companies paid hospital bills without question or hesitation and the bills of patients who had no insurance were subsidized by higher charges for those who did, it wasn't unusual to see people in hospital beds who could not meet today's definition of "really sick." People who needed a break but weren't in a financial position to just take a vacation could check into hospitals for the most trivial of complaints—or for routine checkups. There they could supply themselves with books and magazines, surround themselves with flowers and friends and Get Well cards, and have a reasonably pleasant stretch of R&R. The occasional annoying procedure such as being stuck with a needle was looked upon as a fair trade for the experience. In those days there were enough women working only in the home so that someone was usually around to look after children and pets and plants while this was going on. And hospitals were much safer places then, because the dangerous medical technology we're now familiar with didn't yet exist.

Today only two groups of people for whom sickness-as-vacation is possible exist: desperately poor people who, if they have children, are willing to turn them over to foster care; and people with great wealth. Neither of these groups is large in number or particularly anxious to spend time in today's hospital environment. And elderly people who would in the past have taken to their beds at home and died in peace with family members or neighbors looking after them—an entirely respectable version of The Sick Role—are now hauled off to hospitals and nursing homes against their will because family members and neighbors have to go out to work. Nevertheless, medical students still study the sick role, never mind that it has been essentially extinct since at least 1970, and are ready to accuse you of "assuming it" if they cannot find a reason for your complaints that meets their standards.

Later we will talk about how you can defend yourself when you really *are* sick or injured and medical professionals—using words like "hypochondria, hysteria, malingering, somatization"—insist that you're goldbricking. We will also discuss ways to deal with family and friends and people at work when you haven't been able to convince such a medical pro to label your distress legitimate. In this chapter, however, I want to discuss two related topics:

1. The distant relative of the sick role concept in which people are said to have personalities that somehow attract disease—they are said to be "cancer-prone," for example, or "arthritis-prone."

2. How to investigate for yourself, in privacy and for free, the possibility that you *are* assuming the sick role—that you are *being* sick for personal reasons of your own or of others.

BEING—AND NOT BEING—"X-PRONE"

In the second century A.D., the Greek physician Galen wrote that breast cancer was far more common in women who were "melancholic" than in women who were "sanguine." Galen would not have been surprised by the study showing that joy is a powerful defense against cancer.

More recently researcher Lydia Temoshok was asked to investigate what a number of cancer specialists saw as a possible "personality pattern" in patients with malignant melanoma, and she found that the pattern was real. Remember the hard-working, hard-driving, domineering, tense, highly competitive, aggressive person for whom hostility so often leads to heart disease, who is called "Type A"? The Type A studies also mentioned a relaxed, confident person whose behavior was called "Type B." Temoshok found the melanoma patients so different from either of those types that she decided to call them "Type C" people. They were, she found, people whose primary language goal was to avoid expressing their emotions—especially their negative emotions.

Lawrence LeShan, studying other cancer patients, found that they were consistently people who (a) remembered their childhoods as lonely and bleak, (b) had come out of childhood feeling unable to establish close relationships, (c) had found something as adults that mattered enough to them to inspire a tremendous emotional investment, and (d) had then plunged into depression after losing that something. Here's the description offered for the cancer-prone by Dr. O. Carl Simonton:

> First, a great tendency to hold resentment and marked inability to forgive; second, a tendency toward self-pity; third, a poor ability to develop and maintain long-term relationships; and fourth, a very poor self-image.
>
> (Quoted in "Images That Heal," by Maggie Scarf, in *Psychology Today* for September 1980, pp. 32-45; on page 37.)

Numerous studies have found that even after allowances are made for smoking and other lifestyle factors, people who can be identified on standard tests as *depressed* die of cancer far more often than people who cannot—just as researchers have found far higher death rates for heart disease and stroke in people who test high for cynicism, suspicion, anger, and pessimism. Similarly, researchers have established that arthritis patients—particularly women—tend to show two shared personality traits: an extreme tendency toward self-sacrifice; and trouble expressing anger and other negative emotions. Two things are particularly important when we consider all the available evidence of this kind.

FIRST: much of the most important research is not about who *gets* particular diseases, but about what happens *next*. It's about who, suffering from a given disease or trauma, goes on to die from it or be seriously disabled by it. These studies demonstrate that the way patients *cope* with their illnesses and injuries often determines whether they recover or not, how quickly they recover, how many complications they have during recovery, whether they have relapses, and so on.

SECOND: There is no significant relationship between how *serious* our society would consider a problem that leads to negative emotions and its impact on an individual's health. That is, whether someone becomes depressed after the loss of a beloved spouse or after the loss of a favorite wristwatch isn't the important factor. What matters is how intense the depression is—what many researchers call "the degree of hopelessness"— not how trivial or grave the apparent cause is in the perceptions of other people.

TECHNIQUE #2, CONTINUED-USING SATIR MODES TO AVOID X-PRONE BEHAVIOR

Unpleasant things *will* happen to you—you can't prevent that, or control the form those unpleasant things will take. But you *can* do something about the way you react to them—the way you cope. And you can use your skills with the Satir Modes (introduced in Chapter 2) to achieve this goal. Let's take another look at the information about the alphabetical types just discussed, in *terms* of the Satir Modes. Figure 3–1 will outline what I mean for you.

FIGURE 3–1

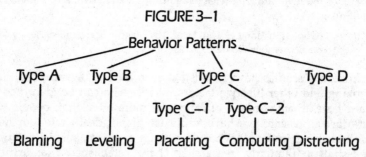

That is, the Type A list of hostility behaviors—exhibiting anger, impatience, distrust, dominance of others, and the like, with body language to match—sounds very much like Blaming behavior. The behavior of the Type B person—relaxed, confident, free of anger and impatience and hostility—sounds like Leveling.

Temoshok's Type C people appear to be of two kinds, which I have labeled *Type C–1* and *Type C–2*. Type C–1s, described by researcher Arthur Schmale as excessively eager to please, sound like people exhibiting

Placating behavior. Type C–2 people lack that characteristic, but share with Type C–1s a determination to avoid expressing their emotions. Type A and Type C people are at equal danger from hostility—but they differ in what they do with it. Type As express hostility openly in Blaming language; Type C–1s express it covertly in Placating language; and Type C–2s turn it inward on themselves, in Computing language. Finally, we have people who can be called Type D (my term, not that of the scientists cited)—people who use Distracting language and shift distractingly from one coping pattern to another.

Let's be very clear here, because the possibilities for misunderstanding are obvious and alarming. I am not suggesting that people who use Blaming language are certain to have heart disorders, while people who use Placating or Computing language are certain to have cancer—nor am I suggesting that if they do have those problems they are certain to die from them. I am not suggesting that in any of those cases those who do become sick are responsible for their illnesses. It's *much* too easy to fall into this error, and our language encourages us to do so. We say to people, "You're just asking for a heart attack, the way you lose your temper!" or "You're just begging for lung cancer, the way you smoke!" We need to listen to what we're saying and be aware of the messages we're transmitting. The message I want to transmit is this one: The match between the medical types and the Satir Modes types is striking—and your choice of which Satir Mode to use is one thing *over which you have very significant control.*

Under ordinary circumstances people are able to shift from one Satir Mode to another at will. But people under stress tend to become locked in to a *preferred* Satir Mode, and that preference can become a dangerous habit. Satir Mode preferences are not something inherently fixed, like eye color; they are learned behavior. They are tied to specific situations and roles, so that an individual who prefers Blaming as a way to deal with conflict at work may prefer Placating for conflict at home, or vice versa. Many people who rely on Blaming in most situations of stress switch to Placating when they are patients interacting with doctors, or when they are dealing with elderly parents. Nobody "is" a Blamer the way someone "is" a diabetic or "is" a Navajo. People *use* Blaming and the other Satir Mode language behavior patterns, and they can consciously decide to use them differently if they wish to do so.

We know with certainty that Type A people are endangered by hostile interactions, and that Blaming language inevitably causes other people to react with hostility. When Mary Jones, Type A heart patient, deliberately and systematically reduces her use of Blaming Mode, she automatically reduces the number and severity of the hostile interactions she is involved in—which in turn reduces her danger of a fatal heart *attack*. From this we can make some reasonable predictions.

We can predict that when Tom Smith, Type C–1 cancer patient, reduces his use of hostility-provoking Placater language, he will in turn improve his chances of recovering from his illness. We can predict that when Anne Wood, Type C–2 cancer patient, makes an effort not to suppress all her emotions with Computer language, she will improve *her* chances of recovery. And we can predict that when patients use Distracter Mode—producing language that frustrates and confuses their listeners as they switch from mode to mode—their behavior will make their recovery less likely.

NOTE: This is not the same thing as predicting that the behavior of any of those people caused them to "get" their diseases in the first place.

When people lie for hours unprotected in the sun, they WILL GET SUNBURN—there is a direct cause-and-effect relationship between the behavior and the condition. When people drive at high speeds on crowded highways they greatly increase their chances of getting hurt in automobile accidents—but the accident is not *guaranteed* by their behavior. For a Type A person to constantly use Blamer language keeps everyone around him or her in a state of tension that makes hostile interactions inevitable. This is like the speeder's behavior. It makes the illness more likely, but it's not like sunburn—illness is by no means guaranteed.

Furthermore, it's a simple matter for an adult to avoid lying in the sun with unprotected skin, and it's perfectly reasonable to tell people who fail to do so that their sunburn is their own fault. Where a hostile language environment is concerned, things are not so simple. The behavior of *other* people is involved, along with many other factors over which a single individual has little control. Type A Mary Jones may make a tremendous effort to reduce her own Blamer language, but if she has to work day in and day out with five other Blamers who make no such effort, and goes home at night to yet another chronic Blamer, it would be absurd to say that she was responsible for her heart attack.

Most of the time, however, the odds against you are not overwhelming in that fashion. (If they are, it's time to consider drastic action, like a job change.) Most of the time you *can* systematically use your knowledge of the Satir Modes to maintain your health and to *regain* it during illness. Use this simple two-part strategy:

1. Stay out of Blamer loops and Placater loops. Don't start them yourself and don't participate when others try to start them. Avoid Blaming and Placating as much as possible.

2. Use Leveler Mode whenever you can—whenever you feel safe doing so. Reserve Computer Mode for situations when you are convinced that

Leveling would be dangerous or entirely inappropriate and for situations when you genuinely don't know what to do. Don't let Computer Mode become your *habitual* language pattern—when you find it to be the best choice, keep it brief.

The major point to remember here is this one: because your own language behavior is something over which you have significant control, it's foolish not to take advantage of the way changes in that behavior can (a) reduce your risk of succumbing to certain health dangers, and (b) increase your chances of recovery when you do fall ill or suffer injury. If you find yourself strongly opposed to making the changes—in spite of the negative consequences—then it's time to take a serious look at two questions: "What's in it for you?" and "Who needs it?"

ASSUMING THE SICK ROLE

Neil Postman (in *Crazy Talk, Stupid Talk*) points out that what happens to you in a medical professional's office is usually very different from what happens when you hire any other professional. You may have an appointment to see the doctor or dentist, but that doesn't mean you won't sit and wait an hour or more past the time when you were required to appear. When you finally are seen, you can't count on an apology for the delay, nor can you be sure that you won't be left to wait some more during your visit while the doctor takes phone calls or attends to other matters. Postman offers us an explanation for this situation. The general perception, he tells us, is that if you hadn't made some kind of stupid mistake you wouldn't *need* a medical professional.

This is a common idea, among medical professionals as well as among patients and the general population. It's not something that people are willing to say openly, of course. But a little determined exploration will get their reluctant admission: they really do feel that when adults have to turn to doctors, it's because they have gone astray in some fashion. Adults get sick because they haven't taken proper care of themselves...or because they've been careless...or because they've sinned...or because they were in the wrong place at the wrong time. And when adults get sick, it's a pain in the neck for everybody involved, with the possible exception of the medical professionals. People take it for granted, by and large, that the only aspect of sickness or injury that could be called positive is the business it provides for doctors and other medpros.

However, this is one of those "obviously the earth is flat" sort of truths. Sickness and injury quite often fill needs and serve positive purposes that go unrecognized or unacknowledged. It's extremely important to find *out* if that's what's going on with you, because your decisions about health care should be based on accurate information. The most common scenarios are these two:

1. Your condition fills a need of your own and gets you something that's more important to you than being well is.
2. Your condition fills someone else's need—usually that of one or more members of your immediate family.

We'll discuss these situations below, one at a time. And I want to stress once again that we're not going to blame any victims. To say that someone's health problem is part of a strategy of his or her own, or a family strategy, does *not* mean that the individual has taken deliberate steps to acquire the problem. We'll be discussing illnesses, but as always, the material applies equally to injuries and trauma.

WHAT YOUR ILLNESS DOES FOR YOU

Every one of us, I suspect, can remember a time when we had something coming up at school for which we weren't prepared—a test, a speech, a role in a play, a big game—and we pretended to be sick in order to stay home from school that day. If we were young enough when this happened, our recovery usually was so swift that we were exposed for the frauds we were; as we got older we became skilled enough to "stay sick" for a logical period of time. And most of us, even as adults, use faked illnesses once in a while as a way of getting out of something we'd rather not do, like staying at a boring party until it's over. The classical "Not tonight, darling, I have a headache" maneuver is another familiar example. With *these* episodes, however, we are fully aware of what we're doing, and we would never think of seeking medical help for such shenanigans. (And parents quickly learn that they can test for fakery by offering to call the doctor or dentist; this often produces almost miraculous and instantaneous improvement.)

If you are assuming the sick role for a specific purpose, if you know what that purpose is and consider it valid, and if you are being careful not to involve yourself in medical treatments for it, that's one thing. If you genuinely believe that you are sick and you're spending time and money and energy seeking a cure—but in reality the sickness is triggered by personal reasons you're unaware of—that's quite another. In *both* cases, the question you should be asking yourself is: "Is there some other way I could accomplish the same goal more conveniently and pleasantly?" But in the second case you are actually endangering yourself, and that's more than just a matter of unpleasantness and inconvenience.

Medicine has a whole array of names used to describe illnesses that are "self-caused." The most common are *malingering, hypochondria, hysteria, conversion disorder,* and *somatization.* The only term in the set that is considered deliberate is *malingering.* This covers the situation in which you know quite well what you're doing and you do it on purpose for a specific personal gain; in adults this is ordinarily considered immoral. For all the others—in which the reasons for your behavior are below the level of your conscious awareness—we will use *somatization* as the cover term here and leave the fine distinctions to the doctors. The question you want an answer to is this one: "Why am I somatizing? What's in it for *me*?" What is the hidden goal that the illness is helping you achieve?

The more important that goal is to you and the greater the need you feel to accomplish it, the harder it will be for you to answer that question. For many people the answer cannot be found without the help of a skilled therapist. I don't suggest that the *Gentle Art* techniques will solve the problem for such people—they should seek help from the appropriate experts. I *do* suggest, however, that you try the strategies described below. Because if your personal reason for somatizing is not deeply buried, there's a very good chance that they will enable you to get at it. I'll be using "headache" in the examples; you would substitute the name of your own problem.

1. Use the three-part message technique, in two steps.

STEP ONE

Write or tape "When I have this headache, I feel _____ because _____" and fill in the blanks. These messages will be negative in content—like "I feel miserable, because I can't go to the office" and "I feel terrified, because it hurts so much." Repeat until you cannot think of even one more.

STEP TWO

Write or tape "When I have this headache, I feel relieved, because _____" and try to fill in the blank. Repeat as many times as possible. If "relieved" doesn't seem to work, try "resigned" or "comfortable," or "safe." BE VERY SURE YOU DO THIS ONLY AS STEP TWO—AFTER YOU'VE GOTTEN ALL THE NEGATIVE MESSAGES OUT OF YOUR SYSTEM.

2. Apply Miller's Law. Assume that the sentence "I am assuming the sick role because it gets me something I want or need more than I need health" is true for you. Now answer the question, "If that is true, what could it be true of?" List as many answers as possible—you're trying to find one that

you suddenly recognize as valid. One that makes you say something like, "Good grief—so *that's* why I have this headache!"

If the result of your investigation is a realization that in fact your illness *does* fill some need that you were previously unaware of, you are in a much better position. Now that you know what you're doing, ask yourself these questions.

1. Is there some way I could fill the same need without having to be *sick*?
2. Would that alternative solution be less difficult and less unpleasant than the illness?
3. Which solution is the best one for me?

If you can find an acceptable alternative solution, your course is obvious: switch to that solution without further delay. But suppose you decide that—Leveling with yourself—the simplest solution for you is the illness. That can happen. Even then, you're still better off. Because now you will be much less afraid of the illness, and you will be reluctant to spend much of your time or energy or money in a doctor's office trying to get it "cured." You'll be less likely to take medications or submit to therapies that have unpleasant side effects. You will know that what you are doing is *your* choice, not a freak of fate or a punishment from Providence. You're a lot safer that way.

WHAT YOUR ILLNESS DOES FOR OTHERS

People who study grammar using a linguistics-based model spend a good deal of time learning about the *roles* that parts of sentences fill. They learn that the quickest way to identify such roles is by finding out what question each part of a sentence is the answer to. Every sentence answers in whole or in part a set of questions like the following: Who's doing the action? Who's in the particular state or condition? Who or what is the action being done to? Who or what is the action being done *for*? With what and to what extent? In what direction? When and where and why and in what way?

Even a fragmentary sentence like "John ate" means at *minimum* "John ate something, in some way, with something, at some time, in some location, for some reason." For a sentence like "John ate spaghetti quickly with his bare hands last night in the Smith's kitchen in Fresno, because he was starving," linguists say that all of those parts have been *lexicalized*. That is, the speaker has given a *surface shape* to all those chunks of meaning. Sometimes this is a matter of choice. You can just say "John ate" and leave out all the rest of that information if you like. Sometimes it's dictated by the grammar—for instance, you can't say just "Ate" or "Ate something." You have to lexicalize the Doer, even if you only say "Somebody ate something." In English you have to do this even when there *is* no Doer, as in "It rained."

In ordinary language, speakers lexicalize two kinds of meaning chunks: those the grammar gives them no choice about, like the "it" that rains and snows; and those for which they feel that it's impotant and appropriate that the information be available on the surface. We have strategies for carefully hiding information when we don't want to express it. We can't say "Spilled oil in the bay" because no Doer appears on the surface—but we can get out of that bind by saying "Oil was spilled in the bay," a sentence pattern that allows us to leave out the Doer subject. On the other hand, we can't leave out the *object*. We can hide away the oil company that did the spilling, by starting with "Oil was spilled," but no simple pattern is available for leaving out the spilled substance without wrecking the sentence. We can't say "The oil company spilled in the bay" or "Was spilled in the bay by the oil company." These rules and patterns are things we know very well; but we know them below the level of our conscious awareness, where it isn't always easy to get at them voluntarily.

We can understand what goes on in the lives of people by analogy with what goes on in grammar. (We'll use the family as our example, but our discussion holds for other groups such as companies, teams, classes in school, church congregations, etc.) In all families there are *roles* to be filled; there is a "grammar" of relationships. Some roles are required; some are optional. Some can be left out or removed or shifted around. Some can't be removed or added or changed without doing violence to the family.

The difference between grammatical roles and family roles is that most speakers of a language agree about the grammatical roles, but different families have radically different understandings about family roles. For some families the obligatory roles include The Weak Person and The Strong Person. Others require The Giver and The Taker, or The Bad Person and The Good Person. Pulling "oil" out of "Oil was spilled" wrecks the structure of that sentence. In just the same way, pulling The Weak Person or The Giver or The Good Person out of a family whose "grammar" requires that there be somebody filling that role can destroy that *family's* structure. It forces the family to change, often when all the other family members have become accustomed to the status quo and are comfortable with it. It's as if you suddenly tried to put on a play from which you had removed one major character—the rest of the cast would be in serious trouble.

I have explained this at such length and in such detail because it's such a difficult concept to handle. If you are a person who is "always sick" and the real reason is that your family needs someone to be The Sick Person, neither you nor your family members are going to want to accept that. It's a horrible thought. Family members will say, "How can you *say* such a wicked thing! It breaks our *hearts* to see him (or her) in pain! There's nothing we wouldn't give to make him well! How *dare* you suggest that we need him sick!" And they will mean that with all their hearts—they are not lying. Nevertheless, they are mistaken. And in such situations everyone unconsciously works together to keep the sick member from getting well, or to make certain that the injured person is so "accident-prone" that a new injury always replaces any healed one.

Please notice that I said they work together *unconsciously*. This is not wickedness or malingering or heartlessness or anything else that requires moral judgment. It's the way that families and other close-knit groups naturally *work*. Let's consider one example that is relatively common. It involves a husband for whom the wife's poor health fills an urgent need; it's just as likely to be the other way around. Neither gender has a monopoly on this behavior.

Tom Winter is a man without much self-confidence but with a very strong sense that he *must* live up to what is expected of him as the male head of a family. He's afraid of responsibility—afraid that if he tries anything new he will fail. On the other hand, his drive to meet his obligations means that he works hard and carefully and would, on a level playing field, get ahead in his career. The fact that his wife Elizabeth has serious multiple allergies that can occur at the most unexpected moments is his safety net. When the boss offers him a promotion, and refusing it would make Tom look bad, he can say how much he appreciates the offer and how much he would like to accept it—but unfortunately his wife can't be left alone at home for the extensive periods of travel the new position would require. People in the firm know about the wife's illness—and they not only do not hold it against Tom when he doesn't accept promotions or transfers or other opportunities, they admire him for his willingness to sacrifice his chances for her sake.

It's crucial to understand that Elizabeth does *not* have allergy attacks on purpose to protect Tom from unwelcome challenges, and that Tom does *not* feel grateful that she's sick because it keeps him from having to face those challenges. Absolutely not. Elizabeth's illness is real. Tom's concern for her is real. And it's possible that if Elizabeth were to get well the marriage could not survive that change. Thus, her illness serves two *positive* purposes that neither she nor Tom is aware of: the protection of Tom's self-image and the preservation of their marriage. In such situations, the end of any one illness or injury threatens the family so drastically that another always turns up to replace it.

I want to be very careful here, because we are talking about things that are extremely serious. I'm a linguist, not a therapist. The *Gentle Art* system is not a therapy. I am suggesting only that you take a careful look at what purposes your illness or injury might be serving in the structure of your family—what role you might be filling in that structure by being sick. If what you see when you take that careful look appears to be a serious threat, I suggest that you get expert help before pursuing the matter any further. (And I suggest that before you get that help you read Chapter 11 in this book, on the subject of surviving encounters with such experts.)

That warning aside, many situations in which your family needs someone playing the sick role are not matters of crisis. If your regular Saturday headache is serving only to give your spouse a reason to stay home from an exercise class, some other solution should be looked for. If your chronic hay fever is serving only to give the whole family an excuse not to move away from Arizona, some other solution should be found. And even if you decide that you'd rather put up with the illness than put up with the consequences of its removal, you will be way ahead in the wellness game. Because once again this new knowledge means that:

1. You won't exhaust your reserves of time and money and energy looking for a *cure* for your illness. This makes it far less dangerous to you.

2. You will know that the illness isn't something that just *happens* to you, out of nowhere. On the contrary, it's something over which you are in control. This makes it far less dangerous to you, too.

Apply Miller's Law here. Assume that this sentence is true: "My family needs me to be The Sick Person—to fill the sick role on behalf of the family." What could it be true *of*?

And use the three-part message strategy. Complete the following sentence in as many different ways as you can.

"When I am sick, my family is relieved, because _____!"

TECHNIQUE #4—FINDING YOUR REAL-SYMPTOM FILTER

A good way to find out what any sentence means is to find the question or questions to which *it* is the answer. In my case the question answered by "I always feel better when I'm gardening" is "What action on your part will distinguish a serious symptom from a trivial one?" I love gardening and tend to lose all track of time while I'm at it. I discovered long ago that when I find myself thinking I don't feel well, gardening will usually make the feeling disappear. And that has served me superbly as a test, providing me with the following reliable rule for my personal health: ANY SYMPTOM THAT DOESN'T GO AWAY WHILE I'M GARDENING SHOULD BE CHECKED OUT. Not one in fifty passes that test, saving me a great deal of trouble. For some people the best filter is laughter; like Norman Cousins, they can make themselves feel better by watching funny movies or television. Others are best served by painting or needlework or carpentry or fishing or computer programming. Some fortunate people's symptoms disappear if they simply go do what they normally do for a living.

To find your own Real-Symptom Filter, keep factual records of your symptoms for a while, to find the patterns. You want to know what the symptom is, the date and hour when it starts, what you're doing at the time, and how long it lasts. You want to know when it stops or becomes less troublesome, and what's going on when *that* occurs. Suppose you're watching the evening news at 6:20 P.M. and you feel a painful twinge in your knee. Grab your note pad or tape recorder and record the facts. "6:20 P.M., April 4th, watching tv news, twinge in knee." Then track the symptom from one activity to another, like this: "9:00 P.M., same evening, working on my tax returns, knee keeps hurting." "April 5th, waking up, knee still hurts; hurts all the time I'm getting dressed and eating breakfast." Put the data into a spread sheet in your computer if that appeals to you. You're not after vivid descriptions or details—you just want a month or six weeks of notes in which you will be able to spot *repetitions* of statements like "April 7th, around noon, weeding the onions—knee stops hurting." Your goal is to be able to fill in the blank in this sentence—

> "ANY SYMPTOM THAT DOESN"T GO AWAY WHILE I'M _____ING SHOULD BE CHECKED OUT."

—as I was able to fill it with "GARDENING." If you can fill it with more than *one* activity, giving you more flexibility, good for you.

Then put that test to use in every case possible. Do everything you can to make that easier. For example, there's no way I can go do much in my garden in the middle of an Arkansas January, or in the middle of the night, or during a thunderstorm. I solved that by installing a couple of fluorescent lights over an empty shelf in my house so that I can garden indoors. Indoor fishing would be harder; indoor flying is out of the question. But give it some *thought*. What can you do that will give you ready access to your Real-Symptom Filter? To the activity that sorts out real symptoms for you and sets them off from trivial ones and from normal (though perhaps annoying) physical sensations?

It's often cheaper to make the modifications you need—buying a computer program that simulates flying, for example—than it is to go to the doctor and spend money on the standard battery of diagnostic tests, trial medications and therapies, hospital stays for intensive observation, and all the rest of the unpleasant apparatus of contemporary "defensive" medicine. (It's certainly pleasanter—always.) Doctors who ten years ago would have told you to go on home and watch the symptom a while and see what happens are so afraid of malpractice suits today that they feel obligated to leave no diagnostic stone unturned.

There are obvious potential sources of confusion. If you almost never exercise and you feel a sudden pain in your elbow the morning after your first session of calisthenics in fifteen years, and that pain stops after a day or two, that gives you very little information. On the other hand, try not to leap to conclusions, especially if you are the sort of super-rational person who always has a ready explanation for everything. Resist the temptation always to produce an explanation like "Oh, I only hurt because I'm out of shape" or "Oh, my headache went away because I wasn't staring at the computer screen any longer." Just record the bare facts and reserve judgment, until you have enough data to make patterns appear. And if you think you already know what your Real-Symptom Filter is, start testing it to confirm or disprove your hypothesis, watching for clarifying items. For instance, if your symptoms always disappear when you play bridge—except that they get worse whenever you play bridge on your neighbor's patio—find out what the patio has that your other bridge locations don't have. A nice stand of ragweed at the edge of the patio could confuse matters considerably.

After you've found your Real-Symptom Filter, *stop* keeping records of your symptoms. It's not useful as a longterm activity. It's far too likely to turn you into someone with the bad habit of concentrating on every smallest physical sensation, which is the yellow brick road to being a fulltime hypochondriac. Keep the records to accomplish the task of finding your Filter, and then throw them away. Should the day come when your Filter no longer seems to work, perhaps because something you once loved to do has finally begun to bore you, you can always start again and find a new one.

Finally, let's suppose that you are genuinely prevented from turning to the activity that is your Filter. For example, if the thunderstorm that's keeping me indoors also knocks out my electric power, the fact that I have plants growing under lights won't help me a bit. In such a situation you might want to try a *mental* runthrough of the activity, using the well-known technique called "visualization" or "imaging." You'll find extensive information on that technique in Chapter 7 of this book and in the bibliography.

USING YOUR DIARY TO REDUCE THE STRESS OF CHANGE

When you're used to behaving in certain ways, giving them up is *hard*, and can create stress of its own. The longer you have relied on the behavior, the harder it will be for you to change and the greater the stress you will face as a result. One useful method for reducing that stress and tension is by keeping a diary, either in writing or on tape. This doesn't have to mean that you sit down once each day and record all of your experiences from the previous twenty-four hours. On the contrary. That may be the *worst* possible way for you to proceed, because what you badly need during difficult change is something that will free your mind for a while from all your negative "I cannot possibly DO this!!" thoughts. In her excellent book, *The New Diary*, Tristine Rainer recommends the use of *lists*, for example, and I endorse the recommendation. Here's a set of lists you might work on when a diary break would be helpful to you, and that you can use as a springboard for other lists of your own choosing.

1. The ten most important events in my life so far
2. The ten things that make me happiest
3. The ten most joyful things that have happened in my life
4. The ten things that I want most in the next year (or five years, or ten years)
5. The ten best things about me (or someone else)
6. The ten best things that could possibly happen in my life
7. The ten things that are hardest for me to do
8. The ten places that matter most to me
9. The ten things I would most like to learn how to do
10. Supposing I could only write one sentence to describe each of the ten people who matter most to me...here are those ten sentences

Another way to put a diary to good use in reducing stress is to use it for taking out some mental trash. For example, you could finish one or more of these sentences...

1. The reason I am so angry right now is _____.
2. The reason I am so hurt right now is _____.
3. The reason I can't _____ right now is _____.
4. The one thing I am most afraid of right now is _____.
5. The one thing I don't understand right now is _____.
6. The one thing I'm having trouble forgiving right now is _____.

7. The reason I keep putting off _____ is _____.

8. What I really wish I hadn't done is _____.

9. What I really wish I could do right now is _____.

10. The one thing that's upsetting me most right now is _____.

11. If _____ happens, the possible negative consequences would be: .

12. If _____ happens, the possible positive consequences would be: .

If you set up talk-loops in your head with sentences like these and go over and over and over them, you are creating your own language pollution. If you dump them on other people, you add to *their* language pollution—and their responses may make things even worse. But if you put them down on paper or tape, you are getting *rid* of them, on your own. That's a positive step. Rainer says that writing something down lets you "get hold of" it. That's true. There it is on your page, where you can go back to it, or tear it up and throw it away, or illustrate it with pictures, or revise it, or just observe it over time. It becomes an existing *object* over which you have some control...after all, you wrote it *down* (or you taped it).

WORKOUT SECTION

1. In *Illustrated Medicine* for June 1987 (page 3), the following definition appears: "Stress may be viewed as the body's response to any real or imagined events perceived as requiring some adaptive response and/or producing strain." Does this seem adequate to you? Is it an acceptable definition? Can you improve on it?

2. Notice that the quotation in #1 defines stress not as the event—real or imagined—but as the *response* to that event. People in our society react very negatively when the power and water goes off in their homes, but spend a great deal of money on an activity called "camping," in which they must live without electric power or running water or sanitary facilities. The events are the same in power outages and camping trips, but the responses are radically different. Why? What is the single factor that makes them so different? HINT: How would you react if someone had the authority to simply order you to go camping, without warning, at any random time of the day or night?

3. In *Journal of the American Medical Association* for March 25, 1988 ("Hypochondriasis and Somatization," pages 1809–10, on page 1809), Michael J. Weintraub MD says that "The term *hypochondriacal* should be reserved for those individuals

who constantly play a sick role by misinterpreting normal physiological sensations as reflecting disease." Think about this in the context of the endless barrage of advertisements and commercials from our media transmitting a single message: FOR EVERY DISCOMFORT, NO MATTER HOW TRIVIAL, YOU SHOULD TAKE A PILL. Are we being *trained* to be hypochondriacs, as Weintraub defines them?

4. Research has proved beyond all question that keeping a diary is one of the most valuable (and least expensive) of all wellness activities. But many people react instantly to the idea of writing with "I *can't* !", usually as a result of their experiences in our schools. If that's true for you, it needs changing—you can't afford to be cut off from a major health resource in that way. Try this method, which we could call "writing with training wheels."

  a. Choose a short piece of writing, no more than a page or two long, that is the kind of thing you'd like to have written yourself. (I recommend choosing something written in the first person, from the "I" point of view, but that's not absolutely critical.) Copy the whole thing *in longhand*.

  b. Go over your copy and underline every seventh word.

  c. Copy the piece again, but this time substitute a word of your own choice for every word you underlined. (If you come to one that seems impossible, don't struggle; skip it and go on to the next. It won't happen often.)

  d. Underline every fifth word in your new version.

  e. Copy again, substituting a word of your own for the underlined words.

  f. Underline every third word and then recopy, making the usual substitutions. AT THIS POINT THE PIECE WILL BE ALMOST ENTIRELY YOUR OWN WORDS.

You may find that doing this once is enough to let you throw away the training wheels. If not, choose another short piece or two and go through the steps again. Of *course* you can write! (This method is one that linguist Leonard Newmark uses to teach people how to write in foreign languages; it works superbly for that, too.)

5. The examples below are typical Satir Mode utterances in health care contexts. Identify the mode being used in each one, and then rewrite it in some other mode. The first sentence has been done for you as a demonstration; there are no Distracter examples.

  a. "You could at least *try*, just *once*, to show some sympathy for the way I'm *suffering!*"

    BLAMER sentence. In Placater Mode, it goes like this:

    "You *never* even *try* to show any sympathy for the way I'm suffering, but *that's* all right—*I* don't mind being neglected."

  b. "Doctors who care about their patients return their calls."

  c. "The food you serve in this hospital tastes terrible."

d. *"Every* time this family wants to *do* anything, you *spoil* it! You *always* have a headache!"

e. "Your father will have a *heart* attack if you do that, dear, but *we* understand... You're entitled to live your *own* life, no matter *how* much pain it causes us."

f. "Using a cane is a nuisance, but sitting home all the time is a lot worse."

g. "If you'd look at what you're *doing* once in a while, you wouldn't always be breaking your arms and *legs* and cutting *holes* in yourself!"

h. "I hate going to doctors."

i. "What's the *matter* with you, *any*way, eating chicken that's been sitting out all night? Are you *crazy?*"

j. "People who walk thirty minutes a day stay fit and trim."

6. Assume that a foundation has offered a ten thousand dollar prize for the best movie script based on a day in the life of your family, and is paying you to help the contestants get started. What would they need to know? How would you describe the setting and the cast of characters? Who would you suggest to play the various parts? What goes on during a typical day in your home?

4

TAKING OUT THE TRASH

INTRODUCTION—WHY LONELINESS AND ISOLATION ARE DANGEROUS TO YOUR HEALTH

> The data have been there for years: People with close, stable, supportive relationships live longer and suffer less illness than loners.
>
> (In "The New American Dream," by Daniel Yankelovich and Joel Gurin; *American Health* for March 1989, pp. 63–67, on page 65.)

Many studies show that people who are lonely and isolated get sick oftener, have a higher death rate, recover more slowly (and with more complications) when they do recover, and are at far greater risk of every consequence of poor health than people with strong social networks. Best of all is a circle of loving family and friends; very good is a devoted spouse or sibling or lifetime companion; surprisingly better than nothing at all is a beloved pet. You'll find references for the social network research in the bibliography; in every case, studies of this category of risk (called "psychosocial risk") report the same simple conclusion: LONELINESS AND ISOLATION ARE BAD FOR YOU.

There are lots of possible reasons for this, and not all of them have anything to do with the new bodymind discoveries. It may be that people who are not lonely have others who look after them when necessary, who see to it that they look after themselves the rest of the time, and who can be called on for help in emergencies. Then there's the old problem of whether the chicken is first or the egg is...it could be that the social networks are there because healthy people simply make more friends and maintain stronger relationships than sick people. It doesn't matter except in formal terms.

As Gabriel Smilkstein M.D. ("Health Benefits of Helping Patients Cope," *Consultant* for January 1988, pp. 56–67, on page 60) tells us: "The theoretical basis for studying psychosocial risk is not that such risk is believed to cause disease, but that *psychosocial risk alters a person's susceptibility to disease*." Whether having social networks keeps you healthy, or being healthy enables you to form social networks, cannot yet be determined absolutely unambiguously. The best bet is that both are true and that they work together. Waiting around to find out the exact contributions of each is unwise, because the basic principle, about which there is no dispute, cannot be ignored: IF YOU HAVE NO FAMILY, NO FRIENDS, NO CLOSE CONTACTS, YOU ARE AT RISK.

This chapter's subject is the use of language to (a) build new social networks and (b) maintain the ones you already have. The strategy is the same in both cases: *using language to be someone that other people will enjoy being around*. This rarely means that you need to add language frills, like a more varied and exciting vocabulary or a repertoire of gripping stories and hilarious jokes. Usually it means getting rid of language *trash*: language phenomena that make others want to be anywhere but with you.

FEEDBACK LOOPS AND SELF-FULFILLING PROPHECIES

We've considered a lot of feedback loops in this book so far, because *all* language interactions are feedback loops. There was the discussion in Chapter 1 of the way hostility feedback loops are like contaminated wells, a source of health problems that just keep on spreading. In chapters 2 and 3 we discussed the various Satir Mode loops and their predictable effects, and the need to avoid all Blaming and Placating loops. We're going to turn now to another kind of feedback loop—the kind that leads to self-fulfilling prophecies. Look at Figure 4–1, please.

Do you see how this works? Like any feedback loop, it has neither beginning nor end. You can start anywhere on the loop and the outcome will be the same. You take it for granted that you won't be liked, which leads you to behave in a way that isn't likable, which causes people to behave as if they don't like you, which is exactly what you predicted. This is the classic self-fulfilling prophecy. Furthermore, it's yet one more source of contamination that spreads and keeps on spreading. The people who don't like you will mention that to others, who will approach you expecting to find out that they don't like you either. You will develop a reputation as someone to be avoided. You won't be asked to go places, which will cut down your opportunities to meet new people and limit your contacts with those you already know...out of sight, out of mind. The less practice you have interacting with people socially, the less skilled at that

FIGURE 4–1

You know people aren't going to like you, and you resent it -- this makes you hostile.

People meet you and sense that you're hostile -- they resent it, and this makes them behave as if they don't like you.

You meet people and they act as if they don't like you -- which is exactly what you knew would happen. And that makes you hostile.

activity you will be, which further aggravates the situation. And it will get worse, as time goes by.

In order to be liked, you have to be perceived as likable. It has to be pleasant to be around you. This has little to do with the popular idea of your "character." Logically, if you are a good person people will want to be your friend; in the real world, this doesn't hold true. Some of the world's most likable people are liars and thieves and murderers; some of the world's most selfless and virtuous people are almost impossible to like. THE CHANCES THAT YOU ARE LONELY BECAUSE YOU ARE WICKED—REQUIRING A TOTAL CHANGE IN YOUR PERSONALITY AND CHARACTER—ARE NEARLY ZERO.

This is also true, despite all the clatter in the popular media, for your physical appearance. There's almost no chance that you are lonely because you are too ugly, or too fat, or too skinny, or too short, or too badly dressed. Such things may interfere with your "image" for a few minutes with people you've just met, but that effect wears off quickly. If you bathe and brush your teeth regularly and dress in a way that doesn't violate local laws, that's all people require of a likable person. If you're *not* likable, losing weight or buying an expensive suit won't change that. Here are the facts, as opposed to the myths:

> Most of the time, if people don't want you around it's because they're not comfortable when they're with you. And most of the time, what makes them uncomfortable is your *language* behavior.

The techniques described below will go a long way toward solving this problem for you.

TECHNIQUE #5—FOLLOWING THE LANGUAGE TRAFFIC RULES

If I gathered fifty people with few social contacts together in a room, I might find two in the group who really *enjoyed* being alone most of the time. These people—the true loners—cannot be described as lonely, feel no need for the company of other people, and so far as I know have not been involved in the studies of social isolation. (And in my experience they usually have at least one dog, cat, or horse as constant companion.) The other forty-eight might make noises about Needing Nobody for a while, but if I were patient they would eventually admit that they were lonely. And their most common complaint would be this one: "I don't have anybody to talk to—nobody ever *listens* to me when I talk!" That complaint is the sure indicator of loneliness, even when it comes from a person who appears to have many social contacts. If the people you live with or work with knock themselves out to avoid talking to you, you're going to feel lonely no matter how many of them you have around.

Lots of things will make people avoid your conversational company—the invariable use of Blamer or Placater (or Distracter) Mode, for example. Talking so loudly that you hurt people's ears, or so softly that they have to struggle to hear you will do it. But perhaps the most common source for this particular problem is a failure to follow what are called "the traffic rules" of language. You can be sure that if you ignored the traffic rules when driving your car, driving at any speed you chose and ignoring such niceties as traffic lanes and traffic lights and stop signs, people would do their best to avoid your company on the road. In the same way, if your language behavior ignores the rules, they will avoid your company in conversational space. If you're convinced that nobody ever talks to you or listens to you and that people go out of their way to keep from getting involved in a conversation with you, the most likely explanation is that you either don't know or don't follow the linguistic traffic rules.

This is easily fixed. The rules have to do with only two things— conversational *turns* and conversational *topics*—and you can handle both with ease. It just takes a little attention, and a little practice.

ABOUT TURNS

Assume that the conversation involves three people. The rules for turns specify the following ideal sequence:

STEP ONE: One person introduces a topic and talks about it for no longer than three sentences. Then she passes the turn on to a second person, giving him clear cues that she's ready to give up the floor and has chosen him as next speaker.

STEP TWO: The second speaker supports the topic that was introduced, talking about it for no longer than three sentences. And then— giving clear cues to his intentions—he passes the turn on to the remaining person, who has not yet had a chance to talk.

STEP THREE: This sequence is repeated, with each person getting roughly the same number of turns, for roughly the same amount of time in each case, until the topic has been dealt with completely or the conversation is brought to a halt by external factors.

In real life things won't be this tidy. Some people will talk a bit less or a bit more than others, some will get a few more turns than others, and the "three sentences" stipulation will be violated a great deal. But the three steps above represent the goal toward which people skilled in conversation are ordinarily aiming as they talk, and will serve as our pattern here. Needless to say, the three sentences should always be of moderate length, so that no one turn goes on for more than a few minutes.

For most American speakers, the way you indicate that you are ready to surrender the floor is by *ceasing to talk yourself.* The way you show someone that you have selected him or her as next speaker is by making eye contact—*and* ceasing to talk yourself. To assume that this is known to everyone is a serious mistake and responsible for much rotten communication.

Many people do not understand that they must STOP TALKING—completely—before anyone else can begin. These are people who grew up in homes where they were never allowed to talk without being interrupted. Often they grew up in homes where *nobody* ever got to finish a sentence without being interrupted. Because the conversational turn was always taken away from them by force, they have never learned (a) how to bring their own turn to a graceful close, or (b) how to hand the turn on to someone else. Similarly, many people do not understand that passing on the turn requires eye contact. Especially if they've grown up in homes where looking the speaker openly in the eye was likely to get only a "Whadda think *you're* looking at?" or "Don't *stare* at people! It's *rude!*" instead of a turn. And because the habits they learned at home guarantee that all their conversational attempts will fail, they never learn what the problem is, even after they're on their own—they just assume that people don't like them. Such people will go on and on and on when they have the turn, even when they aren't enjoying the experience, waiting helplessly for somebody to interrupt and take the turn away from them. Let's call these people the Conversationally Pathetic—CP for short.

This isn't funny. It's as damaging as any physical handicap ever could be. Because people who *do* know the traffic rules and ordinarily follow them take it for granted that *everybody* knows them. When they encounter people who don't pass on the turn—or who take the turn only by interrupting, which is the only turn-taking strategy that CP people know—they assume the worst. They don't pause and think, "Maybe this is somebody who never learned how to carry on a conversation," and then try to help. They leap to the conclusion that they're looking at a monstrous case of *ego*, a case of Being In Love With The Sound Of One's Own Voice, and a total unwillingness to share the conversational space. They then find a way to get *out* of talking to the CP person, preferably till the end of time. And the poor CP still doesn't know what's going on. This goes on for the CP's lifetime, barring miracles, with the linguistically handicapped person growing more and more inept, more and more bitter, and more and more lonely, with every passing year. If you recognize yourself as someone who has not been following the rules for turns, it's important for you to *change* that. Study them, and start using them. It's far better to do that awkwardly than not to do it at all.

ABOUT TOPICS

In the ideal conversation, every topic introduced is fascinating to even the pickiest listener. In the real world, people don't demand that sort of brilliance, but they will *not* tolerate being bored stiff if they can possibly help it. If you have trouble getting people to support your topics in conversation—that is, getting people to talk about what you were trying to talk about instead of changing the subject and talking about something else—chances are very good that a list of your usual topics would be one of these three:

- ☐ The No-Topic List of Topics
- ☐ The All-One-Topic List of Topics
- ☐ The All-Taboo List of Topics

The No-Topic list leads to "conversations" like this one:

YOU: "It's really hot today."

X: "It sure is."

YOU: "I don't remember when it's ever been so hot before."

X: "You don't?"

YOU: "No, I don't. It's unusual for it to be this hot."

X: "Uhuh."

YOU: "Don't you think it's hot?"

X: "I sure do."

YOU: "Well, I do too."

The All-One-Topic List belongs to people who, no matter what the occasion, no matter who is present, talk about a single subject. Often it's their work, or a member of their family. It may be a special gripe they have—like Congress or the homeless or Communism or people who play loud music on their stereos. If other people try to change the subject it may work for a sentence or two, but then All-One-Topicers say, "You know, that reminds me....", and they're back to Congress or Communism or their rotten in-laws again.

Particularly dangerous is having YOURSELF as your one and only topic. Psychologist Larry Schwartz found that "the amount a person talks about himself—how much he says *I*, *me*, and *my/mine*—predicts who dies from heart disease more effectively than cholesterol level and weight do." (In "Minding Your Health: The Pretended Self," by Paul Perry; *Psychology Today* for May 1989, pages 60–62, on page 62.)

People who use the All-Taboo list talk only about surgeries and death and sicknesses and bathroom functions and cannibalism and mutilation and perhaps kinky sex. Only other people who have the same list will listen to that kind of thing for very long, and there aren't many of them in any one place.

Your first step in dealing with this problem is to find out what your own topics inventory is like—by keeping a record for at least two weeks. After any conversation, in person or by phone, make a quick note of the topics that you introduced. Just a word or two will do. And don't *cheat*. If your topic was what a creep Joe is, don't make a note that you introduced a discussion of interpersonal relationships in small businesses. At the end of the three weeks, sit down and compile your list, noting after each topic how often it appears, like this...

What a creep Joe is (17 times)
Why I don't like Ted (11 times)
The dog (3 times)
    and so on...

Seeing your topic list can be a shock, especially if you have always thought of yourself as an interesting conversationalist and you turn out to be a No-Topic, All-One-Topic, or All-Taboo-Topic person. But at least that tells you that if people don't want to talk to you it's probably because of what you talk *about*, rather than a dislike for you personally. Furthermore, it's a problem you can fix rather easily by taking two simple steps.

First, you must begin paying close attention to the *reactions* people have to your topics. That means listening to their responses and making adjustments accordingly. This sounds simplistic, I know. But people whose topic lists fall into the three negative categories are people who have developed a self-protective habit of ignoring bored or frustrated or outraged responses from those they talk to. That habit has to be broken, and it will take deliberate and careful listening, as well as active observation of body language. We'll come back to the subject of listening skills later in this chapter.

Second, make yourself a new list of topics and begin deliberately introducing the items on your list instead of those you're used to introducing. Choose at least a dozen topics that are of general interest and about which you know enough to maintain a conversation; write them down on an index card; and spend one week actively talking about them. The easiest way to do this is to choose them from one of the weekly news magazines like *Time* or *The New Republic* or *Newsweek*, where you will find not only subjects of current interest but basic information about them. When you've come to the end of the list, make a new one.

At first this will seem awkward and artificial and contrived. It *is* awkward and artificial and contrived. But it's only temporary—call it conversational training wheels—until you get the knack of selecting and maintaining topics that other people will enjoy talking about, after which you can safely abandon the list process. When people discover that it's possible to have a pleasant conversation with you after all, they'll stop classifying you as someone to be avoided. This is an essential step toward building the support networks that are necessary for your health and well-being. But be *patient*—the longer you've had the "Rotten Communicator" label in others' minds, the longer it will take them to realize that you have changed your behavior.

Finally, if you can't bring yourself to take this second step, there is one strategy you can fall back on and be sure of success: just support the topics of other people with courtesy and enthusiasm. Most of the time, they'll be more happy to choose the subject of the conversation and will welcome your support as evidence that you are a pleasure to be around.

It's very important to practice following the traffic rules in every situation except life-threatening emergencies. They will never be natural for you, and you'll never be able to use them convincingly, if you decide you'll save them for special occasions and can't be bothered to use them at home or in routine situations. Practice them even when you really *don't* have to do so—practice them even while talking to someone you know you'll never encounter again—so that when you *do* need them they'll be easy for you to use.

TECHNIQUE #6—SYNTONIC LISTENING

Listening ought to be a simple skill, because it's one that will operate automatically as long as you don't interfere with the process. The problem is that so many of us have terrible listening habits that make it impossible for our brains to perform properly. Syntonic listening is *tuning yourself to the person speaking* and giving that person the kind of total attention that allows you to maintain the in-tune syntonic state. (The term "attending" is often used for such listening.) You can't listen syntonically while you....

- □ think about some other subject entirely, paying no attention to the speaker
- □ think about how much better you could say what the speaker is saying, how wrong the speaker is, how badly the speaking is being done, how oddly the speaker is dressed, etc.
- □ sit on the edge of your chair, waiting for a chance to leap in and take the turn away from the speaker
- □ rehearse in your mind what you're going to say as soon as it's your turn to talk
- □ carry out some unrelated activity—taking detailed notes, working a crossword puzzle, reading, doing homework, watching a ball game outside the window, etc.

There's nothing tricky or obscure about syntonic listening. You simply give the speaker your full attention, refrain from trying to do something else at the same time, and allow your brain to function as it is superbly equipped to do. Syntonic listening will then happen without any further action on your part. But your efforts to keep your attention on the speaker, and your irritation when it keeps wandering away, are going to be distracting and may be downright irritating. I recommend, therefore, that you begin retraining your listening skills with a partner that cannot be distracted or insulted: your television set. Like this:

1. Choose a tv show that approximates real talk and on which people talk for at least several minutes without interruption—you want a sermon or a speech or a lecture, not a game show or a situation comedy. If you have access to C-Span and can watch the proceedings of Congress, that's an excellent choice; educational television should provide you with some examples; if all else fails, watch a television evangelist. It doesn't matter if the speaker is boring—that only makes it more of a challenge.

2. Give the tv speaker your full attention. Listen to the words; watch the body language. Every time you realize that your mind has wandered off somewhere on its own, grab it and return your attention to the speaker, as many times as it takes. You may have to do that every thirty seconds or so at first; the tv speaker won't know or care.

3. When you are able to deliberately listen to a tv speaker for roughly ten minutes without having to struggle to keep your attention under control, start practicing with speakers who are present in person instead of on the screen. Be sure to *time* yourself before you decide you're ready for this! When people aren't

interested in what they're hearing, they have a strong tendency to estimate that far more time has passed than is really the case.

Now suppose you feel that this is too much trouble, that you have plenty of friends and relatives who are used to the fact that conversing with you is an ordeal and care enough about you to put up with it. Suppose you are convinced that your support network won't fail you no matter *how* awful it might be to talk to you. I run into that attitude now and then.

In that case, let me tell you about one more health benefit that goes with syntonic listening and that is independent of the social network issue.

Dr. James Lynch heads a blood pressure treatment clinic at the medical school of the University of Maryland. Some years ago, as an accidental byproduct of keeping track of patients who were wearing twenty-four-hour heart monitors, he discovered something amazing. He found that when people listened syntonically—really listened, with full attention to the speaker—their blood pressures dropped and their heart rates slowed. Conversely, when people talked, their blood pressures rose and their heart rates speeded up.

This effect, Lynch found, was independent of the subject talked about. Certainly it was greater when people talked about something that upset or excited them—but even when they talked about the most innocuous things, even when they read a telephone book aloud, it happened. People with high blood pressure showed more dramatic changes when they talked, but it happened to almost everybody. And the exceptions were not people in normal circumstances—the effect turned out not to be present in schizophrenics, for example. For normal healthy people, it was always there. It was the same sort of effect that is achieved by relaxation techniques, and it was clearly good for people. Patients at Lynch's clinic who are unable to tolerate the usual medications and regimes have been able to reduce their blood pressure significantly just by learning to be good listeners.

This means that syntonic listening pays off for you in a big way. Especially if you are a Type A person who ordinarily does all the talking and works hard to dominate every conversation. Do it for your *own* sake, even if you could care less about whether you are liked or not. It's a sound investment in *your personal* well-being.

THE LANGUAGE OF MUSIC

Today it would be a serious oversight to write about the relationship between listening and health without mentioning the new information on what listening to music can do for you. Music is a language, too, and is probably the closest thing we human beings have to a *universal* language. Organized medicine now uses music extensively to reduce pain and tension, especially during and after surgery, dental procedures, and childbirth. It's valuable in the diagnosis of certain mental illnesses. And because many people whose speaking abilities are damaged by illness or trauma retain their ability to sing, music is now used as a method for communicating, with a sort of impromptu opera substituting for spoken conversation.

To put music to use in your own wellness program, you need to understand the basic concept called *entrainment*.

Entrainment is a term from physics, used to refer to the tendency of two pendulums set up side by side to swing exactly together. In this case it means being syntonic with music—matching the tempos and rhythms of your body to those of the music you're listening to. The average heartbeat is about 80 beats a minute, and when we say that something we hear is fast or slow we're using that speed as a reference point. Everybody will agree that "Amazing Grace," at only 60 beats per minute, is a slow song.

Entrainment is a natural consequence of syntonic listening, and you shouldn't have to work at it. Your heart rate and your blood pressure and your breathing rate should all automatically match themselves to music as you listen, without any active effort on your part. But you can help the process along by taking your own music preferences into consideration and by using common sense. If hearing "Amazing Grace" drives you up the wall because you *hate* that kind of music, listening to it will be a struggle—and you can't listen syntonically while you struggle. There's plenty of slow music around to choose from, in every musical style; listen to something that you can enjoy. It doesn't matter whether that means rock music, popular standards, New Age, classical, or any other variety, as long as you listen to instrumental music only—with no words being sung to distract you.

You can buy tapes that are specifically designed to help you relax, and any music store or tape catalog will direct you to those. But you can also make your own "customized" tapes, tailored to your personal needs. For example, if you always come home from work wound up tight, hardly able even to sit still, it won't be easy for you to listen to something slow and stately. For an after-work relaxation tape, then, music therapists suggest that you first record something fast—something that's moving at the same frantic rate as you are, perhaps 100 beats a minute. Add a second selection that's a little slower, and then another that's slower still, so you have a chance to unwind along with the music. *Then* record the slow pieces, for the rest of the tape. If your problem is not that you're wound up too tightly but that you can't seem to get moving, reverse the process. Make a tape that starts with slow music and then add pieces that get gradually faster, to make the change easier. My personal recommendation for an "energizer" tape is one called "Fireworks," by The Empire Brass (from EMI Angel).

If you're facing a painful medical or dental procedure, or a stay in a hospital, a small tape player with earphones that you can take along and use to play your favorite tapes is a good investment.

TECHNIQUE #7—RECOGNIZING THE VERBAL ATTACK PATTERNS

You will be consciously aware of many English sentence patterns, such as the patterns for giving commands or asking questions. Even if you aren't able to state the formal rules for these patterns, you know them perfectly and can demonstrate that knowledge by producing commands and questions unhesitatingly on demand. You probably are *not* consciously aware of the sentence patterns in the grammar of English verbal violence, however—we don't learn them in school and they don't appear in standard reference grammars. Nevertheless, you know them. And you began using them when you were a very small child, in the same way that you asked questions and—to the extent that you could get away with it—you gave orders. Physical abuse requires physical strength and is for the most part carried out by adults and teenagers. Verbal abuse is different, and four-year-old kids can be quite good at it.

THE MELODY OF VERBAL VIOLENCE

It's important to know that *any* sequence of language, no matter what words it contains, can be a verbal attack. I can say "I love you" or "You're the most wonderful person I know" in such a way that you understand immediately that I'm attacking you. The old saw—"It's not what you say, it's how you say it"—is absolutely accurate. And what makes otherwise neutral or affectionate words carry a verbal attack message is the body language that goes with them—especially the tone and intonation of the voice, which lay down the *melody* the words are set to. The most typical characteristic of that melody (let's call it The Attack Tune) is the presence of two or more strong vocal stresses on words or parts of words in a single clause. The meaning difference between the neutral "Why did you tell her that?" and the furious "WHY did you TELL her that?" (or "WHY did you TELL her THAT?") is carried by the stresses on the words written here in capital letters. The words themselves are identical.

Every English clause (a sentence, or a part of a sentence with its own subject and predicate) has to have at least one segment that gets more emphasis—more *stress*—in speech than all the others. Usually it comes at or near the end of the sequence, and it is so taken for granted that no punctuation or graphic frill is used to indicate it. Native speakers of English know where this normal stress should go and place it automatically. Only robots and computers leave out that one obligatory stress, and with current technology even they are beginning to include it. But *two* strong stresses, or a normal stress plus one or more additional strong stresses, should occur only in three situations, as follows.

CONTRASTIVE STRESS:

1. When you are contrasting one item with another, as in "We didn't go to the beach on the FIFTH, we went on the SIXTH." or "It wasn't JOHN, it was BILL."

EMPHATIC STRESS:

2. When you have good reason to be extremely agitated about something, as in "Look OUT, there's a BEAR in the CAR!" or "*I* just WON a MILLion DOLlars!"

3. When you need to indicate the unusual importance of a particular word or words to you as speaker, as in "I never HEARD of vegetarian hot dogs and hamburgers" or "There's no GAS in your new Chevrolet."

Contrastive or emphatic stress in written language is traditionally indicated by underlining or italics.

Except in the situations above, the presence of two or more strong stresses in a sentence or clause should always alert you to the possibility that you are under verbal attack.

Once you get beyond that basic and crucial fact, there are specific patterns that English speakers use over and over again for verbal attacks. These are the VAPs (it rhymes, appropriately enough, with "zaps")—the set of English Verbal Attack Patterns. In this section I'll introduce the concept and discuss it briefly; then we'll take it up again in detail in Chapter 6. We begin here because one of the language behavior habits most likely to drive people away from you and cause them to dislike being around you is the incessant use of VAPs; it's no coincidence that they are also typical of Blaming and Placating language. Every VAP will contain abnormally strong vocal stresses and/or an abnormally large number of stresses. Here are some examples from the set.

"If you REALLY cared about your health, YOU wouldn't SMOKE all the time!"

"EVen a MAN should be able to show SOME compassion for others!"

"WHY don't you ever consider where somebody ELSE might want to go on weekends?"

"HOW could you POSSibly DO such an awful thing?!"

"DON'T YOU even CARE about world HUNGER?"

"YOU'RE not the ONly person with PROBlems, you know!"

Familiar. Yes, indeed. And easily recognized.

If you use these attack patterns, they cause people to try to avoid you, and to dislike you when they can't avoid you. If other people try them on you and you get involved in rows as a result, that also leads to isolation, because nobody you'd want for a friend will stand around and watch your rows. They're language toxins.

PERFORMING THE MELODY OF VERBAL VIOLENCE

The VAPs are *action chains*: behaviors made up of a specific sequence of steps, carried out in a specific order and manner, which cannot be completed if they are interrupted. They contain an open attack, called "the bait," plus one or more *hidden* attacks. The steps in the action chain are:

1. The attacker presents the attack.
2. The victim takes the bait and responds to it.
3. There is a volley of counterattacks and responses that goes on until someone gives up and quits.

For example...

ATTACKER: "If you REALLY loved me, YOU wouldn't cheat on your DIet!"

VICTIM: "I DON'T cheat on my diet! HOW can you SAY such a thing!"

ATTACKER: "I can say it because I SAW you. You ate your grapefruit—and then you went in the hall and ate a DOUGHnut. That's CHEATing."

VICTIM: "I did NOT do any such THING!"

ATTACKER: "SURE you did! Now you're LYing!"

VICTIM: "Well, at LEAST I don't SPY on people!"

ATTACKER: "AHA! So you adMIT it! You DID eat that doughnut!"

VICTIM: "All right, all RIGHT! I'm SORry!" (Leaves the room in distress.)

You see how that goes? The bait was "you cheat on your diet"; the victim grabbed it and ran, just as the attacker intended. Followed by an ugly and undignified volley of abuse until the victim gave up in distress and fled the scene.

This, I am sorry to say, is how many people spend much of their linguistic lives, on one end or the other of interactions like the one above. And this, I am equally sorry to say, is the model that far too many families provide for their children as the proper way to deal with conflict.

The three most important things to remember about the English VAPs are the following:

1. They can be recognized by the presence of abnormal stress patterns.
2. Their purpose is to demonstrate the power of the attacker over the victim by (a) getting and holding the victim's attention and (b) evoking an emotional response.
3. The attacker never is after what would be a normal response to the same words in a neutral sentence; if the attack is a question, for example, the attacker has no interest in the answer.

For example, an attacker who begins with "WHY are you always CHEATing on your DIet?!" has no interest at all in an answer to the question—in an explanation of the reasons for the cheating. And the attacker in the example above who begins with "If you REALLY loved me, you wouldn't CHEAT on your DIet!" would be perfectly contented with a response like "You enJOY being cruel, DON'T you?" or "If I had manners like YOURS, I'D live on a desert ISland!" or even just "DON'T YOU DARE start that again!" It isn't necessary for the victim to talk about either love or diets; the attacker just wants attention demonstrated by emotional language, on any subject whatsoever.

What matters most of all in dealing with such attacks is making sure that the attackers don't get what they want. Which brings us to...

THE ALL-PURPOSE VERBAL ATTACK RESPONSE

Remember that VAPs are action chains. Like handshakes, if they are interrupted at any point they fail. The person who started the chain has to go back and begin all over again from the beginning. In Chapter 6 I will be presenting a number of different strategies for strategic responses to VAPs, but I want to conclude this section with an addition to your linguistic *emergency* kit, called "The Boring Baroque Response." Its purpose is to guarantee the failure of the attack by interrupting it and making it impossible for the volley of counterattacks to take place; its purpose is to make sure that the attacker has *no fun*. Like this.

> ATTACKER: "WHY are you always CHEATing on your DIet?"

> RESPONSE: "You know, that's a good question. I think it's probably because of a movie I saw when I was just a little kid. There was this movie place on the corner of Tenth and Main...no, wait a minute. It couldn't have been Tenth and Main, it must have been on Fifteenth Street. I know because that was the year my Dad opened his shoe store on Fifteenth Street and we used to go right from the store to the movies. At least I *think* we did. It's hard to remember something that happened so long ago, you know? Usually I'm pretty good at it, but..."

(AND SO ON AND SO ON, INTERMINABLY.)

Your strategy is to interrupt the attack by failing to take the bait, while at the same time teaching the attacker that trying VAPs with you is going to be a miserable experience. You are ignoring the fact that you know the attacker doesn't really want an answer to the question, and you are answering it in excruciating detail—the more excruciating the better. You do the same thing in response to a VAP that's a statement rather than a question, but you need a lead-in. Like this.

> ATTACKER: "If you REALLY loved me, you wouldn't CHEAT on your DIet!"

> VICTIM: "You know, I think the reason I do that is because of the way we used to eat at my house when I was a kid. I remember when we lived in Detroit...or no, wait. Maybe it was when we lived in Indianapolis! Sure, because that was the year my Aunt Minerva..." (AND SO ON.)

This won't work if you do it sarcastically. It won't work if you put in a lot of extra stresses—if you say, "The reason I DO that is because of the way we used to eat at my HOUSE when I was a KID." It *will* work if you just talk neutrally, with a pleasant expression on your face. And the verbal abuser will find it extremely discouraging. How interminable you make it should depend on whether you ever want to talk to the attacker again, whether the attacker is someone with the power to do you significant harm, and similar real world considerations. But even if you stop after "I think the reason I do that is because of the way we used to eat at my house when I was a kid"—perhaps because your attacker is a vindictive and vengeful boss, or is a small child without much verbal skill—you will still have caused the attack to fail, because you did not take the bait that allows the volley to begin.

This is not the best or most elegant way to handle VAPs. It does nothing to tackle the problem of poor communication between the two people involved. It decreases the amount of verbal violence in the language environment because it cuts down on the fights and scenes, but it does nothing to build a network of friends and associates who enjoy being around you. However, it's a good place to start and an excellent emergency response to use any time you find yourself facing a VAP and not knowing exactly what to do.

WORKOUT SECTION

1. Much genuinely unpleasant language is not verbal abuse but verbal incompetence. Defending yourself against such stuff is usually a waste of your time and energy. For example: Once I was flying home after a conference, seated between two distinguished linguists. One of them complimented me on the standing-room-only attendance I'd had when I gave my paper. Before I could thank him, the other leaned across me and said, "Oh, they weren't there to hear Suzette's paper! They were all invited to Lakoff's party and they didn't have anywhere to go until it started." This wasn't a verbal attack. It was the typical utterance of a person with the conversational skills of a bull calf. It would have been ridiculous to pay attention to it, and I didn't.

With this example in mind, take a rigorous look at the last two or three times you've thought someone was attacking you verbally. Were they? Or were they like my conversationally handicapped academic up there? Try constructing three-part messages that you could have said in response to the outrageous remarks. Like this: "When you said (OUTRAGEOUS REMARK), I felt _____ because _____" Can you fill the blanks with items that are directly perceivable in the real world?

2. *Saturday Review* for March 19, 1980 (page 13) quoted a doctor who was criticizing people for going to physicians in search of sympathy and listening, saying: "A doctor should absolutely not be used in this way. Doctors are there to provide caring. Not listening." Apply Miller's Law to this speech. Assume that it is true—doctors are there to provide caring, not listening. What could it be true *of*? What sort of reality would it be true for? What other things would have to be true to make it true?

3. For two or three days, behave like a chronic language traffic rule violater in all situations where you can safely do so. Bring up only boring or taboo topics, and

deliberately fail to support the topics of others. When people offer you the conversational turn, pretend not to notice. When you *have* the turn, say only one very short sentence, every time...or deliver a monologue every time. When people talk to you, be careful to avoid making eye contact with them; look at the floor, or the ceiling, or out the window, or at your fingernails. Pay careful attention to the results. At the end of the week, if nobody is even trying to talk to you any more, explain your experiment. If, on the other hand, nobody seems to care, find out why. Is it because this is your *usual* language behavior? Is it because nobody was listening? Is it because they've provided you with an excuse—"You're only acting like that because..."?

4. Theoretically, a statement used in response to a question should be its answer. But it's very common for people to fall into the habit of answering not the question asked but some *other* question. For example:

Q: "Have you done the laundry?"
A: "I mowed the yard today."

"I mowed the yard today" is an answer, but not to "Have you done the laundry?". It might be the answer to "Why didn't you do the laundry?", but that's not what was asked. Countless arguments start this way; it's a pernicious habit that should be stamped out as fast as possible. Check for it, the way you'd check for termites. For one month, pay close attention to the question and answer pairs around you. For each such pair, ask yourself: (a) What question was asked? (b) What question was answered? The two should be the same.

5. There is a cassette tape called "Allelulia," available from Spring Hill Music (5216 Sunshine Canyon, Boulder CO 80302) on which only one thing happens. To the melody of Pachelbel's Canon, a chorus sings the word "Alleluia." *Period.* This tape was produced for use in relaxation and/or meditation, and is very good for those purposes, but you can use it another way. To produce championship listening skills, get that tape and listen to it syntonically. (Be sure you don't do this while driving a car!) Your goal is to keep *hearing* the word being sung, for at least ten minutes, without thinking about anything else and without going to sleep. If you're climbing the walls after thirty seconds, set your goal at one minute for a while and work up from there gradually.

6. Start keeping track of the VAPs in your life. Don't do anything elaborate...you just want a rough idea how high the linguistic pollution level is. For one week, every time you think you hear a VAP, make an X on a scrap of paper; at the end of the week, count the X's for a total. At the end of the week, now that you've had some practice, make your records more useful. Set up your sheet of paper with three columns: A (you were the attacker); V (you were the victim); and O (you were the observer). Go on keeping track of the VAPs that contaminate your language environment for two more weeks, sorting them according to the role you filled in each confrontation. At the end of that time you will have established a good baseline figure that you can compare with the totals for repeat checks six months later and on down the road.

7. If you think you need practice spotting verbal attacks, the situation

comedies on your television set will provide you with plenty of that, at no charge. (So will the children's programs, unfortunately, even the ones on educational tv.) If you're not sure of your skill at this, practice with the tv until you feel more confident.

SIGHT BITES

1. "Scientists have long noted an association between social relationships and health. More socially isolated or less socially integrated individuals are less healthy, psychologically and physically, and more likely to die."

   (James S. House et al., "Social Relationships and Health," in *Science* for July 29, 1988, pages 540–544; on page 540.)

2. "Certainly it would seem that we've created an environment in this country where a genuine conversation is hard to crank up and get going."

   (A.R. Gurney, "Conversation Piece," in *Newsweek* for June 12, 1989, pages 8–9, on page 8)

3. (After describing the "high" many people feel after vigorous exercise): "New evidence reveals that these same emotional and physical changes can be produced with activity requiring much less exertion—helping others."

   (Allan Luks, "Helper's High," in *Psychology Today* for October 1988, pages 39–42; on page 39.)

4. "The researchers found that doing regular volunteer work, more than any other activity, dramatically increased life expectancy (and probably vitality.)"

   (Eileen Rockefeller Growald and Allan Luks, "The Immunity of Samaritans: Beyond Self," in *American Health* for March 1988, pages 51–53; on page 51.)

5. "During a one-year followup assessment of 92 patients discharged from a critical care unit, Katcher and associates showed...that pet ownership was a significant independent predictor of survival: among the patients who owned pets, only 5.6% died, compared with 28% of those without pets."

   (Gabriel Smilkstein, M.D., "Health Benefits of Helping Patients Cope," in *Consultant* for January 1988, pages 56–57; on page 56.)

5

ACHES AND PAINS, MISERY AND DESPAIR

INTRODUCTION—SURVIVORS AND THE BODYMIND

Researcher Sandra M. Levy (Associate Professor of Psychiatry and Medicine at the University of Pittsburgh Medical School) directed a seven-year study of a group of women with advanced breast cancer. All had gone through the standard medical treatments, all had passed the five-year predicted survival mark, and all were still going strong. Dr. Levy wanted to find out what these survivors had in common that could account for their success in beating the odds.

There were a number of likely possibilities. The women might all have followed special diets or exercise regimes. They might have abstained from cigarettes and alcohol. It was possible that they had some shared factor in their family histories—some genetic characteristic. Or the shared factor might have been geographic, with all the survivors coming from a particular region of the country. The list of such possibilities is long, and the researchers expected that one would be the statistical winner, but they were wrong. Instead, what the women had in common was a high score for *joy*, as measured by a standard pencil-and-paper test.

Daniel Goleman, writing about these results, said: "That a joyous state of mind should be so powerful a predictor of survival was completely unexpected" (Goleman 1987). And that is important, because it is not the usual case. In the usual case, scientists select a problem, decide that a particular answer is likely enough to be worth looking for, and then design an experiment to find evidence for or against that solution. Levy's study found the evidence for joy by serendipity—by happy accident.

But how could joy possibly matter so much? Common sense tells us that a happy person will have an easier time during illness than a sorrowful one. But how could that affect the number of years a cancer patient *survives*? Surely cancer is something that happens in your body, while joy is something that happens in your mind!

It's time to take up (and throw out) the idea that the body and the mind are two entirely separate parts of a "set" that constitutes a person (with an extra piece called "the soul" or "the spirit" completing the set for many of us). Here is the basic principle to be remembered:

YOUR BRAIN—WHICH IS RUNNING THINGS—DOESN'T RECOGNIZE ANY SUCH THINGS AS A SEPARATE BODY AND MIND. THERE IS ONLY A *BODYMIND*, WITH BOTH CANCER AND JOY AFFECTING IT DIRECTLY AND AS A WHOLE.

This *does* matter. It matters terribly. When you talk about aches and pains, you can usually say confidently that your body . . . or some particular part of your body . . . *hurts*. Pain in the body, pain in your arm or your ear or your stomach, is easy to talk about and easy to get attention for. You can go straight to the doctor and say, "Doctor, my head hurts something fierce!" and anticipate that an effort will be made to help you get rid of that pain. But when the pain you're feeling can't be located in any body part, matters are not so simple.

Arthur Barsky, author of *Worried Sick*, notes accurately that you can't complain effectively about a pain if you don't have any words for it. If you try to tell someone that your *mind* hurts, you're not going to get the kind of reaction you get when you say your head hurts. To say that your brain hurts would be equally bad, because doctors know the brain is almost indifferent to pain and can undergo surgery without anesthesia—a pain in the brain would be just as hard to talk about as a pain in the mind. We won't even consider the communication problem you'd have if you said to your doctor, "Doctor, my soul hurts like the very dickens!" Things are complicated enough already.

This problem is clearly a LANGUAGE problem. It's not that people don't believe in pain of mind and spirit. When you say "My heart aches" you're not talking about a pain in your physical heart, you're talking about a pain that is not of the body. But whereas "my head aches" will usually get you a physical examination from the doctor plus at least an aspirin, "My heart aches" will not. Doctors, and other people, may express sympathy— IF you can produce some external reason that they feel justifies the discomfort, such as the loss of a loved one. But then you'll hear, "You'll get over it; you just need a little time," or "What you need is something to take your mind off your problem—try to keep busy." And if the external reason doesn't pass the test, you can expect "Oh, come on—don't make a mountain out of a molehill!" instead of sympathy.

You certainly *can* get attention for nonbody pain if you carry on enough to become an annoyance to others around you. Then an expert (for whom we'll use the cover term "therapist") will be brought in to either fix you up or put you away. But people won't send you Get Well cards and flowers while you're getting "mental health care." Your family is very likely to tell people that you're away on a vacation when you are away at a mental hospital. You can lose your job—and your political campaign—for needing care for nonbody pain. And our society makes it absolutely clear that such pain is not "real" pain, using the one measure that is never ambiguous in American life: money. Your medical insurance will pay only a small portion of the costs of your care if it's not care for your body.

This situation has caused most of us, faced with nonbody pain, to feel obligated to grit our teeth and bear it. The penalties for admitting such pain and trying to get help for it are too severe to allow any other choice. Even those rich enough to afford classical psychoanalysis, moving in circles where such analysis is considered chic, have been careful not to let such pain interfere with their functioning. It's okay to go to bed for two weeks with a broken leg. But with a broken mind or spirit you are supposed to "pull yourself together" and go on about your business without inconveniencing other people.

Medical professionals have always talked a pretty good line in this regard. The doctor who told you that your pain was "emotional" was quick to assure you that it was just as serious, and just as important, and just as deserving of care as any bodily pain. But in the real world, faced with three patients screaming in pain from broken legs or stomach cramps and three screaming in pain from something "all in their heads," medical professionals have never hesitated to go straight to the aid of the bodily pain and leave the mental sufferers shrieking.

But pain in your mind *is* in fact just as real as any other pain. And because your brain doesn't recognize any distinction between mind and body, such pain cannot be ignored or suppressed forever, any more than the pain of a broken leg or a ruptured appendix can. What your wise brain often does when the limits of endurance are reached is to find a linguistic solution: IT TRANSLATES YOUR NONBODY PAIN *INTO* BODY PAIN, SO THAT OUR CULTURE WILL ALLOW YOU TO GET HELP FOR IT. Where you started with a heartache, you end up with an ulcer; since ulcers are respectable, you can go off to your doctor confident that Something Will Be Done, and that you won't have to keep whatever is done a secret.

What has now become clear, much to the suprise of conventional medicine, is that your brain is capable of doing this kind of translation in *both* directions. For the cancer patients described at the beginning of this chapter, it has translated something of the "mind"—joy—into a set of "bodily" conditions that are sufficient to hold back cancer.

For the problem of translation in either direction, the solution is not money or gadgets, but LANGUAGE. We would be wise, therefore, to turn our attention carefully to our language and to the way we use it either to get sick or to stay well—that is the purpose of this book. Three terms needed for that task must be made clear here before we go on.

1. Because no valid division can be made between body and mind, we'll use the term *bodymind* to put an end to the artifical divisions that have served us so badly for so long.

2. *Aches* and *pains* are ordinarily terms that refer to the body, while *misery* and *despair* refers to the mind. The single term *pain* will be understood in this book as a cover word for all four.

3. Since any division between the words you speak and the body language that goes with those words is just as artificial as the division between body and mind, in this book the term "language" is understood to mean *anything you do that conveys a message*, whether verbal or nonverbal.

The brain perceives pain simply *as* pain, no matter where it comes from, and must respond to it. It would probably annoy your doctor if you said "My bodymind hurts so much that I can't get anything done," but that is an accurate and truthful sentence. It's time to begin thinking and talking—at least to yourself—in terms of your bodymind and the pain it feels, in order to get your *linguistic* wellness program underway. (In Chapter 11 we will return to the subject of communication with medical professionals.)

Eric J. Cassel, M.D., writing in *The New England Journal of Medicine* for March 18, 1982 ("The Nature of Suffering and the Goals of Medicine," pp. 639–45, on page 640) tells us that

> so long as the mind-body dichotomy is accepted, suffering is either subjective and thus not truly 'real'—not within medicine's domain—or identified exclusively with bodily pain.

You need to be able to say things like "My bodymind is feeling a lot of distress located in my stomach." Never mind how strange that sounds! That's exactly the point. The fact that your language offers you no convenient way to talk about such matters is one of the things that makes that language most dangerous to your health.

THE INTERACTION BETWEEN PAIN AND LANGUAGE

When you hurt, language offers you a multitude of ways to make your pain worse. The familiar principle responsible for this unpleasant truth is once again, ANYTHING YOU FEED WILL GROW. This is just as true of pain as it is of livestock and crops. The more attention you or others give to your discomfort, the longer it will last and the worse it will be. For example:

1. Pain is worse when you talk about it at great length and in great detail—whether you are talking about it to other people or talking about it to yourself. And make no mistake: a constant struggle to keep *from* talking about your pain is just one more way of talking to yourself about it.

2. Pain is worse when you use language like "This pain is killing me" or "I'll die if this pain doesn't stop." Such words are much more than "figures of speech," and they can have dramatic and dangerous effects on you and on those who hear you say them.

3. Pain is worse when you are convinced that you have no way of knowing when or where it will hit you, or how long it will last—when you perceive yourself as its helpless victim. Human beings react far more negatively to problems over which they feel they have no control.

4. Pain is worse when you use body language to resist it—when you grit your teeth and clench your eyebrows and tighten up all your muscles against it. TENSION CREATES PAIN. This is especially true if you are talking to someone who responds by reflecting all this tension back at you. The two of you are then locked into a feedback loop, with the tension and pain growing in both directions and just as contagious as measles.

A first reaction to the list above is that it's time to give up. If you talk about your pain, it will get worse; if you don't talk about it, it will get worse anyway. If you send a pain message with expressive body language—writhing or moaning, or clutching your head—it will get worse. But body language that holds such messages back will make it worse, too. As for having control over your pain, if everything you do is going to make it worse, who needs that control?

But so far we have only talked about what *not* to do. It's true that feeding your pain with constant attention, talking about it incessantly to others and to yourself, guarantees more pain. It's true that *forcing* yourself not to talk about it or think about it is just as bad, because that's only a different kind of constant attention. But those are not your only choices. The way to stop thinking about purple elephants is not to say to yourself, sternly, "Don't think about purple elephants!" but to start thinking about something else entirely, like chocolate ice cream. People tend to think that's not possible. They'll say, "It's not the same *thing*. When you're really in pain, you *can't* think about anything else!" And "Maybe it's possible for *trivial* pain. But not for *real* pain!"

Maybe. But before you label that idea as truth, let's consider a few items of interest here, all of them reported over and over again in the medical literature.

1. Professional athletes—football players, track stars, skiers, you name it—are often surprised when they learn that they've been walking or running on a fractured leg or ankle for long periods of time, because they've been completely unaware of their injuries. Soldiers in battle are often unaware of extremely serious wounds until they're pointed out by somebody else. This kind of "anesthesia" lasts much longer than can be explained by the numbing effects of simple shock.

2. Doctors and nurses constantly see people who are in pain begin to feel relief as soon as they swallow a pain pill, in spite of the fact that the pill won't "take effect" for fifteen minutes or more. In fact, doctors report many patients whose pain becomes less as soon as they are handed a *prescription* for a pain medication.

3. One-third of all patients get adequate pain relief from a placebo—a pill or a shot they believe contains medicine for their pain, but that in fact contains none. A placebo in the form of a shot will relieve their pain better than a pill will, and faster. Placebo pills that are large and purple, or small and yellow, relieve pain more effectively than any other combination of sizes and colors. And for people who respond to placebos, they work just as well for major (for example, postsurgical) pain as they do for minor complaints.

4. Most dental patients have had the embarassing experience of wincing (or screaming) with pain, only to find out that the dentist hasn't *done* anything yet.

That is: pain is not something "out there" that can be weighed and measured precisely, like a tree or a rock. Pain is a perceived sensation—a *feeling*. Whether the sensation is interpreted as pain, and if so, how severe that pain is judged to be, depends on the bodymind doing the perceiving. Examples 1 through 4 demonstrate that you are *not* just a helpless victim of pain, and at its mercy. Nor are you dependent on professionals with the power to prescribe and administer medicines for pain. On the contrary. You are fully capable of taking at least the following steps in response to unpleasant sensations, major or minor.

1. Releasing into your own bloodstream chemicals produced *by* your bodymind, called *endorphins* or *enkephalins*, that relieve pain just as effectively as morphine or aspirin or any other "external" medication—and that require no prescription or permission from anyone.

2. Reinterpreting the sensation as something *other than* pain—as heat, for example, or numbness, or heaviness.

3. Drastically reducing your perception of how bad your pain is and how long it lasts—for example, by reacting to it calmly instead of with the panic that feeds pain and makes it worse.

Pain's major weapon against you is fear. Fear of the unknown. Fear of the mystery that strikes from out of nowhere, cannot be escaped, and destroys the ability to deal with the world normally. The first step toward replacing that fear with confidence is to learn more about it, so that it stops being an unknown.

What *is* "real" pain? There's only one useful answer: REAL PAIN— SERIOUS PAIN—IS WHATEVER THOSE WORDS MEAN TO *YOU PER-SONALLY*. Knowing that the woman next door had a ten-pound baby without so much as an aspirin or that the man across the street had his gall bladder removed with only hypnosis for anesthesia is no help to you. Unless you are a professional athlete or soldier, the fact that athletes and soldiers often handle awe-inspiring amounts of pain with ease may be inspirational, but it's not useful. There is no scientific instrument that will measure pain, no "dolorimeter" against which your personal discomfort can be checked to see if it qualifies for some abstract number on an Agony Scale. Some cultures consider things painful that other cultures don't consider worth noticing, and vice versa. Doctors and nurses are frequently reminded in their professional literature that pain is exactly what a patient says it is and exactly as *bad* as the patient says it is, and that they must take the patient's word for it—they can't send a blood sample down to the lab and ask for a test to verify what the patient is saying about pain.

Experiments with pain in human beings have proved that by and large the *threshold* for pain—the point at which people notice that something hurts—is the same for everyone. The same amount of heat or cold or pressure will cause all the experimental subjects to say "That hurts." Where people differ drastically is in their pain *tolerance*. That is, in how long, after they have noticed the sensation of pain, they are able to bear it, how much pain medication they have to have in order to supress it, and how they cope with it overall. A pain that sends one person to an emergency room may not even keep another person home from work. This is a very personal matter. PAIN TOLERANCE IS NOT A CONTEST.

You need to know, therefore, what *you* mean by "real" pain. Never mind what someone else means by it. What—for you personally—is real pain? You can't begin to deal with it effectively if you don't know what it is. The two language techniques that follow will work together to help you investigate the semantics of pain in your own mental dictionary and begin putting that information to use.

TECHNIQUE #8—DEFINING PAIN WITH SEMANTIC FEATURES

Linguists use a device called *the semantic feature*. These features are units of meaning used to construct definitions, usually with a value of plus or minus. You can define a bird, for example, as [+FEATHERED]; since no other living creature has feathers, that one feature will do it. All birds have two legs, but [+TWO-LEGGED] is not an important part of the definition; people also have two legs, but they are not birds. The feature [+WINGED] is not as reliable as you might expect. Not only are there wingless birds, there are creatures—bats and sting rays, for instance—that look very [+WINGED] indeed.

Students in linguistics are given a simple example like "bird" to make the concept clear, and then are shown a chart called a "feature matrix," like the one below.

SEMANTIC FEATURE MATRIX A

	BIRD	FISH
[FEATHERED]	+	−

This diagram says we can tell whether we have a bird or a fish by checking for feathers—birds have them, fishes don't. Adding a few more animals across the top requires more features, but still looks pretty easy. For example:

SEMANTIC FEATURE MATRIX B

	BIRD	FISH	COW	KANGAROO
[FEATHERED]	+	−	−	−
[TWO-LEGGED]	+	−	−	−
[POUCHED]	−	−	−	+
[HORNED]	−	−	+	−

Once lulled into tranquility by a simple matrix, students are given an assignment something like this: "Prepare a semantic feature matrix for the words "bun, biscuit, muffin, roll, doughnut, bagel." At which point tranquility disappears. Every English-speaking child has gone through the experience of saying, "May I please have another bun?" and hearing, "Sure—but it's not a bun, it's a roll." And "May I please have another muffin?" "Sure. But that's a biscuit." It's clear to the child that there *is a way* to tell them apart, but even the adults have a hard time explaining what it is.

Let's use this technique to begin the investigation of what "real pain" means to you. Write down (or record on tape) the semantic features that define pain in your personal dictionary, and give them their plus or minus values. Figure 5–1 below lists a variety of possible choices to get you started—but don't let them limit you. The features that matter most to you may not be there. And don't worry if your definition differs radically from what you'd find in a traditional dictionary. If pain, for you, has wings and horns and whistles, go right ahead and put those features down.

FIGURE 5–1
DESCRIPTIVE TERMS FOR PAIN

burning	cold, icy
dull	sharp
aching	shooting
stabbing	nagging
agonizing	excruciating
throbbing	stinging
nauseating	pounding
heavy	grinding
crushing	tearing
searing	cutting
endless	sudden
itching	tingling
bearable	unbearable
like a knife	like a fist
like a tight band	like a rock
like an electric shock	like fire

You may find it helpful to use a feature matrix containing additional pain words from your vocabulary. For example, how do you tell an ache and a pain apart? What's the difference, for you, between pain and agony? What factor makes you consider a particular sensation so unpleasant that something has to be done about it, while another is something you just put up with—and what are the labels you attach in each case? Don't settle for "a pain is worse than an ache and agony is worse than a pain." That tells you how you feel about the words, but it doesn't tell you what they mean.

You may want to use a simpler matrix with only "minor discomfort" and "real pain" at the top. Or you may want to expand your matrix to contrast pain words with other trouble words, like "taxes" and "flat tires" and "final exams" and "late airplanes." Use the language tools that work for *you*.

REALITY STATEMENTS

Any semantic feature can also be expressed as a *reality statement*. For example, the feature [+FEATHERED] for birds can be expressed as "Birds have feathers." Making a list of reality statements about the word you're trying to define will help you locate the gaps in your matrix. It will point to features you missed because you just didn't think of them. It will point to features that are missing because your language has no word or short phrase for them—as when you have the reality statement "Rain always falls *after* you wash the car" but English has no name for this curious chunk of meaning. (If you come across one of those in your definition, just call it [+X] and make a note to remind you which reality statement it refers to.) Expanding the features you choose *into* reality statements is also useful, because it will help you find those that aren't really part of your personal definition or are otherwise flawed. Working in both directions this way is much faster than staring at a blank page and hoping for inspiration.

Two important tips:

1. No feature more than about three words long will be useful.
2. There is no "right" answer that you should be trying to find. You're looking for your *personal* answer.

Practice Technique #8A

Another way to hunt for meaning is to construct partial reality statements about pain and then finish them. But you don't want just any kind of statement—you don't want an open-ended one like "Pain is a _____." You've already worked with those. You want a partial sentence in which enough information is included to provide some limits to the possible ways it could be completed. For example, "When I was seven years old, my teacher _____," restricts the possible endings for the sentence to things that were true of you at the age of seven, and that involved your teacher at that time. "While I was learning to drive, I often _____," again specifies the time and the place and reduces the set of possible endings to items true of just those occasions when you were learning to drive, and just those items that happened frequently in that situation.

Here are a dozen suggested statements for you to work with. They will help you fill holes that remain in the information about what pain means to you. Feel free to construct more such statements and add them to the set. Again, there are no "right answers."

1. "When I am feeling real pain, I'm not able to _____."
2. "The thing that scares me most about real pain is _____."
3. "If I suddenly felt real pain while I was giving a speech at a national meeting, I would _____"
4. "My mother always said that when you feel real pain, you should ____."

5. "If George Washington had felt real pain during his inauguration, he would have _____."

6. "The reason small yellow pills work better for pain than middle-sized blue ones is _____."

7. "I would absolutely refuse to admit that I was feeling real pain if_____."

8. "It's okay to scream with pain when you are _____, but not when you are _____."

9. "Until real pain stops, you have to _____."

10. "If I knew I was going to feel real pain at three o'clock this afternoon, I wouldn't _____."

11. "Nobody who is feeling real pain is able to _____."

12. "Until I had my first experience of real pain, I always believed that __."

NOTE: The harder it is for you to complete one of these, the more likely it is that the information it would give you is important for you to have.

Finally: if you get stuck, don't struggle. Stop, and go on to the next technique. It will give you additional information that you need, and then you can come back and finish your definition.

TECHNIQUE #9—FINDING YOUR PERSONAL PAIN METAPHORS.

Metaphors use language patterns to say that two things—often two very different things—share certain semantic features. Consider the metaphor "Life is a bowl of cherries." Logically, that's nonsense—life is no such thing! Why, then, does that *mean* something? Because when you apply Miller's Law to a metaphor that works, you immediately know the answer to this question: "What semantic feature or features do these two things have in common?"

That is: you assume that "Life is a bowl of cherries" is true and you ask yourself what it would be true *of.* You know at once that it would be true of a life that, like a bowl of cherries, is *sweet.* You understand, by the process of metaphor, that both life and a bowl of cherries have the semantic feature [+SWEET]. If your response to the metaphor is, "Well, *my* life isn't!", you're not saying that your life isn't a bowl of cherries because it isn't [+EDIBLE] the way cherries are. You're saying you don't feel that your own life can be described with the feature [+SWEET].

Metaphors that have been used a lot lose their freshness and become clichés. Often they become so familiar that they disappear into the language and we forget that they ever *were* metaphors. There was a time when the idea that "those pieces of wood supporting the table at each corner are *legs*" was new and novel. People heard it and understood that it wasn't intended to mean the pieces of wood had knees or ankles, or would ever walk down to the river. The features shared were understood to be something like [+THIN], [+RIGID], [+ELONGATED], [+SUPPORT]. Today we talk about the legs of tables, desks, chairs, pianos, etc., with no awareness that a metaphor is involved. Only very small children find this process confusing and wonder where the gun is when their father says "You really shot me down that time!"

Metaphors that are less deeply embedded in our language but are no longer perceived as "figures of speech" can be dangerous, especially when they are *unifying* metaphors that add extra context to the situation. The language of violence commonly used to discuss cancer and AIDS, for example, is dangerous because it brings with it the context of death and destruction. When we talk of cancer and AIDS "victims" instead of calling them patients, the word "victim" is not like the word "leg" in "table leg." Talking of furniture legs doesn't add a context in which people expect to hear of table ears and table lungs and table gall bladders. But "victim" still carries metaphorical extra baggage—it marks the patient as someone who has been violently attacked and has *lost*. That's dangerous. We find this everywhere in our mass media, and it inevitably becomes part of our thinking and our expression of our thoughts in language.

Family Circle—a magazine with an enormous circulation, available for about a dollar in every grocery store—had this advice on page 6 of its February 2, 1988 issue: "Think of your immune system as an army constantly on the move, searching for enemy invaders in your bloodstream." *Smithsonian Magazine* for June 1989 ("A molecular code links emotions, mind and health," by Stephen S. Hall, pages 62–71, on page 69) informs us that we can "generate up to one billion different antibody molecules to attack foreign invaders." Philosopher Susan Sontag recently wrote an entire book on the hazards of this Battlespeak habit our culture has fallen into.

But you are under no obligation to accept the metaphor being urged upon you, the one that would have you thinking "My body is a military base on constant Red Alert" and shaping your language in those terms. You are fully equipped to provide yourself with other less toxic metaphors for your use instead.

To construct a metaphor, you begin by identifying the features that define one item—in this case, the features that define "real" pain for you—and then you look for something else that shares one or more of those features. Suppose you have defined real pain as having at least the semantic features [+FIERCE], [+DANGEROUS], [+BAD], [+LOUD],

[+POWERFUL], [+LARGE], [+DESTRUCTIVE]. What *else* has those features, or some subset of those features, in your personal dictionary? A volcano? A tornado? A dragon? A raging fire? A grizzly bear? If you have trouble deciding, set up a reality statement using another kind of metaphor (called a *simile*) with the pattern "X is *like* Y," as in this example:

Real pain is like a(n) _____, because both are fierce, dangerous, bad, loud, powerful, large, and destructive.

Finally, use your answer to complete the sentence below (and similar sentences for any other pain terms you use regularly, such as "ache, torment, misery," etc.) and apply Miller's law to the result.

Real pain is a(n) _____.

Let's assume that you have now decided on the personal metaphor "*Real* pain is an earthquake." If that's true for you, what could it be true *of*? One good answer is that it would be true of a reality in which pain, like earthquakes, is *unpredictable*. A world in which pain can strike at any time, without warning. That chunk of information will let you go back and add [+UNPREDICTABLE]—a feature you hadn't realized was part of your definition—to your matrix defining pain. This is one of the most useful effects of making your mental dictionary more directly accessible. When it brings to the surface personal beliefs you haven't been consciously aware of before, it often clears up mysteries for you. In this example of your definition of pain, it would go a considerable distance toward clarifying the reactions you have to various unpleasant sensations, both for you and for others.

For example, people for whom "real pain" is defined, like an earthquake, as [+UNPREDICTABLE] won't consider the sensation caused by getting a shot or having blood drawn for testing to be pain—because they always know that it's going to happen and they can refuse to permit it if they prefer. They may not like it much, but they would say "It's no big deal." Such people are also likely to perceive those who are seriously distressed by a simple prick of a needle as sissies and weaklings.

That's a moral judgment, and it's one they don't have adequate information to make. All we can know with certainty is that for such people the metaphor "Pain is an earthquake" isn't accurate, and that the feature [+UNPREDICTABLE] doesn't have the importance in defining pain for them that it has for you. My older daughter, whose only experience of real pain has been the pain of childbirth, tells me she could not possibly compare pain to an earthquake; for her, real pain is associated with powerful *waves* that are very predictable indeed. She does not consider a needle stick to be pain, either, but for quite different reasons.

Once you have identified your own pain metaphors, they'll be available to you for classifying distress that you feel thereafter. What is that sensation behind your right eye? Between your shoulder blades? In your left wrist? Does it fit your metaphor or not? You want to be able to use sentences like "This unpleasant sensation I'm feeling right now isn't an earthquake, it's a ride on a bumpy road" or "This unpleasant sensation I'm feeling right now isn't a raging fire, it's a candle flame" or "This strange feeling in my stomach isn't like a dragon, it's more like a large lizard."

If you should ever find yourself thinking, "This unpleasant sensation I'm feeling right now is not an earthquake—it's the end of the *world*!", you will realize that this is a new experience for you, on a scale that is unfamiliar to you. You can then say to a doctor in an emergency room, "This pain is different from any pain I've ever had before, and it's *worse* than any pain I've ever had before," and that will be valuable information for the doctor who is treating you. It is in fact one of the set of statements that doctors (many of whom, unfortunately, have never felt acute pain) listen for and consider significant.

PUTTING IT ALL TOGETHER

The techniques and activities described in this chapter are neither frivolous nor trivial. They aren't evidence of weakness or hypochondria or "being neurotic." They all work together to build in you a confident knowledge that (a) you are not helpless in the face of pain, and (b) you are not dependent on doctors or other health care professionals to manage your pain for you.

Certainly there is an extraordinary kind of pain for which you *must* have expert help—the acute agonizing pain that goes with catastrophes and comes along only once or perhaps twice in most lifetimes. If you encounter that kind of pain you will know you need help, and so will everyone around you. There won't be any question about it. But ordinary, run-of-the-mill pain, although equally real, is different. It's something you can define, investigate, modify, translate into metaphors, draw pictures of, write about.

Don't let the television commercials in which people talk of "When my arthritis pain acts up..." distract you. They should be saying "When I decide to pay attention to my arthritis pain..." instead. Pain is something to which you assign the role of OBJECT. Something you do things to, not something that "acts up" on its own or does things to *you*. The concept of pain as DOER is useful to the American economy, for those who sell pain remedies and those who make their living hammering the idea into our consciousness through advertising. It is not useful to people who must decide what they will or will not do about unpleasant sensations.

Once you have a sense of control over pain—a sense that does not require a prescription or permission from anyone else—two things become possible for you.

> *First:* You will not react to pain automatically with the tense muscles, rapid heartbeat, erratic breathing, and other physical changes that always make it worse. You will not react to pain with *automatic* fear or panic.

> *Second:* When you recognize pain you will be prepared to use one or more of a variety of methods that stimulate your brain to generate your body's natural painkillers—such as "visualization," relaxation techniques, meditation or prayer, exercise, music and art and dance, etc. Some of these methods are discussed in this book; others are discussed in books and materials listed in the references and bibliography.

You may lack confidence in the various endorphin-generating techniques because you've tried one and it didn't work for you. That's a misunderstanding. If your Real-Symptom Filter is trout fishing, you don't give it up because your spouse tried trout fishing and felt worse rather than better. Nor do you decide that the concept of a symptom filter is meaningless because what works for you doesn't work for your spouse. In the same way, if you've tried long-distance running and meditation and neither one had the slightest effect on your pain, that's unlikely to mean that you are one of the very rare individuals who doesn't produce endorphins. You may have been so frightened by your pain that your fear short-circuited your production of endorphins. You may be someone who responds with endorphins to laughter, rather than to exercise or meditation. This is a *personal* matter, requiring custom tailoring to your own needs. Your best move is to investigate further, until you find something you can rely upon to be helpful to you.

It's entirely reasonable for you to ask, in this case, "Why language? Why not just take something, instead of going to all this trouble?" And certainly, if you need a medication, you *should* take it, whether it's something your life depends upon, like insulin, or something your *quality* of life depends upon, like a painkiller. But in spite of the advertising you see and hear all around you, most of the time medicines should be your last resort rather than your first. Because—

> ☐ The less of a medicine you take, the less you will need of it when you really *must* take it.

- [ ] You risk developing allergies to any medicine, and the more you take the higher the risk.

- [ ] You face the problem of interactions not only between one medication and another but also between your medication and such things as the food you eat and the beverages you drink.

- [ ] Every medication involves some expense for you; and all but the over-the-counter ones force you to become involved with our health care system and all its hazards.

When your problem is not severe pain but just discomfort or an unpleasant sensation, you're far better off with language.

You are innately equipped with both the mechanism of pain—without which you could not survive, because you would have no way of knowing when you were in danger—and the mechanism of endorphins produced by your own bodymind to help you deal with that pain. That's a double miracle, and you are entitled to the benefits of both its parts.

WORKOUT SECTION

1. In *Psychology Today* for January 2, 1989 ("The sources of Cooperation," page 72), Wray Herbert reported briefly on the problem of figuring out why some people are cooperative and others aren't. Some recent studies, he said, seem to show that "cooperative people tend in their minds, to evaluate cooperation as good and competition as bad—they see it as a moral issue—whereas uncooperative people see it as a matter of weakness or strength."

This is a good example of a reality gap that can lead to serious misunderstandings. If a group of people all working together in a single project includes three who define cooperation as plus or minus [GOOD] and three who define it as plus or minus [STRONG], the fact that all six are trying to give their best performance may still not be enough to let them work as a team. What about you? In your own mental dictionary, is a person who cooperates with others [+GOOD] or [+STRONG]? Is a person who refuses (or fails) to cooperate [−GOOD] or [−STRONG]? Or do you need different features altogether? If the people you work with can be persuaded to do this exercise too, and then let you compare all the results, you'll gain much useful information for your future reference.)

2. In theoretical terms, it makes absolutely no difference whether you use the feature [GOOD] and mark things you disapprove of as [−GOOD], or you use the feature [BAD] and mark things you feel positively as [−BAD]. This is true for any feature that represents a pair of opposites, like good/bad, large/small, hot/cold, male/female, strong/weak. Logically, either one, marked plus or minus, will do for both. Do you think it makes any difference in practical terms, however? Suppose

you were going to publish a dictionary that defined words by semantic features rather than the way traditional dictionaries do—would you have any objection to defining "man" (and "boy" and "bull" and "stallion" and "ram", etc.) with [−FEMALE]? Why?

3. Read the book by Joan Borysenko called *Minding the Body, Mending the Mind* (Addison-Wesley 1987.) It is one of the finest sources of useful and practical information about body/mind interaction and health for the general reader.

4. One of the techniques for dealing with tension caused by unpleasant sensations that Borysenko and many others recommend is the simple act of *abdominal breathing*. You have a readily available "biofeedback" mechanism available to you for learning how to do this and monitoring your performance: the palm of your hand, and your sense of touch. Like this:

> Put the palm of either hand flat against your abdomen, and keep it there. Take a deep breath, pushing out against your palm with your abdominal muscles. Feel your hand move out as you breath in? Now breath out, still keeping your palm flat against your body...feel your hand move in. Repeat. The report from your palm is your biofeedback monitor.

This is an extreme effective way to relax and to ease pain. Once you learn to do it without the monitoring palm, it's something you can do anywhere, anytime, even in the most public situations. (Oddly, many people tell me they would rather *hurt* than be seen by others "with my stomach sticking out."!) What are the implications with regard to the incessant military instruction to "suck in your gut and stick out your chest"?

5. Another way to deal with pain is to keep the tips of your thumbs gently touching the tips of your index fingers. If your attention drifts even for a moment from this task, the thumb and index finger will separate. Think about it...can you use this as a sort of "Real-Pain Filter?"

6. "Children with Asthma Breathing Easier," (by June Groden, Ph.D., in *Mind-Body-Health Digest* 3:1, 1989, page 3) describes the work of Dr. Daniel P. Kohen, who works with asthmatic children. He shows them a picture of their bronchial system, and makes sure they understand how it works. He leads them through relaxation exercises. And he suggests specific images for them to concentrate on. For example: "Imagine riding a tiny motorboat through the body. You can go over to the breathing tubes and vacuum up all the mucus." Would this metaphor be useful for adults as well? For adults of either gender? Does it need changes? Does it make any difference whether you know what the "tiny motorboat" represents or how the "breathing tubes" look and function? (Dr. Kohen obviously knows the importance of language in health care; he doesn't allow anyone around him to speak of asthma "attacks." Instead, they must use words like "episode" or "event.")

7. For two brief, clear nontechnical summaries on the body's natural painkillers, read these articles: "Anatomy of a Scientific Discovery," by Jeff Goldberg, in *Science Illustrated* for January/February 1989, pp. 5–12; and "A Pleasur-

able Chemistry," by Janet L. Hopson, in *Psychology Today* for July/August 1988, pp. 29–33.

8. The Hopson article just mentioned contains this statement, prominently featured on page 29: "Endorphins, the body's natural narcotics, aren't something we have to run after. They're everywhere." What are the implications of using the word "narcotics" as a name for the endophins? It's correct, in medical and scientific terms, but what kind of semantic freight does "narcotics" carry with it today? What are the semantic features most people attach to that word? Can you make any predictions about effects it might have on a conservative elderly patient's motivation to use exercise or as a way to diminish pain? What if a phsysiotherapist appeared in the patient's room and announced cheerily, "Well, today we're going to learn a new way you can produce your body's natural narcotics!"?

9. Your mother may have told you, when you were small, that you would feel a lot better if you'd keep a smile on your face. For most people, she's correct. A number of researchers, including body language expert Paul Ekman, have found evidence that facial expressions cause many people to feel the emotions associated with them. You can try a quick informal experiment for yourself, following these steps:

    a. Think of something that you personally consider very sad...something worth grieving over...something that happened to you personally or that (like the famines in Africa) you have seen on television in graphic clarity.

    b. Hold that thought.

    c. Now, holding it, smile. Smile your best and brightest smile.

    d. Hold that expression.

What happens? Can you do it? Try it the other way around. Think of something that makes you extremely happy, and then put on your saddest expression.

What does all this tell you about people who are determined to "keep a stiff upper lip" when in pain?

11. Borysenko uses the excellent word "awfulizing" to describe what people do when they take an event and imagine the worst possible conclusion that might result from it, playing it over and over in their minds—when a member of their family is late getting home, for example, and they "awfulize" until they have erected in their minds a detailed image of a horrible automobile accident, with all the associated carnage. Coin a word that will express the *opposite* of awfulizing.

12. One of Ronald Reagan's favorite anecdotes was about the boy who, facing a room full of manure, would say, briskly and cheerfully, "There's got to be a pony in there somewhere!" Once we know that anecdote, we can use it in metaphors—we can say things like "Jack is a real Pony-Finder!" and "One thing about Frank—he's sure no Pony-Finder!" Why do you suppose Mr. Reagan couldn't have managed with the metaphor of Pollyanna, who would have reacted to the room full

of manure in exactly the same way his brisk and cheerful boy did? Can you take your personal metaphor for pain and work it into a story in this way?

SIGHT BITES

1. "As Pert later put it, 'God presumably did not put an opiate receptor in our brains so that we could eventually discover how to get high with opium.'"

    (Stephen S. Hall, writing on Candace Pert and others, "A molecular code links emotions, mind and health," in *Smithsonian Magazine* for June 1989, pages 62–71, on page 67.)

2. "Comic Relief: 'Let's draw your blood.' Comment by a Bozo lookalike as he offered a crayon and sketch pad to a pediatric patient at New York's Columbia-Presbyterian Medical Center."

    (From a brief note about the "Clown Care Unit" of the Big Apple Circus and its visits to hospitalized children, on page 60 of *Medical World News* for February 27, 1989.)

3. "Diseases whose cures have been found become just diseases; those we do not yet understand become metaphorical carriers of fear and loathing."

    (Michael Ignatieff, "Modern Dying: The soul returns to the sickbed," in *The New Republic* for December 26, 1988; on page 30.)

6

KEEP THE HOME FIRES BURNING

INTRODUCTION—THE HOME AS TOXIC WASTE DUMP

> Publicly, at least, we think of the family as a loving, tranquil, peaceful social institution to which one flees *from* stress and danger....Privately, the family is perhaps society's most violent institution. Except the military, and then only in time of war.
>
> (Richard Gelles, quoted in "The Puzzle of Child Abuse," by Ann Finkbeiner, *Science Illustrated* for June/July 1987, pp. 14–19.)

That's a chilling quote, I know. And absolutely acccurate. People with sentimental natures like to remind us that Robert Frost defined home as the place where, if you go there, they have to take you in. But Frost, who was not always kind to his family, wasn't being sentimental. Home, he knew, is the place where, if you go there, they have to take you in no matter how cruel you are, no matter how great a torment it is to live with you. You can't hit another person with your fist in a restaurant and get away with it; you can't shove somebody down the stairs in an office and get away with it. You can do those things and far worse in your home and often you will get away with it for many years—you may in fact never pay any penalty for it except that of having to look at yourself in the mirror every morning.

The article from which I quoted focuses on physical abuse and physical neglect in the home, which is epidemic in the United States today. My focus in this chapter will instead be on verbal abuse in all its forms; on the words which the National Council for the Prevention of Child Abuse rightly says "can hit as hard as a fist."

When I was a child and had punishment coming, I would plead for a spanking, because that was quick and when it was over it was over. What I

99

dreaded was being lectured and berated, and I feared punishing words far more than punishing hands or implements. As an adult I am still inclined to think that a lifetime under the lash of cruel words is as bad as one spent under any physical lash. But it doesn't really matter whether I'm right about that or not, because the question is irrelevant to the larger problem. The simple truth is that the roots of physical violence are in verbal violence, and if we are ever to get the epidemic of violence in America under control, we have to start with verbal violence. By the time someone feels free to *hit*, it's too late. You can lock such people up to protect others from them, at a terrible cost to society, but only very rarely can you make them less violent.

Children, we know from much careful research, are naturally caring and compassionate. The stereotype of the wicked selfish infant savage that must be tamed is totally wrong. If a child begins to cry in a room full of children, infants just able to crawl will go at once and try to offer comfort, and if they can't help they will join in and cry too, in sympathetic distress. Only children who come from abusive homes behave differently—such children will go to the crying child and *hit* it to stop its noise, and they will do that when they are as young as nine months old. Children are not naturally cruel. They have to be *trained* to be violent. But they learn quickly, and they learn in the home, figuring out the rules for human conduct from the data provided to them as a model by others.

In this chapter we will not be concerned with crude open insults and curses and epithets of the "You jerk!" and "You bitch!" and "I'm going to break your head, you little brat!" variety. That sort of thing is not verbal violence, but the stream of sound that goes with *physical* violence. Physical abusers who for one reason or another feel they cannot hit in a given situation will substitute that kind of language for the hitting, and they will use that kind of language when they *do* hit. It is properly part of the pattern of *physical* abuse. Instead, we are going to return to the verbal attack patterns of English. They are the vehicle for such large amounts of verbal violence that just eliminating *them* from the language environment in your home is like getting rid of two-thirds of the toxic substances in a contaminated landfill. Furthermore, it's like getting rid of those specific toxic wastes that are the breeding ground for all the others, because so many scenes that escalate to the shouting and physically violent stage begin with the VAPs.

You already know how to recognize VAPs—by the presence of their unusual melody of numerous strong stresses on words or parts of words—and you have learned one all-purpose emergency response to them. You recognize them easily because they are as much a part of your internal grammar as the rules you use for forming questions or putting plural endings on nouns. Now we are going to move on to the technique of responding to VAPs with *skill*, in ways that are useful for chronic as well as emergency situations.

TECHNIQUE #10—MANAGING THE VERBAL ATTACK PATTERNS OF ENGLISH...RESPONDING TO THEM AND GETTING RID OF THEM

The English VAPs ordinarily contain two parts: the open and obvious attack that I call "the bait," which is the part intended to get the hearer's attention and cause the hearer pain; and one or more far less obvious attacks hidden away inside *presuppositions*. A presupposition is anything that native speakers of a language know is part of the meaning of a sequence of words even when it it isn't present on the surface. For example: if I say to you, "I'm so glad you've stopped worrying," that sentence *presupposes* another sentence that isn't present on the surface—the sentence "You started worrying." If I tell you I'm glad you "managed" to get to work on time, it presupposes that you had difficulty doing that, even though I don't say openly "You had trouble getting to work on time." In some VAPs the bait and the presupposed attacks are clearly separated; in others they are mingled in complicated ways. We'll start with one that has the clear separation.

ATTACK PATTERN #1

"If you REALLY cared about your family, YOU wouldn't waste MONey like you do!"

BAIT: "You waste money."

PRESUPPOSED: "You don't really care about your family."

That is, the words "YOU wouldn't waste MONey like you do" contain the open insult and are the bait. And every fluent speaker of English knows that the words "If you REALLY cared about your family" carry the message that "you don't really care about your family."

There are a number of variations on this basic attack. For example:

VERBAL ATTACK PATTERN #1-A

"A person who REALLY cared about his/her children wouldn't neGLECT them!"

Pattern #1–A has been shifted into Computer Mode. But when it's addressed to you, you know perfectly well that it's only a camouflaged version of #1.

Then there are variations in wording alone, like these—

"If you really CARED about your children, YOU wouldn't neGLECT them!"

(The strong stress has shifted from "really" to "cared.")

"If you [truly/actually/genuinely] CARED about your children, YOU wouldn't neGLECT them!"

(Other words similar in meaning to "really" have been used.)

Finally, because mainstream English requires a form of "be" in sentences without verbs, we have examples like these—

"If you were my REAL father, YOU wouldn't neGLECT me!"

"If you were a REAL woman, YOU wouldn't neGLECT us!"

Children learn this pattern very early. A child of three knows how to say "If you REALLY loved mè, YOU'D buy me a comPUTer like all the OTHER kids have got!" Here the bait is "All the other kids except me have a computer" and the presupposed attack is "You don't really love me." Don't let the fact that the bait in this case seems so trivial distract you—this child is *attacking*. And what happens next is critically important. Here's what the child has planned.

CHILD: "If you REALLY loved me, YOU'D buy me a comPUTer like all the OTHER kids have got!"

ADULT: "Oh come on—Tommy doesn't have a computer."

CHILD: "Yes, he does, TOO—UP in his ROOM."

ADULT: "Well, if he does, he only just got it. And I know Mary Ellen doesn't have one."

CHILD: "She DOES! I SAW it!"

ADULT: "Don't *lie* to me."

CHILD: "I'm not LYing! I SAW it! YOU just don't KNOW anything, THAT'S all! She does TOO have one!"

ADULT: "All right, that's *enough!* You go to your ROOM, young man, and you STAY there until you're ready to behave like a decent PERSon!"

CHILD: (Runs from the room, crying.)

A standard analysis of this interaction would be that the child started out being annoying, progressed from annoying to downright rude and insolent, and got exactly what he deserved—that is, the parent was the winner. (The structure of the VAP action chain always demands that there be a winner and a loser.) That standard analysis would be wrong. What really happened is this:

1. The child wanted the parent's total attention for at least five or six minutes—and got it.

3. The child wanted to provoke the parent into an emotional response—and succeeded in doing so.

3. The child's presupposed attack—"You don't really love me"—not only was not attended to, it wasn't even heard. It therefore stands as true by default.

4. The child has learned that this technique *works,* even on supposedly intelligent and sophisticated adults.

What really happened here is that in the struggle between child and adult, the adult was soundly defeated—and the child was given another lesson in being a skilled verbal abuser. The punishment received is only additional evidence for the child that this language behavior is an effective way to "get to" the parent and demonstrate power over the parent. When this kind of thing happens over and over again between parent and child, and when (as is typical) the child observes similar exchanges between the two parents time and time again, the message received is that this is how you are supposed to deal with disagreements in the real world—no matter how trivial—and it's *okay.*

You would not allow your child or your spouse to pollute your home with rotting food or a can of dioxin. You would consider that a total neglect of basic hygiene and safety; you would consider it very stupid. It is equally stupid, and equally dangerous, to allow your home to fill up with *linguistic* garbage and trash and toxins. That stuff makes people sick and makes them accident-prone, and it needs to be dealt with and gotten rid of just like any other kind of trash.

Here are the rules for responding to the VAPs.

RULE ONE: Ignore the bait.

RULE TWO: Respond directly to a presupposition.

> RULE THREE: No matter what else happens, always transmit the message that VAPs won't work on *you*.

Here's how you would apply those rules in the altercation about who does or doesn't have a computer.

CHILD: "If you REALLY love me, YOU'D buy me a comPUTer like all the OTHER kids have got!"

ADULT: "Of *course* I really love you!"
— or —
"When did you start thinking I don't really love you?"

Both of these responses ignore the nonsense about every child but this child having a computer; both respond directly to the presupposed "You don't really love me" instead. Both serve the primary goal of interrupting the action chain and demonstrating that this tactic won't work on you. And both are obviously preferable to a Boring Baroque Response in this situation. Both acknowledge that the adult has heard the presupposed attack and realizes its importance. The difference between the two is a strategic one: you use the "when" question only if you have time to listen to an answer and are willing to do so.

One of the most important rules of communication, taught to me by rehabilitation counselor Curtis Berry, is "Never ask a question unless you're willing to listen to the answer." (Doctors routinely ignore this rule, and get malpractice suits in return.) If you don't have time to listen to the attacker, or don't have the patience—or if the situation is one in which such a conversation would be inappropriate, like a dinner party with a dozen guests waiting while you talk—use the statement. Say firmly and calmly, "Of *course* I really love you!" and go on to something else.

If you respond with the question, it's important to use "when" instead of some other question word. "When did you start thinking I don't really love you?" presupposes only what the person has just said to you. It's neutral rather than confrontational. The other possibilities—"Why do you think I don't really love you?" and "What makes you think I don't really love you?", for example—carry other messages that only create semantic clutter. A great deal of the time the "when" question will allow you to find out what is *really* going on with your attacker. For example—

HUSBAND: "If you REALLY loved me, YOU wouldn't SMOKE so much!"

WIFE: "When did you start thinking I don't really love you?"

HUSBAND: When you forgot my birthday last week, *that's* when!"

Notice—this attack wasn't about smoking at all. It was about a forgotten birthday. If the wife had taken the bait and gone into a long argument about whether she smokes too much, how much smoking is too much smoking, and whether it's any business of her husband's, she would never have known he was hurt about the forgotten birthday. And he would have had an ugly argument to add to his reasons for being angry and resentful.

Notice also that this pattern is so powerful, so much a part of the grammar of verbal violence, that it has what we might call a "metapresupposition": that whatever comes after "If you REALLY" section is *in itself* negative. It's not surprising to hear that "If you REALLY loved me, YOU wouldn't BE an axe murderer!" is negative and offensive. But consider this sentence: "If you REALLY loved me, YOU wouldn't WANT a Nobel Prize!" (Or "YOU wouldn't SMOKE!") By themselves, "you smoke" or "you want a Nobel Prize" are not insulting; inside this VAP, they become so. That's why such uninformative examples as "If you REALLY loved me, YOU wouldn't DO the things you do!/BE the way you are!" can start arguments. "You do the things you do" and "You are the way you are" turn into bait because they are part of the pattern, not because of logic.

Let's look at one more variation on VAP #1, this time with an elderly parent involved.

VERBAL ATTACK PATTERN #1B

> PARENT: "If you REALLY cared about your family, YOU wouldn't WANT to smoke!"

The addition of the heavily stressed "want" to the pattern adds yet one more chunk of presupposed meaning. It says "People can control their desires by will power alone." And it puts the potential victim in the quandary that therapists call a "double bind." Whether you quit smoking or not, you haven't proved you love your family, because even if you quit you still *want* to smoke. Far too may typical American households handle such interactions like this:

> PARENT: "If you REALLY cared about your family, YOU wouldn't WANT to smoke!"
>
> ADULT CHILD: "Dad, all that stuff about smoking hurting your family is just a lot of propaganda and scare tactics—there's no real evidence for any of it!"
>
> PARENT: "Oh, yeah? What about that study they were talking about on TV last night? The one where—"

ADULT CHILD: "Hey, I don't want to talk about my SMOKing, oKAY? My smoking is MY business, I'm all grown UP now, and I'm tired of HEARing about it!"

PARENT: "That's a fine way to talk to your father."

ADULT CHILD: "I'm sorry, Dad, but you STARTED it!"

PARENT: "*I* STARTED IT? *I* wasn't the one who was smoking at the dinner table!"

(AND SO ON, FAR INTO THE NIGHT.)

There are two ways to respond to this pattern that will avoid such outcomes:

First: You can ignore the part about *wanting* to smoke and treat the attack just like the very first one. Say "Of *course* I care about my family" or "When did you start thinking I don't care about my family?" The question may well provoke "When I saw you smoking at the dinner table" from your parent, but that's still an improvement. It interrupts the action chain, it acknowledges the first presupposed attack, it's not an emotional response, and it ties the discussion down to a specific incident. You would then say, "Oh, I understand," and wait for your father's next move. If he wanted to carry out a verbal attack, he'd have to start over again with a new one.

Second: you can respond with either a "when" question or a statement directed at the new presupposition, like this: "When did you start thinking people can control their desires by will power alone?" (Leveling) or "The idea that people can control their desires by will power alone is an interesting concept" (Computing). Your attacker will still be unable to complete the action chain. He will have to join you in a discussion of the philosophical issue of will power and desire, or start over with a new attack.

All four responses demonstrate that you won't play this stupid game. And they do so without loss of face either for your attacker or for you, which goes a long way toward dispelling the tension in the air. Other people in your home—especially children—will have an opportunity to observe that there are other ways to handle conflict besides arguing. That's taking out the trash. That's cutting off violence at its roots.

People tell me that they have two problems with this technique. One problem they express as "I just couldn't let him/her get away with it!" (Because the bait was so outrageous or so cruel or so wrong or whatever applies.) The other problem is expressed as "I just felt so *guilty!*" We'll come back to the problem of guilt later in the chapter. But let's put that "getting away with it" matter to rest immediately.

Any time you take the bait in a verbal attack and make it possible for the attacker to complete the action chain with its volley of attacks and counterattacks, *that* is letting the attacker get away with it. No matter which of you comes out of the volley as apparent winner, the *real* winner is the attacker. He (or she) has decided to demonstrate that he has the power to tie you up in an emotional interchange for ten minutes or more and to get and hold your full attention for that period of time. And you've gone along with that. She (or he) has decided to prove that she can set up a program for your next quarter of an hour and insert an unpleasant intrusion right into the middle of whatever *you* had planned for yourself. And you've gone along with that, too. It makes no difference whether the attacker ends up in tears or apologizing profusely or out cold on the floor— the victim loses. And let me point out something very important:

YOU CAN ONLY BECOME A VICTIM BY TAKING THE BAIT.

Because the attack fails automatically when you refuse it, there *is* no victim.

Here are some more examples of attack patterns, with suggested responses and comments as needed. All of them will be familiar to you: all of them are verbal toxic waste.

VERBAL ATTACK PATTERN #2

"EVen a WOMan should be able to balance a CHECKbook!"

Here the bait is mingled with the presuppositions. One chunk of bait says "You can't balance a checkbook"; another says, Women are inferior and second-rate." The power of the pattern set up by "EVen a(n) X..." is so great that it's almost impossible to construct a neutral example. Even (there's that word again!) if you leave out the abnormal stresses—for example, "Even a woman knows that going bald is traumatic for a man"— the sentence still has faint negative overtones. This is unusual. For all the other VAPs, there are neutral sentences that contain the same words without the abusive melody. VAP #2 is so powerful that it provides linguists with classic (and bizarre) examples for teaching semantics, like: "EVen an EAGle Scout can tie a KNOT!" or "EVen a FISH can SWIM!"

SUGGESTED RESPONSE:

"The idea that a woman is somehow inferior is something you run into once in a while—but I'm amazed to hear it from *you*."

Above all, don't answer with "I CAN balance my checkbook!" Similarly, don't say, "Listen, there are LOTS of men who can't balance checkbooks! And you're no financial genius yourSELF, buster!" Those are the responses the attacker is after; providing them means you lose, every time.

VERBAL ATTACK PATTERN #3:

"WHY don't you EVer LISTEN to me when I try to talk to you?"

"WHY do you ALways igNORE me when I try to talk to you?"

This pattern, like #1, is one that children learn early. The critical elements are the use of "EVer/ALways" and the very strong stress on "why." "Why"—with no strong emphasis—presupposes "you have a reason and I am asking you to tell me what it is." But "WHY" presupposes "you have a reason, I'm demanding that you tell me what it is, and I'm telling you in advance that it's not good enough." And this one word serves as an excellent explanation for the need to have both italics and capital letters as punctuation showing vocal stress. Look at this set.

(a) "Why did you buy that?"	Neutral question wanting information. May be rude, but no attack.
(b) *"Why* did you buy that?"	Still asking for information, but with the additional message that the questioner is a little surprised by your choice.
(c) "WHY did you buy that?"	Potential attack—even with just the one strong stress. The more the "why" is emphasized, the more hostile the sequence is.
(d) "WHY did you BUY that?"	Overt verbal attack.

There are two basic strategies for responding to the "WHY do you ALways/WHY don't you EVer" pattern, depending on the situation. If your primary purpose in responding is to break your attacker of the habit of using VAPs with you, choose the Boring Baroque Response introduced in Chapter 4. If that's not appropriate, construct a response that makes the "always/ever/never" presupposition false. Let's look at an example of both strategies.

PATIENT: "Why don't you EVer LISTEN to me when I try to TELL you my SYMPtoms?"

BAIT: You never listen to me when I try to tell you my symptoms.

PRESUPPOSED: Your reason for never listening to me when I try to tell you my symptoms is totally unacceptable.

Now suppose you are a doctor who has reached the limit of your tolerance for this patient, a doctor who indeed *does* listen to descriptions of symptoms, and who has decided that it's time to make sure this power play no longer gets the patient the desired attention and investment of time from you. In that case, use the Boring Baroque Response, like this—

DOCTOR: "You know, it's probably because there are so many important and exciting new developments in medicine today....I'm sure my attention *does* wander once in a while. Take the article I read in the *New England Journal of Medicine* yesterday on the new studies they're doing at Bleekmark Medical School on liver diaphoresis. According to the authors, we now know....No, wait a minute. That wasn't in the *New England Journal*, it was in *JAMA*. I know it was, because I loaned my copy of the *New England Journal* to Dr. Wiggins before I'd even read it, and she hasn't given it back yet. Or maybe it was the..." (AND SO INTERMINABLY ON).

Alternatively, suppose this patient is clearly in real distress, is not a chronic complainer, and has surprised you with this attack—suppose you would like to defuse the attack and demonstrate your real concern. In that case, respond to the unlikely presupposition behind "ever/never" and "always" that is folded into the bait: the presupposition that there are NO exceptions to what is being stated. It takes only one exception to make that false, and you can provide it on the spot. Like this—

PATIENT: "WHY don't you EVer LISTEN to me when I try to TELL you my SYMPtoms?"

or

"WHY do you ALways igNORE me when I try to TELL you my SYMPtoms?"

DOCTOR: "Tell me—which symptom is bothering you the most right now...right this minute?"[1]

And then *do* listen, attentively, to the patient's answer. Notice that you haven't said "Tell me *about* the symptom that's bothering you the most right

---

1.Parents can easily adapt this same strategy for complaining children (or other family members.)

now." Doing that would obligate you to listen to the entire description. You have only asked the patient to *identify* the most urgent symptom. When the answer comes back—"It's this terrible pain in my right leg"—you have another pair of choices. If you have time to listen, you say, "I understand. Tell me about it, please," and you give the patient your full attention. If you don't have time, you make immediate arrangements to schedule the discussion for another time, like this—

> "I wish I *could* talk to you about that, but I can't—I've got a patient waiting in the emergency room and I have to leave. But I promise you I will call you tomorrow afternoon before four o'clock and we'll talk about it as long as you like." (Or "I'll come back this afternoon..." if the patient is in the hospital. Or whatever is suitable for the situation.)

Then be sure you follow through on whatever arrangement you make, or you will have lost this patient's trust for good.

The same strategy works in the home. Suppose your spouse comes at you with "WHY don't you EVer do anything to make ME happy?" If this is a constant and chronic and unjust complaint, you may want to use the Boring Baroque Response. If not, make an immediate offer to do something to make your spouse happy, choosing something that (a) you think will be refused, but (b) you're willing and able to fulfill if accepted. You want scenarios like these:

> WIFE: "WHY don't you EVer do ANYthing to make ME happy?"
>
> YOU: "Okay...let's go visit your sister in Newark this weekend."
>
> WIFE: "Good grief! I don't WANT to go to Newark this weekend!"
>
> YOU: "Well, then, you certainly don't have to."

or

> WIFE: "WHY don't you EVer do ANYthing to make ME happy?"
>
> YOU: "Okay...let's go visit your sister in Newark this weekend."
>
> WIFE: "Could we? I'd really like to do that."
>
> YOU: "Sure we can. I'll plan on it."

You can also try offering the famous "illusion of choice." Suppose your teenager wants to watch a movie on tv this afternoon and is attacking you because you've reserved the set for the football game instead, and he has used this VAP to accuse you of never considering what *he* might want to do. Offer him a choice between two things that meet the conditions above, like this—

> "I hear you. Well, after we watch the football game this afternoon, would you rather I dropped you off at the library or at Frank's house?"

Not only are you offering to do *two* things for your youngster that represent attempts to consider his wishes, you are letting him choose which one of them he prefers. This is infinitely better than the usual "Whadda you MEAN, I never consider what you might want? How about YESterday, Mr. Smartalec, when you spent the WHOLE DAY listening to that STEREO of yours and nobody could hear themselves THINK around here? And how about TUESDAY, when...." And so on.

As always, be very careful not to respond with sarcasm, or with anything except your most neutral and courteous manner. And use your common sense. If the attacker is someone whose company you value and the attack is "WHY have you always HATed me?", sailing into a Boring Baroque Response is not self-defense but an overt counterattack. The same thing is true if the attacker is a small child and the attack is the most basic "WHY"-VAP—something like "WHY do you hate me?" without the additional "never/always" presupposition. In such cases you would be wise to fall back on the reliable "when" question. Respond with "When did you start thinking that I hate you?" And listen carefully to what your small attacker says next.

VACUOUS VAPS

Several of the most common VAPs are logically absurd. They shouldn't work on anyone, but they do. For example:

> "YOU'RE not the ONly person who has PROBlems, you know!"

> "SOME kids would run away from HOME if their parents treated them like CATtle!"

These patterns contain empty logical presuppositions like "There exists no person such that that person has no problems" and "There exist some kids such that, if treated like cattle by their parents, they would run away from home." The chances of these statements being false are so nearly zero that they're not worth considering. The best way to deal with such drivel—and with any verbal attack of this kind—is to respond directly to the empty presupposition and agree with it. Just say "You're absolutely right!" and wait for your attacker's next move.

There are of course more Verbal Attack Patterns, although the complete set is probably not larger than twenty-five. But the principles for recognizing them and responding to them will now be clear to you, and you will know them when you hear them—by their distinctive abnormal stress patterns. They are all handled in exactly the same way.

TURNING THE VERBAL ATTACK PATTERNS ON YOURSELF

You can easily make your own life miserable by using VAPs on *yourself.* Other people who want to attack you verbally have only limited access to you, but you are under no such restriction. You can torment yourself incessantly with VAPs that you play over and over in your head like repeating tape loops; the sentences below are typical examples. Notice that the *bait* in a self-VAP is likely to be some real-world fact that you know is true and find difficult to deal with, while the presupposed attack is likely to be false.

a. "If I REALLY were a good parent, I'D be able to HELP this child."

BAIT: I can't help this child.

PRESUPPOSED: I'm not a good parent.

b. "If I REALLY cared about my family, I'D WANT to go back to work."

BAIT: I don't want to go back to work.

PRESUPPOSED: I don't really care about my family.

c. "I'M only HAVING this headache because I HATE parties!"

BAIT: I hate parties.

PRESUPPOSED: I don't have any acceptable reason or excuse for this headache; it's my own fault.

d. EVen *I* ought to be able to stay on a DIet!"

BAIT: I can't stay on a diet.

PRESUPPOSED: I'm stupid and inferior and second-rate.

e. "SOME people would have brains enough to be GRATEful for a good job like mine."

BAIT: I'm not grateful for this good job I have; I don't even like this good job I have.

PRESUPPOSED: People with brains, intelligent people, are grateful for their good jobs; I'm not smart like they are.

f. "EVERYbody KNOWS why I keep having one stupid accident after aNOTHer."

BAIT: I keep having stupid accidents.

PRESUPPOSED: People know I have stupid accidents all the time because there's something really wrong with me, and they all know that it's (X).

Start listening for these in the dialogue you carry on with yourself, and when you spot one, remind yourself not to use it. Say to yourself, firmly, "I don't *say* that to myself. Ever." If that doesn't keep it from popping into your head, write it down or record it on tape, discussing it in complete detail until you understand it better. It's *personal* trash; letting it pile up is bad for your health.

VERBAL VIOLENCE OVERVIEW

CODEPENDENCY—IT TAKES TWO TO TANGO

The term "codependency" is a buzzword these days, and it's used with a variety of meanings. What I mean by the term is that two people must participate in the dependency. People who are addicted to alcohol or other drugs often involve others in their addictions, but they don't *have* to have partners. They can drink or do drugs all by themselves and get the gratification they seek. Verbal abusers don't have that option. What they are after is *attention,* and that can't be found in a bottle or a pill. Their need can only be satisfied by another human being—by someone who will take the bait in their verbal attacks and be their partner in the verbal violence action chains they set up. Someone who will play the role of Victim for them. It is not possible to be a verbal abuser *without* a living human victim.

This makes abusers dependent on their victims, and it makes the victims truly codependents. And that is why the "I couldn't do it because I felt so guilty" objection to the *Gentle Art* system for dealing with VAPs isn't valid. When you start breaking out of the codependency and refusing to play the verbal abuser's game any longer, you can count on protest in the strongest terms. The abuser will be at first astonished, then outraged and then hurt. If the abuser is someone you love, the effort to lay a guilt trip on you may work. What you need to remember is that feeding a dependency is not loving or kind or nice or nurturing. In the same way that handing a drink to an alcoholic is doing that person harm, providing verbal abusers with their linguistic fixes is doing *them* harm.

VICIOUS CYCLES—TRAINING OTHERS TO BE VERBAL ABUSERS AND VICTIMS

When you insist that a child have a vaccination for tetanus or smallpox, you know the shot is going to hurt. The child will beg you not to insist on the shot, and will cry and protest and ask you how you could possibly do such a terrible thing. The child will try very hard to make you feel cruel and heartless and guilty. But you proceed with the vaccination all the same, because the child risks greater suffering if you don't. The situation with regard to verbal violence is exactly the same. Sure, it will make your verbally abusive family member miserable for a while if you withdraw the attention, but the alternative is much worse. Here are the three inconvenient facts that must be faced.

☐ Every time you participate as verbal victim with someone, you are *training* your attacker to be a better abuser and rewarding him or her for abusive behavior.

☐ Every time you participate as verbal victim in your home, you are providing all family members present with a model of what appears to be *your* preferred method for handling verbal disagreements. Your children will model their verbal behavior on yours, and will go on to perpetuate that model for your grandchildren. This becomes a vicious cycle that is carried on generation after generation, destroying the health and the well-being of everyone involved.

☐ As is true for any dependency, the more attention the verbal abuser gets with verbal abuse, the more attention the verbal abuser wants. All that happens when the need for attention is satisfied is that it grows larger.

There's one thing you can do to help, however, that rarely has a corresponding option in other dependencies. You can go out of your way, when the abuser is someone you care about, to provide attention that is *not* the result of verbal abuse.

ONE SMALL STEP—THE CONNECTION BETWEEN VERBAL VIOLENCE AND PHYSICAL VIOLENCE

Earlier in this chapter I said that children have to be *taught* to be cruel. I want to end this section by making that statement as clear as possible. I'm not referring to the kind of training children get in families where they are urged—literally—to do violent things; that's a rare situation and one for the mental health experts. I'm not referring to the training in homes where physical violence is common and children routinely see it happen or are its victims; much as I deplore such situations, they are not my subject here. I'm not even referring to the seeming encouragement for violence that children get when parents take them to wrestling or boxing matches and make a family event out of watching Rambo movies on the VCR. (I don't think that's where the unhealthy habit of violence toward self and others is born, any more than taking children to see Westerns in the past encouraged them to shoot and hang people.)

In my opinion, there are two specific ways we teach our children the habits of toxic language. First: by the models that we provide them; and second, by the open statement that it's okay to cause people pain with words. Most of the time, unfortunately, the adults teaching these lessons are unaware that that's what they're doing.

Adults (and other children) in the home serve as the *models* from whom children learn the use of language. If what the kids see modeled day in and day out is language behavior in which every disagreement, large or small, is dealt with by verbal confrontation, they learn that there is no other way to handle disagreement. If what they see modeled day in and day out is language behavior in which every disagreement must result in a clear winner and a clear loser, they learn that this is important to our culture—and they concentrate on mastering the techniques that make them the winner. If their adult models are not themselves aware that winning an argument in the usual sense is losing the war in every other sense, it's totally unreasonable to expect the kids to understand that. This produces children who have training only in those verbal skills needed for confrontation and abuse. And it is just as true in the home or school where all arguments are "polite" arguments—that is, where no one ever curses or yells or uses open insults—as it is in less elegant situations.

As for the license to do verbal violence, consider these very common scenarios...

CHILD: "Daddy, I was playing with Tommy and now he's crying!"

ADULT: "What did you do to make him cry?"

CHILD: "I didn't do anything! We were just talking and he started crying all of a sudden!"

ADULT: "Did you call him names or something?"

CHILD: "No, we were just *talk*ing!"

ADULT: "Well...don't worry about it, honey. You know how Tommy is. He's always getting his feelings hurt over nothing. He'll get over it."

or

CHILD: "How come Aunt Janet's not eating with us?"

ADULT: "Your Aunt Janet isn't happy with us at the moment."

CHILD: "Why not?"

ADULT: "Oh, I suppose we said something that hurt her feelings....Your Aunt Janet has no sense of humor."

It's a rare television sitcom that lacks at least one scene a month in which some woman reacts to the words of a man by running from the room in tears, whereupon the man looks at the others present and says with varying degrees of disgust or amazement, "WOMen!" And it's a rare home in which children don't hear, over and over again, sentences like the following, all in the context of one individual responding with pain to someone else's words:

"Only an idiot would pay any attention to something like that."

"You're just getting yourself all upset over nothing."

"Hey, if you let every little thing make you cry, nobody's going to want to be around you."

"Only sissies make a big deal out of a little teasing."

"Look, I was only kidding—don't be so touchy! You're acting like some kind of neurotic, you know."

"Nobody meant to hurt your feelings, dear. You've got to learn how to take a joke."

"She only acts like that to get attention—just ignore her and maybe she'll grow up."

These statements, and the thousands of others like them, contain one crystal-clear message:

WHEN PEOPLE ARE HURT BY THE WORDS OF OTHERS, IT'S BECAUSE SOMETHING'S WRONG WITH *THEM*.

Most of the time, these things are said with the best of intentions. We don't want our children to be at the mercy of others' teasing and insults; we know that if they "act like babies/sissies" the other kids will take advantage of that. We're trying to teach them to be invulnerable to such tactics.[2] But instead of teaching children to be invulnerable because their communications skills are so good that they never are *involved* in verbal battles, we teach them that verbal victims are to blame for the pain they feel, and that feeling pain in response to verbal abuse is a sign of incompetence or worse.

The basic skill taught is indifference to other's pain, and the constant note of that background message is inescapable. For many children, it leads only to their carrying on the family tradition of verbal abuse; for others, the callousness is extended to physical abuse. Either way, the lesson we're teaching is this one: PEOPLE WHO GET HURT—NOT PEOPLE WHO DO THE HURTING—HAVE SCREWED UP.

You can change this, and make the quotation that opened this chapter only a memory, by openly teaching your children and any other children you're involved with that they are responsible for their language and its consequences, and by providing them with the *Gentle Art* model for language interactions. There are very few things you can do that will make a greater contribution to their health and well-being, or to your own. This doesn't mean that your children will grow up to be wimps and sissies and doormats. It means that they will grow up to be so highly skilled with language that they will never have any *need* for verbal violence.

WORKOUT SECTION

1. The sentences below are typical examples of VAPs people hear as they navigate the turbulent waters of our health care system. Using the examples in this chapter as a reference, identify the open attack (the bait) and the camouflaged (presupposed) attack or attacks in each one. The first one has been done for you as

---

2. There are schools of therapy that continue this toughening process with adults—Rational Emotive Therapy is perhaps the best known example—labeling a reaction of hurt to another's words "irrational" and making it the victim's responsibility to learn a different sort of reaction.

a demonstration. I recommend reading each VAP aloud, stressing the parts that are in capital letters, before you analyze it.

a. "If you REALLY cared about your health, you'd at least TRY to stop smoking!"

BAIT: You're not even trying to stop smoking.

PRESUP: You don't really care about your health.

b. "EVen someone YOUR age should be able to remember that medications have to be taken every day."

BAIT: _____

PRESUP: _____

c. "EVeryone underSTANDS why you're convinced that the nurses don't LIKE you, you know."

BAIT: _____

PRESUP: _____

d. "A person with seVERE eMOtional problems can't be exPECTED to be reasonable about test results."

BAIT: _____

PRESUP: _____

e. "Some doctors would be extremely anNOYED if a patient ARgued with them constantly the way YOU do."

BAIT: _____

PRESUP: _____

_____

and

There exist some doctors who, if a patient_____

_____

_____

f. "You KNOW I would never give a patient ORders—that's not what nurses are *for*—but I REALLY think YOU take too many VITamins."

BAIT: _____

PRESUP: _____

g. "WHY do you always carry on like a little CHILD when people are doing their best to HELP you???!"

BAIT: _____

_____

PRESUP: _____
_____.

NOTE: In the next three examples, the bait and the presuppositions are mingled in complicated ways; the divisions are approximate.

h. "EVen if you DO refuse to have the surgery you need, *I* won't consider you a coward."

BAIT: _____
_____.

PRESUP: _____
_____.

i. "DON'T you even CARE if your constant smoking is endangering the health of your whole FAMILY?"

BAIT: _____.

PRESUP: _____
_____.

j. "YOU'RE not the ONly patient we HAVE, you know!"

BAIT: _____.

PRESUP: _____.

and

_____.

2. Now, using the examples in the chapter and the rules on pages 103-4, construct a possible *response* to each of the VAPs you analyzed in #1.

3. If you plot the pitches of a musical melody by making dots above and below a base line as the notes rise and fall, and then draw another line connecting all the dots, you have a waveform representing that melody. Scientist Manfred Clynes has spent a lifetime studying the emotions that such musical waveforms evoke in the human brain, and has found reliable correlations between particular waveforms and particular emotions. One generalization that can be made from his work is that the wave patterns for positive emotions follow pleasant curves, while those for negative emotions have angular jags and peaks or nearly flat lines. How can you relate these findings to the facts about the "melodies" in the English VAPs? (Remember that we learn the melodies—the intonation of the patterns—long before we learn to put words to them.)

4. Begin keeping a diary record of the VAPs in your life, with an entry for each day something like this:

DATE AND TIME: _____

PLACE: _____

VAP USED: _____

_____

I WAS THE ATTACKER ☐   THE VICTIM ☐   AN OBSERVER
ONLY ☐

WHAT WAS SAID: _____.

_____

WHAT HAPPENED: _____

_____.

NOTES: _____

_____.

At the end of each week, make a note of the total VAPs for the week, as well as the totals for You As Attacker, You As Victim, and You As Observer. When you've been using the *Gentle Art* techniques for a couple of months, you should see those totals grow steadily smaller.

5. After you have a dozen pages in your diary of verbal confrontations, go back and rewrite them, using the techniques you have learned in this book to reduce the hostility and avoid the row.

6. For practice in using the techniques in this chapter, try some role-playing. You'll need three people. One plays the attacker and says the verbal attack; one plays the victim and says the response. And one plays the observer, watching and listening while the other two talk and then reporting to them afterward on how they did. Rotate the roles so that everyone gets plenty of practice in all three.

SIGHT BITE

1. "a 22-year study...found that young bullies are far more likely than other children to become adult criminals and to have more aggressive children. That's why psychologists are exploring a range of prevention strategies that might break the cycle..."

> (D.R., reporting on the work of psychologist Leonard Eron: "Why Is Everybody Always Picking On Me?," in *New Age Journal* for January/ February 1988, pp.9–10. On page 10.)

7

THROUGH A GLASS DARKLY

INTRODUCTION—IS THERE ANYTHING OUT THERE?

Once upon a time it was taken for granted that there was indeed something "out there." There was a real tree that fell in a real forest and made a real noise, whether any living thing was around to perceive all that or not. Today matters are not so simple. We do have to behave a lot of the time AS IF reality were something independent of perceptions, because we couldn't carry on our daily lives in any other way—but it's becoming difficult to decide what is or is not "real."

Certainly you can't trust the evidence of your senses. Your senses tell you that the floor you stand on is solid and that the ground beneath it is flat and stable and still. But you know that those are illusions. The floor you stand on is composed mostly of "empty" space, inside which particles you cannot see are whizzing about on errands of their own. The ground beneath the floor is in fact part of the curved surface of the enormous sphere that is Planet Earth, which is not only rotating at 1038 miles per hour but moving through space at 66,700 miles per hour. And the planet you stand on is itself part of a solar system circling the Milky Way galaxy at 605,000 miles per hour while roaring out through the universe with hundreds of other galaxies at one *million* miles per hour! Which, then, is "real"? The solid floor through which you cannot shove your fist or your foot? Or the cavernous space through which the particles are flying? The stable flat ground? Or Spaceship Earth, maintaining its position within the multigalactic fleet?

You cannot trust the evidence of your feelings—your internal perceptions—either. Whether you perceive people as good or bad, beautiful or ugly, intelligent or dull, talented or inept, tall or short, fat or thin, rich or poor, friendly or dangerous, depends heavily on such things as what you have been told about them in advance, what is fashionable at the time, whether they are part of your culture and ethnic group, and what power relationships exist between them and you. None of which has anything to do with "reality." Like "real" pain and "real" illness or disability, the specifications depend upon the perceiving individual.

We can't settle this question here. Philosophers have been trying since the beginning of recorded history at least, and they have made very little progress. In this book, then, let's compromise, for the sake of practicality.

Let's agree that although we cannot know what, if anything, is really "out there," what we have to *deal* with in our daily lives is the evidence gathered by our perceptions. We need to keep those perceptions as accurate as possible, by being willing to perceive things with an open mind and being careful to pay things the kind of attention that will yield adequate data.

We need to remember that the evidence of our personal perceptions may be drastically different from the evidence of some other person's, so that when we talk we are not talking about the same "realities" at all. And we have to realize that our bodymind reacts to what it *perceives* as real, whether it is "out there" or not. That's why you don't feel obliged to cling to the nearest tree or pole so you won't fly off the planet as it hurtles through space.

THE SENSORY MODES

The mechanisms we use to process information from both our external and our internal environments are our *sensory systems*—the most familiar of which are our senses of sight, hearing, touch, smell, and taste. We all have one sensory system that we prefer to the others, one with which we know that we can understand and learn and remember more efficiently. Some of us learn best if we can look at printed materials, pictures, charts, maps, and other "visuals." Some of us are less interested in relying on our eyes and prefer to *listen* when we have something new to learn. Still others need "hands-on" contact if they are to process information at their maximum potential. And we express these preferences in our language choices, using what are called *sensory modes*.

Suppose a new service is about to be introduced to the market, and market researchers have described the service to a group of people and asked for their opinions. In such a situation, a typical breakdown by sensory modes would go like this:

> SIGHT: "That looks terrific! The way I see it,
> it's something we really need."

> HEARING: "That sounds great! It sounds like something we really need."
>
> TOUCH: "That feels exactly right to me! You've put your finger on something we really need."

Because we know very little about people whose preferred sensory system is taste or smell, we will focus on the systems of sight and hearing and touch in this discussion. But if such people exist, they would respond to the market researchers with language like that in the examples below. It's a peculiarity of English that plausible sensory statements using smell vocabulary tend to be negative ones. And because these two systems overlap significantly, we often find them mingled in a single statement, as in the final example.

> TASTE: "That absolutely makes my mouth water—what a sweet idea! And it's something we really need."
>
> SMELL: "In my opinion, that idea *stinks*. And we don't really need anything like that."
>
> TASTE-AND-SMELL: "That smells funny to me—it almost turns my stomach. And we don't really need anything like that."

One of the basic *Gentle Art* techniques is that of *matching* sensory modes, which builds trust and rapport between speaker and listener. The doctor who responds to a patient's "How bad does it look?" with "It doesn't look serious" or "I don't see it as anything serious" is matching sensory modes. The teacher who responds to a student's "I don't get it" with "Look, I don't see any reason why you should have trouble with that problem," is *mis*matching sensory modes. In casual conversation people can shift from one mode to the other with ease. But just as with the Satir Modes, people who are tense and under stress tend to become locked into their preferred sensory mode and have difficulty communicating in any of the other modes. Unfortunately, where sensory modes are concerned we don't have an equal opportunity culture; the bias toward sight and hearing is so strong that a preference for touch mode is actually a severe handicap.

Human beings can't change the way they process information from the external and internal environment, because it's part of what *makes* them human beings. We are hardwired in precisely that way. But we can take what we know about the system and use it to our advantage. And we can learn to work around the problems caused by our society's extraordinary reliance on visual information. The technique described below—*percepting*—is one of the most useful ways to put our human information-processing capabilities to work toward improved health and fitness. We'll take up the problems of adapting it for all sensory systems as we go along.

TECHNIQUE #11—PERCEPTING: "VISUALIZATION" AND THE SENSORY MODES

Unless you pay absolutely no attention to the mass media, you are aware that something called "visualization" (or "creative visualization" or "imaging") is getting a lot of attention in the United States today. You will have seen brief medical news stories on television about cancer patients who've gotten significantly better by concentrating daily on mental images—images of their cancer cells being gobbled by giant dragons or attacked by armies of valiant knights. You will have heard that tennis is an "inner game" and that Olympic athletes show dramatically improved performance when they spend time daily going through a *mental* practice session for their upcoming events. You will have seen at least one article or heard at least one news brief suggesting that the newest way to diet is to simply *think* yourself thin. Reports in the media on this imaging process range from the stodgiest and most tentative articles in medical journals to the seminars and writings of the "New Age" celebrities like Shakti Gawain, with an astonishing variety in between.

I'll make no attempt to tell you who *originated* this idea. No one knows. It most assuredly was not anyone recent. Napoleon, for example, is known to have sworn by mental rehearsals for battle. Books and systems for self-improvement based on the technique can be found going back hundreds of years, even if you stay within Western civilization. I am therefore going to begin, arbitrarily, with a Pentice Hall book published in 1960—that's far enough back to serve our purposes and to demonstrate that visualization techniques are not new. And then I'll move on to the practical question of how you yourself can put them to work. If the history of the technique interests you, you will find ample references in the bibliography for exploring that subject.

The book in question is *Psycho-Cybernetics*, written by Maxwell Maltz, M.D. The book sold well, but you usually found it in the same section of bookstores where you found books on astrology and numerology and telling fortunes with cards or tea leaves. Nevertheless, the following sentence from page xii is still an accurate statement of the most important principle of visualization:

Experimental and clinical psychologists have proved beyond a shadow of a doubt that the human nervous system cannot tell the difference between an "actual" experience and an experience *imagined vividly and in detail.*

That is, what your brain does when you vividly *imagine* that your airplane is about to crash is what it would do if the plane's bucks and wobbles were the beginning of a crash instead of the normal result of turbulence. What your brain directs your body to do in response to your sudden conviction that you've heard a prowler downstairs is exactly the same thing it directs your body to do when the prowler is actually there. Vividly imagining that your teenage children are at this very moment being injured and perhaps killed on the highway—because it's three o'clock in the morning and they're not home yet—causes the same set of negative events to take place in your body that you would experience if the phone rang and the highway patrol actually gave you the report you have spent the last two hours dreading.

Going into a surgical operation convinced that you will die, complete with a mental rehearsal of the grief your family will feel and a play-by-play rehearsal of your funeral, gives your body the same "prepare for death" message that a genuine threat of death provides. Lying awake at night imagining the awful things your boss will say to you tomorrow, and the inadequate things you will say back, and what your family will say when you have to come home and tell them you've been fired, starts the same unhealthy series of physical effects in your heart and your stomach that an actual firing would initiate. The more strongly you "just know that X is going to happen," and the more you dwell on that X, the more your bodymind experiences X and responds to it as if it *were* happening.

There are two problems with this information, even for people who have seen the research results and respect the science involved. First, there is the strong tendency to believe that although it may be true for some people, it is not true for you personally. And second, there is the difficulty of accepting the idea that positive results from imaginary events are just as likely as negative ones.

The simplest test I know of your personal ability to "visualize" (and the classic one) is something you can do yourself, immediately, like this:

Imagine that you have a fresh ripe lemon in your hand. See its yellow color. Feel the firm, slightly bumpy sky. Imagine that you are holding it up to your nose and taking a long deep breath...smell that sharp sour smell? Now you are going to bite into that lemon—*hard!* Your teeth are going right through the peel and into the juicy fruit inside, with a *crunch.* The cold juice is tart on your tongue, and it's filling your mouth as your hand presses against the fruit. Now you're going to swallow....you feel the juice going down your throat. And now you are opening your mouth to bite into the lemon again....

ENOUGH? Does your face hurt? Notice: no real lemon is involved here, but your brain has gone right ahead and directed your mouth and tongue and cheeks—especially your cheeks—to do exactly what they do when the sour raw lemon you bite into is a real-world lemon.

You see—you *can* do this, and very expertly indeed! And what matters, now that you have proved that to yourself, is to realize that just as you have the power to create imaginary *negative* experiences for yourself, with inevitable negative consequences for your health and your well-being, you have the power to create imaginary *positive* experiences, with corresponding positive results.

There's nothing "mystical" or "psychic" or even mysterious about this process. Your brain is programmed to release a variety of messenger substances and impulses in response to what you perceive, whenever the perception is *vivid* enough to be interpreted as "real." And the effects of those substances and impulses on your body are exactly the same, whether the perception has its source in the outside world or is "only" imaginary.

THE EYES HAVE IT: SIGHTISM

There are many books and cassettes and videotapes on visualization, especially now that its routine use by athletes has made it respectable. Athletes are not viewed as flaky misfits with bizarre ideas. If your preferred way to process information is by using your eyes—by reading, by looking at films, by studying charts and maps and diagrams and graphs—you will probably find many of those materials useful. But most of them reflect a curious prejudice of our society—sightism—that makes them useful *only* to people who learn and understand and remember best with their eyes. I'm sure that sightism is responsible for the failures many experience when they try to put information about visualization to work. Sightism is a prejudice against people who process information best through hearing or through touch, and it is a bias perpetuated by *language*.

Consider the names given to the technique. "Visualization" and "imaging" are actions of the eyes only. For people who learn best when they hear information rather than see it, and people who have to get "hands-on" experience in order to really learn, those two words and all their related words raise barriers to success before they even begin. Those two words carry the message, "This is not for you—this is for *eye* people!"

An article by Sally Squires in *American Health* for July 1987 had a sidebar titled "How to Use Guided Imagery," meant to be helpful and informative. Here are a few representative quotes—they're typical of all such materials. I've underlined the sightist words.

> "As you begin the *imagery, picture* a place where you feel safe..."

> "...make yourself a participant in the *vision*, not just an *observer.*"

> "...*picture* the setting you are trying to change..."

> "Try to *'see'* this svelte new you."

Instructions like these may contain an occasional suggestion that you hear or feel something (or smell or taste something). But the bias toward the eyes is overpowering. An amazing example arrived in my mailbox the other day. It's a handsome catalogue of cassette tapes—audio tapes. Everything from tapes for small children to complete novels and nonfiction books recorded for adults is represented, and every item offered is intended to be *heard*. However, the title on the catalog is "The Mind's Eye"! It is simply taken for granted that people who listen to a tape will process the information as *pictures*. People who try to "visualize," but who cannot easily create internal pictures, find the whole process so frustrating and unrewarding that they give up.

Betty Edwards's two excellent books, *Drawing on the Right Side of the Brain*, and *Drawing on the Genius Within*, seem to have been written without attention to the fact that sight is not the only sensory system in human beings. Edwards's proposal that people have trouble expressing their perceptions of the world in art because they rely on stereotyped "alphabets" of the way they think things *should* look is tremendously valuable. But there is no hint that people might also have stereotyped inventories of sounds and textures standing between them and creative expression.

I don't think any of this is *deliberate* bias. Instead, it has its source in two facts about our culture which we know so well that we have forgotten all about them.

First: A majority of people in our society *do* prefer sight to the other senses, and this is strongly reinforced by our educational systems and all our media. Touch is so strongly *dis*preferred that we bring up our children in a constant barrage of antitouch orders, telling them "Don't touch!" and "Keep your fingers to yourself!" from morning to night. Touch-dominant children are forbidden to run their fingers along the line of print when learning to read and are required to master the basic skills by eye and ear alone—though we would never require the sight-dominant child to learn those skills while wearing a blindfold. It's probable that the people writing the materials are eye people themselves, and they fall into sightist writing without any conscious intention or awareness.

Second: The English language reflects this cultural preference by lacking an adequate *vocabulary* for presenting the material without sight bias. There are no hearing or touch words that correspond easily to "visualize"—there is no "hearize" or "auditize" in the everyday vocabulary, much less "touchize" or "feelize" or "tactilize." (If those hypothetical words sound slightly ridiculous to you, that is precisely my point.) This means that even writers who are seriously concerned about eye bias and would like to avoid it are hampered by a lack of vocabulary for that purpose. And saying, as some of them do, that when they use sightist words they *mean* them to include all the senses is like using only masculine pronouns with a note saying you mean them to include both genders: it doesn't work.

The first thing to do, therefore, to make visualization techniques useful for everyone, instead of just the dominant eye people, is to give the process a new name that will be sensory-system neutral. There is one from which we can work—the word "perceive." In a novel I once wrote about problems of perception, my characters were careful to express understanding of others' speech with "I perceive" instead of "I see", in order to avoid sensory bias. I suggest that we take this perfectly good English word and call the process of deliberately creating internal perceptions *percepting*. (Less awkward on the tongue than "perception" or "perceptization.") And when I provide instructions, instead of telling you to "picture" something I will suggest that you *perceive* it.

CONSTRUCTING VIVID PERCEPTIONS

Suppose you are down with a rotten case of bronchitis and you want to perceive something unpleasant happening to the bacteria prowling in your chest. The eye person can construct a vivid perception of those bacteria as monsters being zapped by the rayguns of fierce immune system warriors. Or—like the priest describe in that same article in *American Health*, who didn't want that kind of violent perception in his head—such a person can construct a vivid perception of a garden where those bacteria are bothersome weeds that go unwatered and get pulled up by the roots. But people who prefer other sensory systems can't do that. That is:

THEY CAN'T CONSTRUCT SUCH PERCEPTIONS *VIVIDLY* ENOUGH FOR THE BRAIN TO ACCEPT THEM AS REAL AND ISSUE THE NECESSARY INSTRUCTIONS TO THE BODY IN RESPONSE TO THEM.

Suppose you forget about "visualizing" and "imaging" and try "percepting" instead. How do you proceed?

IF YOU ARE AN EAR PERSON....

You can perceive the bacteria as musical instruments that are badly out of tune and are making awful noises. You can perceive the helpful cells in your immune system as big powerful drums playing so loudly that the squawking bacteria are simply drowned out. If your good cells themselves are not functioning well, perceive them as *out of tune*; then you can perceive other cells equipped with tuning forks and tuning instruments that tune up these cells until you can hear them all playing in perfect four-part harmony.

IF YOU ARE A TOUCH PERSON...

You can perceive harmful bacteria as sharp little points sticking up where they should not be, and perceive the helper cells hammering them into nonexistence....or you can perceive damaged cells as blocks of stone with rough hurtful surfaces and perceive other cells as stonemasons polishing them until they are satin-smooth like healthy cells ought to be.

(Notice, by the way, that the impoverished English touch vocabulary has no convenient touch equivalent for "eye" and "ear." I can't say "If you are a skin person'.... ")

People who *do* prefer hearing or touch for obtaining and expressing information will find that they can percept just as well as eye people can, once they stop struggling to "picture" and "see" and "visualize" things. And if you should happen to be someone who has an even more rare sensory preference—a preference for smell or taste, for example—you would construct perceptions made up of odors and flavors, in exactly the same way.

Success Magazine for December 1988 had a multi-authored special section titled "Beyond Positive Thinking: New Facts Confirm Ancient Wisdom" (pages 31–38). It opens with the statement that "today, far from representing naivete; belief in the power of a positive mental attitude represents the utmost in sophistication." Then, after descriptions of the percepting routines of weight-lifter Mario Martinez and gymnast Doe Yamashiro, there is this paragraph:

> Most of us rely on feedback from others to let us know how we are doing. Athletes such as Martinez and Yamashiro are instead engaged in a sort of "feedforward": They create powerful images of a future reality they desire...

It is typical of the high quality this magazine consistently shows in its writing that it quotes author/psychologist Charles Garfield (*Peak Performance* and *Peak Performers*) instructing would-be visualizers with these words: "If there's something to smell, then smell it. If there's something to feel, then feel it...Do this over and over to create in your mind the reality you want to create in the world." You perceive....this is a man who is aware that "visualization" can't be restricted to the sense of sight alone.

Percepting—constructing perceptions of yourself as healthy or free of pain or happy or successful or loved by one and all or any other positive characteristic you choose—provides you with at least the following two benefits:

1. *Specific positive thoughts* that you can think, to replace dangerous negative thoughts about failing and being sick and suffering and having accidents and so on. With the additional payoff that other people will enjoy your company more because you're not such a downer, and will be more willing to provide you with the advantages of a strong social support system.

2. The knowledge that there is something you can *do* about areas of your life that are unpleasant....the knowledge that you are not a helpless victim. THIS SENSATION OF BEING IN CONTROL HAS BEEN PROVED TO BE ONE OF THE MOST CRITICAL OF ALL FACTORS IN STAYING WELL.

There are two percepting strategies. In one, you construct an internal perception of the *outcome* you are seeking—hearing the doctor tell you you're in perfect health, hearing the boss tell you you're being promoted, seeing your ideal weight in the numbers on your scale, hearing the applause as you accept the award. This can be helpful and is certainly better than negative thinking; the more vivid the perception you construct, the more likely you will benefit from it. Brief materials in the popular press frequently rely on this method. But there's a better way. In "Sporting Life: Using Psychological Tools to Improve Your Game" (*Psychology Today* for May 1989, pp. 23–25, on page 23), author Jerry R. May describes the disappointment of a man he calls "Bill," who tried "visualizing" himself scoring a birdie on the first hole of an important golf date, and failed dismally. He goes on to say that Bill's mistake was in rehearsing only his final goal—the birdie—instead of...

> concentrating on the specific steps of addressing the ball correctly, centering his weight carefully and swinging completely through the ball.

That is, in order to get the full benefit of your positive perceptions, you need to vividly perceive every step on the *way* to your goal. Your bodymind can't work at its full potential if you rehearse only the *outcome*;

for reliable results, you need vivid perceptions of the entire sequence from beginning to end. Olympic skiers don't expect improved performance as a result of many mental rehearsals of arriving safely at the bottom of a mountain; they begin their rehearsals at the top.

Here are the steps you follow to get the most benefit from the technique of percepting:

1. Select your goal and state it in specific terms. For example, you might choose this goal: To go one full day without smoking.

2. Make a list, in writing or on tape, of the steps involved in achieving your goal. For example...

a. Get up, shower, and dress, without a cigarette.

b. Eat breakfast without a cigarette.

c. Drive to work and go to my desk, without a cigarette.

d. Work until lunch without a cigarette.

e. Go down to the cafeteria and have lunch, and then return to my desk, without a cigarette.

— and so on through the day.

3. Now begin percepting: Construct a vivid image of each of the steps on your list. You are getting out of bed and heading for the shower; there's no cigarette in your hand. What do you see? hear? taste? smell? feel? Now you're in the shower, with no cigarette. What do you see? hear? taste? smell? feel? Rehearse your day, one step at a time, as vividly as you can, letting your perceptions come from the sensory system that is most important to you, until you come to the final perception of yourself falling asleep at the end of an entire day without cigarettes.

4. Repeat as often as needed.

Suppose your goal is to run one mile, in your own neighborhood, without stopping. The steps toward your goal would then be something like these: to run from the front walk to the intersection of Plane Street; to run from the intersection to the elementary school; to run from the corner of Pine and Fourteenth to the Dunkin' Doughnuts Place—which is one mile. And as you ran in your mind through each of these steps, you would construct the most vivid possible perception of the things you would see or hear or feel or taste or smell, to make the mental run *real* to you. If you wear special clothes and shoes for running, add a first step in which you change into those clothes; if you have an after-run ritual, add that step at the end. In either case, the effect will be that when you do the actual one-mile run—or go through the actual one day without a cigarette—it will be a familiar experience about which you feel confident.

You will have noticed that mental rehearsal for the day without a cigarette is going to take a lot of *time*. Percepting for the run would take a long time, too, if you were going to run twenty miles instead of one. Doctors who use percepting (by any of its names) in their treatment of cancer patients report that patients who achieve good results often spend two or more hours a day with the technique. What if you don't *have* the time?

In that situation, break up your goal into subgoals and do them separately. Turn the cigarette-free day into three parts: from waking up until lunch; from lunch until dinner, from dinner until you go to sleep. Don't start working on the time from lunch until dinner until you can get through the cigarette-free morning with ease. If you need to make even smaller divisions, go right ahead! There will be times when you're up against a deadline. If you find out on Monday that you have to have a wisdom tooth pulled on Tuesday, you only have twenty-four hours to rehearse an internal perception that takes you from the moment you enter the dentist's waiting room until you step back out on the street with one less tooth, all without becoming nervous or being frightened or suffering any serious discomfort. In that case, you can't afford to work on subgoals and sub-subgoals. But the rest of the time you can set your own deadlines—including one that you define as "as long as it takes."

If you're dubious about the value of percepting, or about your own ability to do it, start *small*. Start with something for which the outcome isn't critical. Choose a minor task or activity that you do frequently, that usually takes you fifteen or twenty minutes to do, and use percepting to take five minutes off your time. Choose a routine interaction that you always come out of in a frazzled state—a monthly half-hour with a relative whose company you don't enjoy, for example—and use percepting to get through it without the usual distress. Prove to yourself that you can do it and that it's worth doing—then move on to apply it to more important matters.

You may find it good practice to prepare a detailed account in your diary (taped or written), using the strategy of working in the third person, as if it were information about someone else. For example, for a woman whose preferred sensory system is hearing, and whose goal is a morning without smoking, a diary entry might go like this:

> She wakes up, and she realizes that it's not going to be a pretty day; she can hear the sound of rain blowing against the window. From down-stairs she can hear the kids already squabbling about who's going to get into the bathroom first; somebody must have started the coffee, because she can hear it perking. She turns on the radio, to listen to the news while she's getting dressed....

...and so on, until noon.

The more practice you have at percepting, the easier it will be for you to do and the better the results you will obtain. That makes it worth your while to use it in preparation for small tasks and minor unpleasantnesses. So that when you need it for something really serious you will already be skilled at it and you won't have to lose precious time learning *how.*

CASE STUDY

Much of the "visualization" research has been done with very serious illnesses such as cancer. The work of the Simontons and that of Bernie Siegel are particularly well known. You may never need to deal with illness on that scale. But before you can do any useful percepting even for minor health problems you have to have some data to build your perceptions with. You have to know how your bodymind, faced with a threat, *works.* Just constructing an internal perception of yourself, perfectly healthy and fit, isn't good enough; you need adequate information to create vivid perceptions of the steps involved in reaching your goal.

Your body's immune system is the major factor in both the prevention of illness and recovery from both illness and accident. But the human immune system is *complicated.* Learning about it is a hard task for medical students, and keeping up with the rapid flow of new developments is a burden for practicing doctors. I'd like you to take a look at it with me now, nevertheless. Not with the idea of becoming an expert on immunology, but with the reasonable goal of acquiring enough information to enable you to build vivid perceptions of the system and work with those perceptions. For the nonspecialist, the major barrier to understanding is a long list of new *vocabulary* that has to be learned; you'll find Figure 7–1, which provides an overview, helpful.

Most of what you need to know involves your white blood cells—your *leukocytes.* (Like most medical terms, this one is transparent if you know a little language history; it's made up of "leuko," meaning "white," and "cyte," meaning "cell.") These are of two basic kinds: the *phagocytes,* which can't deal with viruses but are otherwise very much all-purpose trouble-shooters; and the *lymphocytes,* which deal with cells troubled by viruses, fungi, parasites, and tumors, and are highly specialized.

Roughly 80 percent of your white blood cells are phagocytes, divided into about 65 percent neutrophils and 35 percent macrophages. You send them to the site of the problem, where they surround the threatening item (called an *antigen*) with their own bodies and destroy it by eating it—they are scavengers. Neutrophils tend to die in this process, forming the unpleasant substance we know as *pus.* Macrophages, fewer in number but

FIGURE 7–1

YOUR WHITE BLOOD CELLS (LEUKOCYTES)

NONSPECIFIC (PHAGOCYTES)

SPECIFIC (LYMPHOCYTES)
**can become memory cells
**clone multiple copies of themselves
when activated

NEUTROPHILS   MACROPHAGES   T-CELLS   B-CELLS

*scavengers
*deal with bacteria
*often die (forming pus)

*scavengers
*deal with bacteria
*eat anything
*put remnants of item killed on their surface to attract lymphocytes
*produce messenger hormones

*deal with viruses, fungi, parasites and tumors

*become plasma cells that produce and secrete antibodies

(MAST CELLS)
*related to phagocytes
*react to allergens by releasing histamine and causing allergic disorders and reactions

EFFECTORS (KILLERS)   HELPERS   SUPPRESORS   NATURAL KILLERS (NKS)

*kills cells with viruses or tumors, by punching holes in them

*observe action; carry info

*observe action; call it off

*kill tumor cells, and cells with viruses, fungi, and parasites, by poisoning them much larger than the neutrophils, tend to survive and do additional tasks. They clean up after the neutrophils, eating anything and everything. They produce messenger hormones needed to let other parts of the immune system know what's happening. And perhaps most important of all, they *display* on their surfaces remnants of the antigens they kill, which attracts lymphocytes programmed specifically to tackle those antigens.

You also have a special kind of cell related to the phagocytes called a *mast* cell. Mast cells react not to antigens but to *allergens*, and they do it by releasing *histamine*, the substance largely responsible for the symptoms of hay fever, hives, poison ivy, asthma, drug reactions, and other allergic conditions. It's tempting to say that mast cells are more trouble than they're worth, frankly; when you take an *anti*histamine, its purpose is to counter the activity of your mast cells.

Your lymphocytes are divided into 30 percent B-cells and 70 percent T-cells. When a B-cell encounters a macrophage trimmed with a remnant of the antigen it specializes in, it turns into a *plasma* cell and does two remarkable things: it starts producing and secreting antibodies against that antigen; and it clones itself into many copies, all doing the same thing. Your T-cells are grouped in several different classes; like the B-cells, once they're activated they begin cloning themselves to produce copies— up to a thousand of them—that work together to deal with the threat of the moment. Here's a list of your most important groups of T-cells.

a. Effector T-cells (also called killer cells); they destroy tumor cells and cells taken over by viruses, by punching holes in them and causing them to rupture.

b. Helper T-cells; they observe the action going on and carry information as needed.

c. "Natural killer" T-cells (NK cells); they are on constant patrol for tumor cells and for cells that are carrying viruses or fungi or parasites. They kill these cells by poisoning them, and survive the process to kill many more.

d. Suppressor T-cells; they observe the action and fill the critical function of calling it *off* when it's over.

Both B-cells and T-cells can become "memory" cells—cells you use to remember an antigen dealt with previously and to recognize it if it turns up again. They set the countering action going so quickly and forcefully in such cases that there's no time for any symptoms to develop—this is what it means to develop *immunity* to a particular threat. The reason you're more likely to "catch a bug" when you're traveling is that your B and T cells run into antigens they've never dealt with previously and have no memory cells for.

Finally, a few words about the antibodies and hormones just discussed. The antibodies secreted by your plasma cells are tailored to specific antigens and allergens. They are shaped like a Y, and they attach themselves to antigens and allergens by the two prongs of the Y, leaving the leg of the Y free. They're there to attract the phagocytes that will eat the offending item and get rid of it for you. Sometimes they can do this alone; sometimes they need the help of a set of proteins called *complement*. As for the hormones, they carry two kinds of messages, without which none of this could happen—messages that stimulate the immune system, turning it on, and messages that suppress the immune system, turning it off.

All of these cells are born in your bone marrow (as are the red blood cells that carry oxygen for you) and "trained" for their roles in the bone marrow or the thymus. You then store them in various sites—particularly your spleen, your lymph nodes, and (if they haven't been removed) your tonsils. Like every other cell of your bodymind, they wear an ID badge that says "I *belong* here." It's the absence of that badge that alerts your immune system to the presence of antigens and allergens.

In describing this for you I've been trying to play down the metaphor people ordinarily use to remember the details: The Military Metaphor, in which your body is a battlefield, where you keep your white blood cells on alert as the standing army that fights an incessant war with invading antigens and allergens, from the first instant of your life to the last.

That very dangerous metaphor has been used so much that it has taken on a life of its own. People I talk to about it ask me, "Well, what other metaphor could you *use*?" and they add that it's the only "natural" one. Its prevalence means that you can't avoid coming into contact with it—like the rest of life's hazards, it's everywhere. We might just as well see how it's laid out, therefore. An excellent example appears in a book I recommend, Michaud et al.'s *Fighting Disease: The Complete Guide to Natural Immune Power* (Rodale Press 1989). Except for calling the commanding officers of the armies generals instead of admirals (a minor glitch in the Michaud et al. book), I am using the authors' terms in the paragraph below; you'll find the same set or a very similar one in anything you read on the subject.

THE MILITARY METAPHOR

On the body's battlefield, the phagocytes are the main fighting force. The neutrophils are the shock troop foot soldiers, first on the scene and throwing themselves into battle without concern for their own survival. The macrophages are the tank corps. Your lymphocytes are the elite troops and officers. There are the B-cells, who are the generals. There are the T-cells, including your Green Beret force of natural killer cells. T-cells are contact troops armed with swords and poisons; some are involved in the top levels of command, providing intelligence information and planning strategy. B-cells do their killing at a distance, using the missiles and spears that are the antibodies (sometimes with help from complement, which fills the role of chemical warfare specialist.) And the mast cells are like small bombs, already primed and always ready to go off at a moment's notice. These cells are deployed to fight the invading armies of antigens and allergens. And all of these armies do what armies do anywhere, using the standard military vocabulary. Like any other armies, they remain in constant contact with central headquarters—your brain—using hormones and neurotransmitters to carry information back and forth.

This is the standard line. Often gripping illustrations are added to reinforce it. It carries a perverse and self-contradictory metaphorical message: *Health is slaughter.* Its semantic baggage is the baggage of carnage and pillage and war, and the whole thing constitutes a dangerous linguistic antigen.

In the next chapter, we're going to construct a new metaphor to replace this Body-As-Battlefield mess. You will now have a reasonably vivid perception (in its G.I. version) of your bodymind's method for dealing with threats to your well-being. Hold on to it—it will serve as a foundation on which we can build something better.

TECHNIQUE #12—SETTING UP MINDFILES

Finally, let's begin the process of using your percepting skills to set up *mindfiles*: self-contained perceptions you have created and stored in your memory. Like a computer file, you can open a mindfile, run it, change it, close it, and use it in a variety of ways—*if* you have it properly indexed so that you can get to it with ease.

For example: because you have encountered it so often both in this book and elsewhere, you undoubtedly have opened a mindfile named something roughly like "Eating a Raw Lemon." Chances are, the word "lemon" alone is not your index (although you have a much larger "Lemons" file in your memory which, if you listed its contents, would eventually bring you to "Eating A Raw Lemon.") You are not likely to have made any effort to set up an index for that file, because aching cheeks and a salivating mouth are not pleasant enough to make repetitions of the experience it provides desirable. If you *had* wanted to index it, however, you could have used any of the following—

1. The word "lemon"
2. The sentence "Imagine that you are holding a raw lemon"
3. A picture of a lemon
4. The smell of lemon
5. Beethoven's Third Symphony
6. The sound of a door slamming
7. The number 4

—and an infinite number of others. Some would be obvious to anyone; others would be so personal that nobody but you would ever make the connection between them and the raw lemon experience.

You set up an index for a mindfile by giving yourself instructions, in ordinary language. You say to yourself, "From now on, every time I ————————————————, I will perceive that I am holding a raw lemon in my hand, feeling its cool bumpy skin, smelling its sharp sour odor, putting it to my mouth and biting into it...(etc.)." You fill the blank in your instructions with the index you have chosen.

This works very well—so well that caution is required. You don't want an index so common that your whole life begins to revolve around that lemon mindfile! You want the indexes for your files to be under your control, not turning up constantly in your environment the way real and pictured lemons do, or the way the number 4 does. Beethoven's Third Symphony, which may have struck you as an unlikely choice, would in fact be a good one for most of us. Because we have nearly total control over when and where we will hear that piece of music.

Let's choose a more pleasant perception than lemon-eating and go through the process of setting up a file for it. I'll get you started; add as much additional material as you like, as we go along. The more details you add (as long as the perception doesn't become so overcrowded that you can no longer keep track of it) the more vivid the perception will be, and the easier it will be to remember. If you don't *want* the file I've chosen as an example, on any long-term basis, don't feed it data.

DEMONSTRATION: SETTING UP THE "SMALL POOL OF WATER" MINDFILE

1. You are sitting at the edge of a small pool of water. It's exactly the same size and shape as the circle you would make if you held your arms out in front of you,

open palms toward you, and curved your hands around until your fingertips touched...do that now so that you will know the size and shape of the pool well. (If you're reading this book in public...on a bus, for example...do it mentally.) Look at the circle your arms make, feel the circle your arms make, until you have a good strong perception. Good. Now relax your arms and be comfortable.

2. Look at your pool of water now. It's absolutely clear water, in a basin scooped out of rock; the bottom is lined with clean, white sand. You can see every grain of the sand, because the water is so clear and so clean and so pure.

3. On the surface of the water, a single autumn leaf is floating. It's a beautiful bright red....just floating there...barely moving at all...on the water.

4. Put your hand in the water now. First, lay it on the surface, near the floating leaf, and feel it against your palm. It's very cold against your bare skin...feel the way it presses back at you. Now, let your hand go on into the water, all the way to the bottom....it's just deep enough to reach halfway to your elbow, no deeper. Touch the sand that covers the stone surface below. Draw your fingers through the sand, very carefully and gently so that you don't stir it up and cloud the water. Touch the rock bottom...explore it with your fingertips. There are wavy depressions in it, where the water has worn it away; feel them with your fingertips. Put your other hand in the water, now....feel how cold the water is all the way up past your wrists....good. Now, take your hands out of the water and feel the air drying your skin...relax and be comfortable.

5. The pool of water is from a natural spring. If you are very very quiet you will be able to hear the sound it makes under the ground. Listen carefully....hear that? Such a soft sound! Just a murmur of water down under the ground. Just a whisper of sound, slow and rhythmic...lucky for you, it murmurs in exactly the same rhythm as your breathing. Listen to it carefully.

6. Now taste the water in the pool. Cup your hand and take out just a little of the water. Feel your hand dipping the water out and lifting it to your face. Smell it? That fresh cool smell? Sip the water from your palm...feel it cool on your tongue...feel it cool as it goes down your throat. If there's any water left in your hand, drink that too.

7. Enjoy your pool. Admire the red leaf floating in the water...breathe deeply so that you can smell the water...listen to the sound the water makes, hidden under the ground.

Now we have the file opened and there is enough information in it to make it useful. We just have to give it an index. Say aloud the sentence, "Every time I ————————————————, I will go to the Small Pool of Water and be comfortable there." Fill the blank with the index of your choice, selecting one that will give you as much control as possible. An index made of your own body language is one good choice. For example: "Every time I tap the back of my right wrist with the fingertips of my left hand three times, I will go to the Small Pool of Water and be comfortable there."

I've given the pool a generic name; give it some other name of your choice if you prefer. Put plants and trees around it if you like; add the sounds of birds or insects. If you prefer a water lily floating on it instead of a red leaf, remove the leaf and add the lily; if you'd rather have a leaf of a different color, make that change. I've chosen a pool from a spring; if you'd be more comfortable beside a formal pool in a garden, fix the details. The more often you call up the file and examine its contents, the more easily you will be able to put it to use. Add as much information as you need to make the perception vivid—but not so much that it loses the quality of being self-contained, of being a single experience that can be enjoyed all together at one time as a whole.

Because so much of the population——especially the reading population—has a strong preference for the sensory system of sight, I began the Small Pool of Water mindfile with *eye* data. If you're not an eye person, you will want to rearrange the language to put ear or touch data first. If you're an ear person, you may want to put the whole file's language on a tape so that you can listen to it. (Be sure not to listen to it while you're driving a car, or using power tools, or anything requiring you to be fully alert.) You can strengthen the perception by adding things from the outside world like pictures you have drawn, photographs clipped from magazines, one of those handy tapes of woodland and/or water sounds. Touch people may find a small bowl of very cool water, with sand in the bottom of the dish, a useful reinforcement. You don't need any such "real" items in order to *use* mindfiles, but they can be helpful to you in setting files up and making your perceptions sufficiently vivid.

Now you have this example mindfile. You have opened it, you have filled it with information, you have indexed it. And you have stored it, closed for now, in your memory. From now on, whenever you choose, you can use the index to re-open it and enjoy it for as long as you like. And you can use this technique to construct *other* mindfiles for your own use.

In Chapter 11, we will take up the subject of creating mindfiles specifically for use in unpleasant healthcare situations. In the meantime, practice using the demonstration file. You'll find it extremely helpful as a way of relaxing when you are tense, and for dealing with minor aches and pains. It would also be useful as a way of going to sleep, but be warned—if you use it for that purpose, you won't be able to use it for anything else, because it will always make you sleepy. You might prefer to set up a new and different file specifically to help you go to sleep at times when that's not easy for you.

WORKOUT SECTION

1. *Brain/Mind Bulletin* for August 1989 reported on a research study done by David Spiegel of Stanford University Medical School, in which a group of women with breast cancer who received group therapy and lessons in self-hypnosis lived an average of almost twice as long as a similar group who were given only traditional medical treatment—36.6 compared to 18.9 months. According to *Brain/Mind*, Spiegel was stunned by these findings and explained that the investigators' intention was "to refute the popular notion that state-of-mind plays a major role in the course of diseases, which he had termed potentially destructive." ("Group therapy support increases cancer survival," on page 1.) Why do you suppose Spiegel was "stunned"? Why would he have considered "the popular notion that state-of-mind plays a major role in the course of diseases" potentially dangerous? Is it surprising to you that an association professor of psychiatry at a major medical school *refers* to the concept as a "popular notion" instead of as "the leading edge of medicine"?

(I recommend *Brain/Mind Bulletin*, by the way, as a good source of news in this field. It has brief accounts of developments, plus all the necessary references and sources for exploring stories in more detail.)

2. In "The Body's Inner Voices" (*New Times* for 6/26/78, pp. 45–59, on page 59), Ruth Rosenbaum discusses the hypnosis studies in which people falsely told that they will be touched by something very hot develop blisters, or bleed where they've been falsely told they will be stuck with a pin. She tells us that "In each case the subjects are controlling (though unconsciously) the flow of fluids in and out of the membranes of cells covering a very small area." What is the implication of that quoted sentence? What does it demonstrate that people *know* about the workings of their bodyminds? Would it be useful for people to be able to construct vivid internal perceptions of the "membranes of cells" involved in this process?

3. In "The Healing Power of Imagery," (*New Age Journal* for March/April 1988, pp. 46–56), author Martin L. Rossman, M.D. says that although we don't understand everything about the way percepting works, we do know that the construction of internal perceptions is "the natural language of a major part of our nervous system" and his candidate the right hemisphere of the brain. That is, he proposes that for most people the left hemisphere does its thinking in words and logical formulas, while the right brain does its thinking in "images." Does this strike you as plausible? Is a "natural language" composed of "images" a contradiction in terms? If Rossman is correct, what would it mean for persons whose preferred sensory system is touch—what sort of inventory of "images" would their right brains find most useful? Do you find it hard to "imagine" such an inventory yourself?

4. People sometimes object to the term "percepting" proposed in this chapter, even when they agree that words like "imaging" and "visualizing" are obviously biased in favor of the eye. When I point out to them that the alternative is to accept the idea of *seeing* smells and tastes and sounds," they don't like that either. There's nothing unusual about "percepting" as an English word. It's based on an existing word; it's not hard to pronounce; it's not assembled from initial letters as "laser" was or borrowed from another language the way "chaise" and "pizza" were; it's not just invented from scratch. Still, it's unfamiliar and seems odd at first.

Let's assume that you don't care for "percepting" yourself; can you propose an alternative word? It's *very* hard to think about something you have no word for. It's clearly unfair to reserve an entire territory in semantic space for people who prefer to process information with their eyes. On the other hand, I have no interest in trying to impose my new words on others. If you have a suggestion, I'd be pleased to hear about it.

5. In "Mind Openers: Possibly Yours" (*Psychology Today* for April 1988, pp. 8–10), Pamela Adelmann describes an experiment in which students were asked to imagine themselves as future successes or future failures. Student's constructed perceptions ranged from "working at a mindless job and living in a rat-infested apartment" to "becoming a successful Southern California lawyer with her own swimming pool." Researcher Hazel Markus and her colleagues then had the students work on difficult mental tasks and found that those who had imagined themselves as future successes performed better. Put this to use in your own life. Construct a vivid perception of yourself succeeding at an upcoming project or goal. Pay careful attention to what happens. Does it help you with the project or goal? Does it seem to spill over to other things you're doing and help with them as well?

6. For the items listed below (and others you may want to add), go through the following simple percepting exercise:

a. Perceive the item in your mind.

b. Describe what you perceive as vividly as you can, either on paper or on tape, for all your sensory systems. What do you see? hear? smell? taste? feel?

c. Go back and perceive the item again.

d. Repeat until the item is vividly present in your mind.

□ A single glass marble, in your favorite colors

□ A silver or golden bell, ringing

□ One bright new yellow pencil, freshly sharpened

□ A big wooden sign with your name written on it in giant letters, in whatever colors you choose

□ A big comfortable chair, where you are sitting

□ Your own face

☐ One tree, going through the seasons: bare in winter; then just budding out; then in full leaf; then with the leaves in brilliant autumn colors; and finally bare again

7. For a thorough brief account of processes in the brain during percepting, read "Aspects of a Cognitive Neuroscience of Mental Imagery," by Stephen M. Kosslyn, *Science* for June 1988, pp. 1621–6.

8. When you set up your mindfiles, it's often useful to reinforce them with what are called "affirmations"—brief sentences that sum up your goal in a few positive words, such as "I am at peace" or "I am completely relaxed." Try constructing a few of these that will be meaningful and compelling for you. Be very careful not to word them *NEGATIVELY.* That is, instead of "I am not in pain" you would use "I am completely comfortable." You may be surprised at how difficult it is to find exactly the words you need *without* including negatives.

9. For an excellent nontechnical article on the way your immune system operates, with dramatic illustrations that will be helpful, read "Stop That Germ!", by Leon Jaroff, in *Time Magazine* for May 23, 1988, pp. 56–64. For an account of psychoneuroimmunology research read "A molecular code links emotions, mind and health," by Stephen S. Hall, in *Smithsonian Magazine* for June 1989, pp. 62–71.

10. Find out which is your own preferred Sensory Mode—you may be surprised. Ask yourself some questions like this one: If you had only twenty-four hours to learn to pack your own parachute before jumping out of a plane, would you rather learn from looking at written directions and diagrams, from listening to a skilled instructor's lecture, or from working on an actual parachute with an already-packed one as a model? Pay attention to the sensory language you use, and make notes in your diary; also make notes of sensory language used by other people that strikes you as something you would *never* say. Try deliberately using each of the Sensory Modes one at a time, for a day or two each: which one seems most natural and which makes you feel tongue-tied? Imagine that you had to take a semester's worth of courses with (a) a blindfold over your eyes, (b) tight earplugs in your ears, or (c) thick mittens on your hands; which would you choose?

SIGHT BITES

1. "Imagery is a flow of thoughts you can see, hear, feel, smell or taste....Imagery is the interface language between body and mind."

(Martin L. Rossman, M.D., "The Healing Power of Imagery," in *New Age Journal* for March/April 1988, pp. 46–56; on page 49.)

2. "...scientific research supporting the mind/body link dates back to 1929 when researchers demonstrated that thinking strongly about a particular body movement activated motor neurons in corresponding muscles."

(Will Stapp, "Imagine Yourself Well," in *Medical Self-Care* for January/February 1988, pp. 27–30; on page 27.)

3. "It is my contention that modern medicine is heavily biased toward seeing and therefore is susceptible to missing or devaluating what can be learned through hearing."

(G. Gayle Stephens M.D., "On Seeing and Hearing in Medicine," in *Continuing Education* for November 1 5, pp. 754–6; on page 754.)

8

I'VE GOT YOU UNDER MY SKIN

INTRODUCTION—HOW METAPHORS CAN BE DANGEROUS TO YOUR HEALTH

In Chapters 5 and 7 we discussed the poisonous nature of the military metaphor for illness. And the danger of frequently saying such things as "This job is killing me," which is just another way to express the metaphor "This job is a killer." That danger is very real—but let's be clear about its sources. *It's not the words themselves that make metaphors so dangerous.* I'm not suggesting that "This job is killing me" or "Cancer is attacking my liver" are evil spells and incantations, the very whispering of which endangers the speaker. Nor am I suggesting that when you say "My white cells are mighty and triumphant warriors" you are pronouncing a magic charm for health. Two things make metaphors a signal of danger, and neither one is magic.

First: People who say "This X is killing me" are all too likely to be expressing their true feelings about their personal "X"—their job, or their marriage, or their farm, or their asthma, or their family. And the feeling *behind* the metaphor, the feeling that they are the helpless victims of an intolerable situation that they can't escape, is dangerous. The constant use of the "killer" statements turns the metaphors into a language habit that reinforces and strengthens the negative feelings already present. Anything you feed will grow, and those statements feed the metaphor.

Second: Metaphors are a bit like holograms. Mentioning one part of a metaphor tends to generate the whole. When someone says "Wagons—Ho!" to you, you're likely to think of the entire unifying metaphor from which that comes. Cowboys. Covered wagons. Indians circling on their ponies. Oxen yoked together. Salt flats and endless plains. The U.S. Cavalry riding to the rescue. The whole thing is called in your mind by those two otherwise innocuous words. In the same way, "This job is killing me" will fit into a unifying metaphor for you.

Such a metaphor may be so compelling that it serves as a *filter* for all the perceptions you have about the situation. Whether the killer in question is a berserk butcher holding an enormous chopping knife or a tiger prowling through a jungle in search of prey or an evil wizard cooking up fatal poisons, or worse, depends entirely on your metaphor. The metaphor brings all its semantic trappings with it, usually at a level well below your conscious awareness. You then perceive and express your perceptions about your situation through the perceptual filter created by the metaphor—and you tend to perceive only those things that confirm the filter's specifications.

Suppose the job that you're calling a killer is the work you do as homemaker and parent, and your metaphor is The Mad Butcher. The butcher is like "Wagons—HO!", only a part of the whole. What are the other details that are clustered with it in your mind? What is the knife? The white apron? Where is the cutting board? Where does all the blood go? Are there flies? Maggots? What's going on *behind* the butcher?

Suppose the job that's "killing" you is your work as a lawyer or a mechanic or a nurse, and your metaphor is The Stalking Tiger. How large is that tiger? How hungry? How sharp are its teeth? Where, in your mind, does the jungle it prowls through begin? What other perils, does the jungle contain? Are there snakes? Are there spiders?

Note: There's a *difference* between The Butcher As Killer and The Tiger As Killer: only the butcher is insane. This matters. Because a tiger's behavior is predictable, but a mad butcher might do *anything*.

Here are some other typical contexts in which metaphors can lurk without you being aware of them.

- "My supervisor is really a pain in the neck."
- "That kid is driving me out of my mind."
- "Every time I drive by that place my stomach turns over."
- "Talking to him takes all the starch out of my spine."
- "They're really getting under my skin."
- "I don't think I'll ever get on my feet again."
- "It's just one headache after another around here."
- "I can do anything if I just put my back into it."
- "This place is a stinking swamp."

□ "If they ever stop bleeding me dry down there, I'm going to buy a new car."

□ "The way he talks to me makes my blood boil."

And so on, by the thousands.

It's important to remember that *using metaphors like this now and then really IS "just figures of speech."* We use metaphors to express ourselves more vividly and efficiently, to make what we say more clear, and to keep our speech from being boring. We use them to avoid having to be specific when we feel that others wouldn't be interested in details. Metaphors have many entirely beneficial uses in language. They're dangerous only when they become linguistic habit patterns, tapes that we play over and over again for ourselves until they become a permanent part of our mental environment. If you enjoy your work most of the time, but two or three times a year you tell your spouse that it's killing you, that's not dangerous. That's just life, with all its warts on. It's the *chronic* metaphor that is a threat.

You need to be able to work with metaphors systematically and skillfully, so that you can spot those which pose a hazard and replace them with something less toxic. The techniques introduced in this chapter are designed to make you a metaphor expert, able to accomplish those two tasks with ease.

A metaphor is just an equation—X equals Y—using language instead of numbers. The critical difference between math examples like "2 × 3 = 6" or "a + b = c" and language examples like "Time is money" is that language examples have lots of *give*, while number examples have no give at all. Two times three is *always* six; once the values of a, b, and c are established, a plus b is *always* c. Language isn't like that. Time equals money linguistically, in the sense that you can spend it and waste it and budget it, but you would never try to put twenty minutes in your billfold or three hours in your checking account. Even linguistically you can't take the equivalence for granted: time may be money, but it also flies and marches on, things that money never does. And you may be able to convince someone that $2.98 is close enough to $3.00; no amount of argument will make 2 × 3 = 5.8 suffice.

However, the metaphor I started with—A METAPHOR IS AN EQUATION—is something we can work with and get good results, despite the fact that linguistic equations can never achieve the absolute precision of mathematical ones. "Slippage" in language is something you know well and are accustomed to dealing with every day of your life; it will hold you back in managing metaphors no more than (and no differently than) it does in managing your business affairs.

TECHNIQUE #13—METAPHOR MATH

METAPHOR ALGEBRA—PLAIN VANILLA

1. Choose a common metaphor and write it down or record it.

Life   is   a bowl of cherries.

X   =   Y

2. Now substitute some other chunk of language for either X or Y, staying as close to the original as you can.

For X:

> Life   is   a bowl of salted peanuts.
>   a bowl of chocolates.
>   a bowl of salted peanuts.

For Y:

> Marriage   is   a bowl of cherries.
> A promotion
> Saturday

3. Each time you make the substitution, check it—is it as close as you can make it, or are you headed toward 2 × 4 = 6? For example: "Death is a bowl of cherries" won't work, because the original metaphor is [+HAPPY], and "death" in our culture is usually a cause for sorrow. "Life is a bowl of flowers" is cheerful enough, but it won't fill in the equation, because cherries are [+EDIBLE] and flowers aren't.

Never settle for just "a feeling" that a substitution won't work. Decisions like those I made in the previous paragraph train you in the finding and use of metaphors. The harder it is for you to decide *why* you feel that a metaphor won't work, the more important it is for you to find out. Such decisions will give you valuable information about what words really mean to you—information that you are ordinarily not aware of.

In the examples above, I've kept the bowl and changed its contents. There are other ways to do it. I could change the container instead, as in "Life is a spoonful of cherries" or "Life is a bucket of cherries." Then there's the option of treating "a bowl of cherries" as something indivisible and making substitutions like "Life is money" or "Life is a horse race." All of the possibilities are useful, as long as you're *consistent*, making the same kind of change every time.

METAPHOR ALGEBRA—ZIGZAG

1. Start with a common metaphor as in Plain Vanilla.

Life	is	a bowl of cherries.
X	=	Y

2. Substitute something new for X, and then for Y, and then for X again, alternately. Again, stay as close to the original metaphor's intention as possible.

	X	=	Y
	Life	is	a bowl of cherries.
For X:	College	is	a bowl of cherries.
For Y:	College	is	a bowl of chocolates.
For X:	Marriage	is	a bowl of chocolates.
For Y:	Marriage	is	a bowl of salted peanuts.

(And so on, for as long as it's productive.)

3. Analyze your metaphors as before. When one doesn't seem to work, find out *why*. What is it in your mental dictionary that makes the metaphor fail? If one choice seems better than another—if equating marriage with a bowl of peanuts works for you, but doesn't seem as "correct" as equating it with a bowl of chocolates, what does that tell you about the way you define marriage, or peanuts, or chocolates? What semantic features are involved for you?

As you use these techniques, even when you are working seriously and with the best of intentions, you're going to find some strange things popping into your head—"Life is a bowl of chickens" will do for an example. If it happens only once, it's just your mind at play; let it pass. But examples that occur to you more than once should get your attention.

Don't work with them in the middle of these techniques, because they'll distract you. But make a note to come back to them later. If you keep thinking "Marriage is a bowl of catsup" or "College is a slice of toast," or "Death is a bowl of cherries," you'll learn a great deal from finding out why.

METAPHOR ALGEBRA—STIR-FRY

1. Begin with a common metaphor again, as before.

Life   is   a bowl of cherries.

2. Now make substitutions, but make them as *outrageous* as possible. Throw in anything at all that comes to mind.

Life   is   a kangaroo.   ??

A bulldozer   is   a bowl of cherries.   ??

3. Apply Miller's Law to each of your stir-fried metaphors, to find out what they *mean* to you.

"Life   is   a kangaroo."

Assume that that's true—what could it be true *of*? It could be true of a life in which you're always having to make giant leaps from one thing to another and never get to stay in any one place or activity long enough to enjoy it.

"A bulldozer is a bowl of cherries."

What could it be true of? It could be true of a life in which you've always wanted to drive a bulldozer, ever since you were a little kid, and you finally get a chance to do so.

APPLIED METAPHOR MATH

When you've become comfortable with this technique, it's time to start applying your skill to your health and wellbeing, using the steps below.

1. Start keeping a metaphor log in your diary. Observe your own metaphors (get someone else to help you, if you like), until you spot one with negative implications. Sometimes these will be very obvious. But don't be misled when they're not in a perfect "X is Y" form. Watch for other figures of speech that have

metaphors hidden inside. Just as "This job is killing me" is hiding "This job is a killer," "My son is breaking my heart" hides "My son is a heartbreaker."

And sometimes you will use metaphors that are very hard to spot *as* metaphors. There's nothing metaphorical about saying "I do well in my job when I really put my back into it" if you dig ditches for a living. But if you're a lawyer or a broker or a musician, ask yourself why you say that. Is it a way of saying "My job is a backbreaker"? If you often say "When I see that place my stomach turns over," is that a way of saying "That place is a nausea-producer?" Don't let the fact that English has no common word for one half of your metaphor keep you from spotting what you're trying to express.

2. Once you've found a negative metaphor, look carefully for consequences in your life. If you are forever "putting your back into" things, do you have frequent back pain? Does chest pain go with things that "make your heart ache"? If you don't find anything like this, congratulations; if you do, go on to #3.

3. Work with the metaphor you found—using the techniques you've learned—until you find a *positive* metaphor that you can substitute for it. For example, consider:

"My new job is a killer."

Why? What is it about your job that causes you to use that word? Suppose it's because you find yourself in a work situation in which you have to do things in a way you've never done them before. Suppose there are so many changes that it's hard to keep track of them, and you find that threatening. What could you say about a situation of newness and change that would be positive instead of negative? What metaphor would give you that result?

"My new job is a breath of fresh air."

4. Now use the new metaphor deliberately and systematically. Anytime that you would have said "My new job is a killer," say "My new job is a breath of fresh air" instead. Yes, it will feel artificial and contrived and hokey and ridiculous—do it anyway and observe what happens.

What if you find that you *cannot* go on to Step 4? You may detest whatever lies behind "My new job is a killer" so much that you can't make yourself say it's a breath of fresh air, even as a temporary exercise. That's not necessarily all bad. Just having identified the "killer" metaphor in your speech habits will make you more alert to it, and you will now be conscious of it when you use it. That's useful in itself, and will help prevent the metaphor from taking over your entire perception of your work. However, there's one more technique to try before deciding that the substitution is impossible.

TECHNIQUE #14—SEMANTIC MODULATION

Musicians sometimes want to change from one key to another inside a single composition. If the two keys are closely related in musical space the change can be made directly, in a single step. But when the keys are far apart the step would be a shocking leap for the listener. That may be fine in an orchestral composition or a concert of avant garde music, but it won't do in music intended for general consumption. In such cases, the musician turns to the technique of *modulation*, building a bridge from the base key to the target key by moving briefly through one or more keys in between. We can adapt this musical strategy for our purposes by saying that when Metaphor N and Metaphor Z are so far apart in our perceptions that going directly from one to another seems impossible, we can use semantic modulation to bridge the gap.

Here are the steps to follow, with a demonstration example. (Because the process is unfamiliar, I strongly recommend reading all the way to the end of the demonstration before trying it.)

STEP ONE:

Use all the skills you have developed for working with metaphors to do a semantic feature analysis of Metaphor N and Metaphor Z. Work back and forth between features and reality statements if necessary. Don't worry about technicalities.

STEP TWO:

Complete the semantic feature diagram for each metaphor by filling in the plus and minus values and adding *extra* ones when they more accurately represent your personal perceptions. If [+HEAVY] isn't quite heavy enough, add more pluses; if a single minus sign on [ETHICAL] won't do it for you, add as many additional minuses as you like.

STEP THREE:

Compare the two diagrams to find out where the differences are. Which features occur on one diagram but not on the other? Which features have a plus on one diagram and a minus on the other? Which features differ in the number of pluses or minuses? If you can reduce some of these differences by making minor changes, do so.

STEP FOUR:

Now construct a *bridge* metaphor. Ask yourself: what *else* has semantic features shared by Metaphor N and Metaphor Z, but is less drastically different from N than Z is? Construct a bridge metaphor to serve as Metaphor R.

STEP FIVE:

Begin deliberately substituting Metaphor R for Metaphor N in your speech.

STEP SIX:

Once Metaphor R has become familiar and comfortable, move on to substitute Metaphor Z in your speech.

NOTE: If you need more than one bridge metaphor to get from N to Z, repeat the process as often as necessary.

DEMONSTRATION EXAMPLE

METAPHOR N: The human immune system is AN ARMY IN COMBAT.

METAPHOR Z: The human immune system is A GARDENER AT WORK.

For me, a list of semantic features to describe an army in combat includes [+ACTION], [+MANY], [+DANGEROUS], [+CRUEL], [+KILLING], [+HURTFUL], [+FRIGHTENING], [+NOISY], [+DIRTY], [+WICKED], [+WASTEFUL], [+TRAGIC]. (This will explain why I would not be happy saying "My immune system is an army in combat, attacking the cancer cells or bacteria or viruses that might threaten my health.") There are many people for whom armies in combat would carry semantic features like [+HEROIC], and [+NECESSARY] and [+COURAGEOUS] and so on ... people who view soldiers in combat very differently. My husband belongs to that group. But that's not relevant for this demonstration. That is, there is no "correct" set of features that I must work out. To find out what is in my own mental dictionary, I have to express my own perceptions.

If I were preparing a formal semantic analysis of "AN ARMY IN COMBAT" for a scholarly article, or as a basis for a corporation's advertising campaign for a new mouthwash, my list of features would be much too sloppy. If formal analysis were my goal, I would have to choose more carefully. But in using semantic modulation for your personal life, concern for such technicalities is counterproductive and may keep you from turning up the one feature that would give you the most useful information. It's like worrying about your handwriting in your private diary. We can therefore move on to my list for "A GARDENER AT WORK," which includes these features:

[+PEACEFUL], [+NURTURING], [+SAFE], [+ECONOMICAL], [+USEFUL], [+GOOD], [+QUIET], [+ACTION], [+DIRTY], [+PLEASURE].

Looking over these lists, I can see some possible changes that might improve matters. For example, I chose [+WASTEFUL] as a feature for the army metaphor and [+ECONOMICAL] as a feature for the gardener metaphor. Since economical is the opposite of wasteful, I only need one of the two features. I can just use [+WASTEFUL] for the army and [−WASTEFUL] for the gardener. Safe and dangerous are also opposites; I can reduce the number of features by using [+DANGEROUS] for the army and [−DANGEROUS] for the gardener. Nurturing and hurtful are another such pair. Theoretically, I could change to [+HURTFUL] for the army and [−HURTFUL] for the gardener—but in my perceptions that loses something. Logically it's right, but in real-world terms "not hurting" is not the same thing for me as actively caring for a garden and nurturing it systematically. I will therefore keep both those features. I will also want to decide what features should be given more than one plus or minus. For example, I would put three pluses before [HURTING] and [CRUEL] for the army metaphor.

At this point I will begin to notice some problems. For example, it's not accurate to say that gardeners *never* kill things, because they are constantly killing weeds and insects. This tells me that in a formal analysis I would have to make clear that the word "killing" in "killing weeds and bugs" is not necessarily the same word as the word "killing" in "killing enemy soldiers." But I will put problems of this kind on hold for purposes of this demonstration. When I come to end of the tidying-up process, my list for comparing the two metaphors is as shown in Figure 8-1.

Now I can compare my two lists to find out what they have in common. And I can see at once that of sixteen features listed, only one is a perfect match: [+DIRTY]! On all the other features the values are completely opposed. In some cases the opposition is not just plus or minus—and it's a long semantic distance from one minus to three pluses or from one plus to three minuses. It's obvious that if I were accustomed to thinking of my immune system as an army in combat (perhaps as a result of encountering that metaphor constantly in all the media), it would be difficult for me to substitute the gardener metaphor all at once. It's equally obvious that perceiving my immune system as defined by the list of

FIGURE 8–1

AN ARMY IN COMBAT		A GARDENER AT WORK	
1.	+ + ACTION	+	ACTION
2.	+ MANY	−	MANY
3.	− − PEACEFUL	+	PEACEFUL
4.	− − NURTURING	+	NURTURING
5.	+ + + HURTFUL	−	HURTFUL
6.	+ + + WASTEFUL	−	WASTEFUL
7.	+ DIRTY	+	DIRTY
8.	+ FRIGHTENING	−	FRIGHTENING
9.	+ NOISY	−	NOISY
10.	− − − GOOD	+	GOOD
11.	− PLEASURE	+	PLEASURE
12.	+ + + DANGEROUS	−	DANGEROUS
13.	+ + + CRUEL	−	CRUEL
14.	+ + + KILLING	−	KILLING
15.	− USEFUL	+	USEFUL
16.	+ TRAGIC	−	TRAGIC

features that—for me—identify an army in combat could not possibly be good for my health.

Clearly, an army in combat can be summed up as [−GOOD] in my mental dictionary, while a gardener at work is a [+GOOD] thing. To get from the bad to the good, I need to find something in that internal dictionary that (a) I perceive as less bad than a fighting army, (b) I perceive as less different from the army than a gardener is, and (c) I perceive as sharing some of the features of both army and gardener.

There are a number of possibilities; for this demonstration I will choose a *road crew* at work. Like the army, it involves a number of people carrying out an action that is dirty and noisy and dangerous. Like the gardener, a road crew is useful and peaceful. And road work is not ordinarily tragic or cruel or harmful; on the contrary, it is another *good* thing. I can now insert this bridge metaphor between the original two. Figure 8-2 will make that more clear.

Now you'll notice that there truly is a semantic bridge being built. The road crew has five features in common with the army and twelve features in common with the gardener, and the differences in numbers of plus and minus signs are smaller. It should be possible for me to begin thinking and speaking of my immune system as a road crew, stationed in the various systems of my body, working usefully to deal with potholes of

FIGURE 8–2

	ARMY	ROADCREW	GARDENER
1. ACTION	+ +	+	+
2. MANY	+	+	–
3. PEACEFUL	– – –	+	+
4. NURTURING	– – –	+	+
5. HURTFUL	+ + +	–	–
6. WASTEFUL	+ + +	–	–
7. DIRTY	+	+	+
8. FRIGHTENING	+ + +	–	–
9. NOISY	+ +	+	–
10. GOOD	– – –	+	+
11. PLEASURE	–	–	+
12. DANGEROUS	+ + +	+	–
13. CRUEL	+ + +	–	–
14. KILLING	+ + +	–	–
15. USEFUL	–	+	+
16. TRAGIC	+ +	–	–

infection and virus and cancer, clearing away dangers, making all the paths of my body safe and clean and whole. Dangerous, dirty, noisy work, to be sure—but nothing to be afraid of or sorrow over. And then, after that metaphor has begun to feel natural in my mouth, I could try to eliminate the noise and danger as well and shift to the gardening metaphor. But if I never were able to make that final shift, the change from army to road crew would *still* be a major improvement.

*   *   *

When the media and the powerful institutions of culture decide to make a single metaphor all-pervasive—like the military metaphor in illness—they use it as though the words it contained had the *same meaning* for everyone who speaks the language. In the real world, this conclusion is far from safe. What an army in combat means to me is radically different from what it means to a person who has actually experienced combat. Or what it means to someone who has never fought in war but thinks of combat as exciting and patriotic and an adventure to be admired. When Oliver North uses the words "an army in combat" it means one thing; when Ronald Reagan uses them it means another; when my friend Elizabeth Ann Scarborough, who was a nurse in Vietnam during that terrible war, uses it, it means something else; and none of them means the same thing by those words that I do. That is why it's important to examine metaphors you frequently encounter and use, to find out what you may be carrying along in the way of dangerous semantic baggage.

It's easy to add a metaphor to your habitual speech patterns just because you hear it often, or because someone you admire uses it, or because you find it vivid and interesting, without giving it any further thought. Easy; but not wise. If you think of your cancer as an invading army with tanks and bombs and napalm and hordes of soldiers bent on killing, you are going to fear it more than if you think of it as a single tiger. If you think you are a *victim* of your arthritis, you are going to fear it more than if you think of it as a nuisance—nobody becomes a victim of a nuisance. If you think of doctors as magicians or high priests, you are going to be far less willing to question their decisions and actions than if you think of them as skilled engineers or mechanics. Which of those metaphors the doctors themselves subscribe to will have drastic effects on the way they relate to you as a patient, and on their interactions with your nurses and other caregivers.

Metaphors are powerful. Yes, indeed. But they are not beyond your control. Learn to work with them so that the power they exert in your life is something you understand and can deal with. Something you can use—deliberately, systematically, and strategically—to achieve your personal wellness and fitness goals.

TECHNIQUE #14—USING THE LANGUAGE OF YOUR DREAMS: DREAM-MAPPING

The analysis of dreams is a subject that gets mixed reviews. For some people it's eminently respectable; for instance, it is a major therapeutic technique in Jungian psychotherapy. Others, perhaps unaware that any dream analysis exists beyond the "Dream Books" sold at grocery checkout counters, think of dream analysis as silly nonsense. I'm going to ask you here to set aside your preconceptions about it long enough to try the technique I call *dream-mapping*. You can do this in privacy and at your own convenience. If it doesn't prove useful, you can drop it at once, and you will have invested very little of your time and energy in the experiment.

Dream analysis is important because so much of the information needed for using language wellness techniques is below the level of your conscious awareness, in what is usually referred to as your *subconscious* mind. Your dreams, which rely heavily on metaphors, are one of the few readily available sources you have for access to your subconscious. The data they provide to you can be extraordinarily valuable. Even when the data don't seem directly relevant to a current problem, the practice you gain in interacting with your subconscious pays off in the long run. And often clues to what is making you sick or causing you to have accidents, or clues important to your recovery from illnesses or trauma, can be found in your dreams but not in your conscious thinking.

Let's begin by assuming that you've remembered a dream and are ready to map it. (We'll come back to the topic of what to do if you rarely remember dreams.) To prepare your map, you need a copy of page 159, an ordinary black pen or pencil, and two differently colored pens or pencils. I recommend copying the dream-map page on a sheet of paper that you can put in a three-ring binder; graph paper is good because it gives you lines to write on, but anything that works for you will serve. Fill in the date and time of the mapping at the top of the page and then work through the steps below. As with Technique #13, a demonstration example follows, and I recommend reading it before trying the technique.

STEP ONE:

Choose a set of key words (or phrases) from your dream and write one in each of the ovals on the dream-map, using your black pen or pencil. If you dreamed that you flew to New Jersey by hang glider with your Irish setter as passenger, you might choose "fly, hang glider, New Jersey, Irish setter, high, I, cold." It's all right to leave one or more ovals empty if you don't have seven key words; it's all right to add more ovals if you need them.

STEP TWO:

Choose one color for Level One of the analysis, and begin writing words or phrases or sentences around the ovals to record things you *associate* with the key word inside. For example, the key phrase "New Jersey" might trigger the set "beach, Uncle Bill's house, Elsie the Cow" for you. You would write those near the "New Jersey" oval.

Work quickly as you do this. Don't struggle; don't worry about being logical; just put down whatever comes to your mind. Don't reject puns and metaphors—they are the language of your dreams. When you've written associations for each key word, circle the items and connect them by a line to the oval they go with. If you notice any cross-connections—where a word associated with one oval seems related to a word associated with another—draw a line connecting the two. If you have an oval for which nothing occurs to you, just leave it blank.

FIGURE 8–3

DATE _____ TIME: _____

DATE OF DREAM (IF NOT THE PRECEDING NIGHT): _____

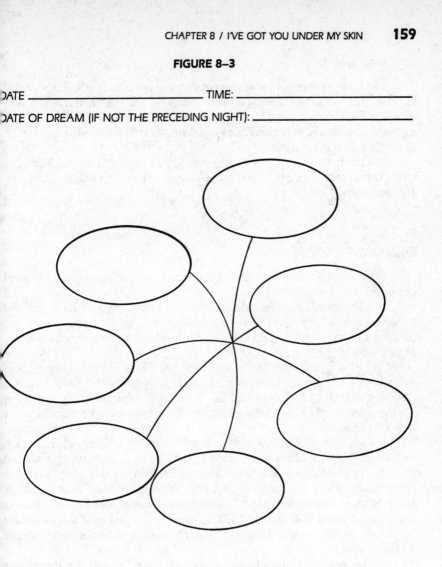

STEP THREE:

Repeat the process in Step Two, using the remaining color to identify Level Two of the analysis for you. Go around the map again and fill in new detail. This time you're looking not only for more associations to the original key words, but also for associations to items you wrote down in Level One of the Analysis.

NOTE: If you get stuck at any point, just go on to the next step or level. When things occur to you from an earlier level, switch to that color and add them.

DEMONSTRATION

Figure 8–4 is one of my dream-maps, for your reference; it's a typical example.

The key words/phrases on this map are "I, dog, pillar, blue, tears, old woman, cactus." My Level One associations are in white circles, Level Two in light gray circles. We'll go through the work around just one of the key words—the word "blue."

"Blue" triggered six associations for me: "Blue Hawaii, Sweet Little Alice Blue Gown; cool; sadness; Christmas (especially the Virgin Mary's clothing); the blues." This looked like a motley jumble, unlikely to tell me anything interesting. But when I added the second layer of associations I was surprised.

"In My Sweet Little Alice Blue Gown" is a song from my childhood—its connection with Mary's traditionally blue gown is obvious. It made me think of "little Alice, in blue," which made me think of the Alice of *Alice in Wonderland*, who swam around in a pool of tears. (Notice that "tears" is another key word on the map.) This reminded me of Mary's tears during the birth of Jesus and during the Crucifixion. I noted that the blues are "cool," in another sense of the word, and sad. I drew connecting lines for all these items.

At this point I thought I was finished and that "Blue Hawaii" was just a leftover. I had already gone on to another oval when I suddenly remembered. "In My Sweet Little Alice Blue Gown" was a song my father used to sing—and so was a popular song about Hawaii, called "Sweet Lelani." Which reminded me of the Hawaiian queen associated with the song and, in turn, of the fact that the Virgin Mary is often referred to as "Queen of Heaven." In the midst of this, another thought came to my mind, and it was once again a song—"Had a Dog, and His Name Was Blue." Since "dog" was another key word, I added this as a cross-connection.

FIGURE 8–4

DATE ___June 11, 1989___   TIME: ___7:30 a.m.___

DATE OF DREAM (IF NOT THE PRECEDING NIGHT): _____

Blue." Since "dog" was another key word, I added this as a cross-connection.

*　　*　　*

The reason you record the date and time of dream-maps is so that you can keep them as an ongoing database; knowing which ones were done at which times is helpful. You're watching for *patterns* that will provide you with reliable translations for your personal dream language. You're gathering data that gives you access to levels of your mind not ordinarily available to you. For example, when "blue" turns up in my future dreams I will be aware of the potential connection with my father; before doing the example dream-map I would not have suspected such a connection.

It would be more convenient if the subconscious would be less indirect and provide translations for you automatically, but it won't. You have to find the connections and the cross-connections, one association at a time, and your conscious mind is often *flabbergasted* at what turns up. Dreams are your best and most accessible clues for this process, and are far less expensive than psychoanalysis.

When I discuss the dream-map process, people always begin to talk of the "right brain/left brain" information that has had so much attention from the popular media. Much of that information should be taken with several grains of salt, because (a) so many of the brain's functions are redundant—duplicated in more than one location, and (b) because popular accounts of brain research tend to oversimplify grotesquely. But if you would like to think of the dream-map process in right brain/left brain terms, you might say that it is a way of translating right-brain information into left-brain information.

Now ... what if you are someone who doesn't remember dreams? That's all right. Take a blank dream-map and put down any set of seven words or phrases that occurs to you, even if it seems entirely random. Use words with some semantic content—you won't get far with words like "to" or "at" or "the." Then work *as if* the words were key words from an actual dream. Go ahead and make a dream-map. After you complete a few of these hypothetical maps, you will probably begin remembering actual dreams for analysis. How long it takes for that to happen will vary from one person to another; in the meantime, even hypothetical dream-maps will provide you with interesting information about the language enviornment below the level of your conscious awareness. I should also point out that for dream-maps you don't have to remember the entire *story* in a dream, as you might for psychoanalysis. You only need enough fragments to give you a set of key words.

Don't hesitate to make much larger dream-maps if a standard page is too small for your needs. You may find that you want a very large space for your maps—perhaps because you want to add more levels of associations—and that being crowded interferes with the work.

FOR THE EAR PERSON:

If you are a person whose preferred sensory system is hearing rather than seeing or touching, *talk to yourself aloud* as you work through the technique. Tape record what you say, if possible; if you can't do that conveniently, make notes when something you say surprises you or gives you information worth remembering.

FOR THE EYE PERSON:

If you're an eye person, take a finished dream-map (or one that has only the key words or phrases filled in) and redo it using *pictures* instead of words—drawings or doodles of your own, or illustrations cut from other materials.

FOR THE TOUCH PERSON:

As so often happens in our culture, it's hard to find an alternative for the person who prefers the sense of touch, but I do have two suggestions. Take a dream-map that has the key words filled in and redo it using clay; you may find it easier to link three-dimensional shapes to the key words to express the associations you feel. Or use textures—scraps of cloth or paper or other materials that are rough or scratchy or slick or patterned to the touch in other ways.

WORKOUT SECTION

1. You can learn a lot about the people you spend your time with by comparing your semantic feature definitions for significant words—and your reality statements based on those definitions—with theirs. You're not likely to find people who disagree with you about defining the word "bird" with just the features [+ANIMATE], [+FEATHERED], but when you move beyond birds matters get complicated. For each of the nouns listed below, construct a semantic features definition, using the minimum number of features possible. Then have family members or associates prepare definitions of their own to compare with yours. Be prepared for surprises.

a. LIE
b. FAIRNESS
c. GAME
d. WORK
e. CHEATING

(You'll also find this process useful whenever you realize that the reason a discussion is going nowhere is that the people involved are using the same words but are giving them different meanings.)

2. One of my favorite metaphor examples is by Eric Korn, from page 874 of the *Times Literary Supplement* for August 14, 1987: "The river of information is pumped and ... facsimilated and satellite-bounced around the world, but high up in the mountains the source is polluted by the same old dripping excrement, the same old dead sheep." Take this sentence as a pattern and do some substitutions to turn it into quite different metaphors. How about modulating from "the river of information" to "the jungle of information" or "the river of politics" or "the orchards of education"? What if, instead of saying that the source for "the river of information" is polluted, you say it is strengthened or stolen or stored?

3. Many people whose work involves the process called "free association" have developed techniques like the dream-mapping presented in this chapter. Examples you might want to take a look at appear in *Using Both Sides of Your Brain* (by Tony Buzan, E.P. Dutton 1983), *The Everyday Genius* (by Peter Kline, Great Ocean Publishers 1989), and *Writing the Natural Way* (by Gabriele Lusser Rico, J. P. Tarcher 1983.)

4. Most dream researchers and specialists advise people to keep paper and pencil (or a tape recorder) by their beds so they can easily and quickly make notes of their dreams when they first wake up, while the memories are fresh and vivid. Psychoanalyst Robert Langs disagrees, suggesting that the forgetting of dreams is a natural protective strategy of your mind, which tries to keep you from having to deal with emotional issues you're not ready to face. What is your opinion on this issue? Do you feel that you want or need protection from the possible contents of your subconscious mind?

5. For a very good and thorough account of traditional dream analysis, read *A Little Course in Dreams*, by Robert Bosnak (Shambhala 1988). Also worth reading are the following two brief articles on dreams: "The Stuff That Dreams Are Made Of," by Sharon Begley, in *Newsweek* for August 14, 1989, pages 41–47: "Dreams: Now you can make them work for you," by Lynne Lamberg, in *American Health* for July 1987, pages 50–55.

6. Much of American life is presented in metaphors of games—usually team sports. Robert Keidel, author of *Game Plans: Sports Strategies for Business* (E.P. Dutton 1985), has suggested that our businesses can usefully be classified in terms of whether their governing metaphor is football, basketball, or baseball. In an interview in *Inc. Magazine* for November 1985 (pp. 35–58, on page 36), Keidel said: "My argument at its simplest is that football represents control and baseball

represents autonomy, while basketball represents voluntary cooperation." What are the implications for business if this is true? For example, in all three of these sports it's perfectly all right to pretend you have the ball when you really don't, or vice versa. Could you apply these three metaphors to the American health care system, or would you need to add some other sports?

7. After you have mapped at least twenty of your dreams, go over the maps and make a list of all elements and keywords that turn up in them repeatedly. Then use that list to prepare what we might call a "Dream Metamap," with the recurrent elements as your keywords. Use exactly the same technique that you've been using for the individual dreams.

SIGHT BITES

1. "Some truths are probably available only through metaphor. They are literally unthinkable without the figure of speech that explodes into an entirely new world view."

   (Joanne Troutman Banks, "Suffering and sentimentality: A thematic essay on literature and medicine," in *Medical Humanities Review* for July 1987, pages 16–24; on page 18.)

2. Alcohol is the AIDS virus of injury control. It lowers the defenses and immunity to injury, leaving people vulnerable to what would otherwise be nonthreatening situations."

   (William H. Foege M.D., "Highway Violence and Public Policy," in *New England Journal of Medicine* for May 28, 1987, pages 1407–8; on page 1408.)

9

AS YOU (AND OTHERS) SEE YOU

INTRODUCTION—THE INACCURACY OF PERCEPTIONS

In Chapter 7 we discussed the fact that we cannot trust our perceptions to reflect accurately what—if anything—is "really out there." We agreed that for daily living we have to ignore that and behave *as if* our senses could be trusted. We know in theoretical terms that the bridge across the creek is mostly empty space and anything but solid; in practical terms, we also know we must behave as if that were false or we will never dare set foot on the bridge. And we know that we can get as much practice in crossing a bridge by crossing an "imaginary" one as a "real" one, provided we have enough information to recreate the crossing vividly in our minds.

This is all just as true of people as it is of lemons and bridges. The difference between real and unreal is a difference of perceptions. But it's not a *trivial* difference. For human beings, one crucial and inconvenient principle must be remembered:

FALSE PERCEPTIONS HAVE REAL CONSEQUENCES.

The January/February 1988 issue of *Hippocrates* carried a feature by Lisa Davis ("The Height Report," pages 90–91) about a research study in which 585 district superintendents were asked to rate hypothetical applicants for the job of school principal, based on resumes—*identical* except for height, weight, and gender—constructed by researcher Carl Bonuso. The results were amazing. Davis tells us on page 90 that:

> Nearly 90 percent of the superintendents said they would consider the 6-foot man, and about 84 percent were interested in the same man at 5-foot-9. Only 54 percent said they would consider the 5-foot-6 candidate.

Davis adds that the study showed far greater prejudice against shortness than against female gender, demonstrating clearly the importance of height for our culture. But it's critical to realize that we react to *perceived* height, not "real" height. Americans have consistently perceived George Bush as a short man, for example. He finds this surprising, because he is two inches taller than Ronald Reagan, who is always perceived as a *tall* man.

Davis quotes psychologist Irene Frieze saying, "Height is really a kind of basic form of nonverbal communication. We speak of looking up to someone, and I think that has a literal meaning." In her studies on this subject Frieze found that every extra inch of height in men translated into $600 a year more in earnings.

How can we use this information to an advantage as we make decisions about our own appearance and its approximation to our culture's ideal? Consider the case of George Bush again. Bush already *is* the "ideal" male height: six feet two inches. But he appears to fall short (note the metaphor!) when it comes to transmitting the messages that people *perceived* as tall transmit. Consider also Meryl Streep, who misses the specifications for a beautiful woman in our culture by some distance—she is nevertheless perceived as beautiful. Because she knows how to transmit "I AM BEAUTIFUL" messages.

It's absurd to have to function in a culture where a man's height and a woman's weight matter more than how intelligent either one may be. It's barbaric to have to function in a culture where the ideal woman is not only eternally thin but eternally young. But it's the only culture we have, and since we *must* function in it, let's at least understand what we're up against:

> Beyond any shadow of a doubt, for the average person it is not facts but *perceptions* that must be dealt with.

It's hard for someone a foot shorter than average to be perceived as tall, or for a person a hundred pounds heavier than the average to be perceived as thin. Absolutely. But for most of us—only an inch or two, only fifteen or twenty pounds, off the ideal—the primary goal should be *behaving* as if we were tall or thin. The same thing holds for perceptions of beauty. If your facial features differ drastically from the norm, it may be difficult for you to be perceived as beautiful or handsome. But for most of us the differences are very slight. A millimeter here; a centimeter there; no more. Most of us would get a greater real-world return from learning to transmit "I AM HANDSOME/BEAUTIFUL" messages than from putting our resources into attempts to change the physical facts.

No amount of dieting or cosmetic surgery or working out with exercise machines or massage—no quantity of pairs of expensive elevator shoes and silk shirts and padded jackets—nothing that money can buy—will make others perceive you as attractive if you are personally convinced that you are not. SUCH THINGS WILL WORK FOR OTHERS ONLY IF THEY WORK FOR YOU AS WELL. And they will never work as well as the skill called "projecting" the quality you're after, which can be acquired far more cheaply and quickly and which, unlike "real" characteristics, has great resistance to the normal changes associated with aging. There are three steps in learning to project the qualities of your choice—

1. Identify and characterize your own self-perception.
2. Improve your own self-perception.
3. Move to make others' perceptions of you match your own.

You can do this. It's not easy, because you have to swim upstream all the way against incessant messages from our culture designed to force you to accept a self-image chosen for you by others—but you can do it. We'll begin by discussing ways to use language (which you have in abundance and for free) to analyze the messages you are now transmitting about yourself.

SELF-PERCEPTION ... YOUR INTERNAL IMAGE

How do you perceive *yourself*? I'm not asking how you describe yourself to others, with all the complicated constraints about not sounding conceited and not being accused of false modesty. How do you describe yourself *to* yourself? The quickest way to find out is to write or tape a self-description detailed enough to let a stranger identify you in a crowd—and to do that using the third person, as if you were writing about someone else. Start with your name and go on, being as clear and truthful as you can. When you get through, check your description over. Make any changes that are needed to help out that hypothetical stranger. That is, if you've said that you have "The Mergautroidde nose," remember that the stranger has never seen your family nose and clarify that. If you've used a lot of vague terminology, make it more specific—"a little bit heavier than he used to be" won't tell your stranger much about your size.

Now take your finished description, identify each descriptive word or phrase, plug those items into the sentences below, and finish each sentence completely. You can switch back to saying "I" and "me" and "my" now.

TRIGGER SENTENCES:

"The reason I know that I am _____ is because _____."

"The reason I know that I have _____ is because _____."

"The reason I know that my _____ is because _____."

For example:

"The reason I know that I am too fat is because...."

"The reason I know that I have an enormous nose is because...."

"The reason I know that my eyes are too close together is because...."

The harder it is for you to complete one of these and the more you are tempted to finish it with "because I just *know*!", the more important it is to get that one done. Why *do* you think you have lumpy thighs or that your stomach sticks out too far or that you have ugly teeth? What is your evidence for those perceptions?

Some things can be verified because there is an accepted standard for them about which everyone agrees in general terms—your eye color, for example. You know you have blue eyes or black hair because all native speakers of English would agree with you about the color terms you use. But most of your reasons won't be like that. If you are truthful, you'll find that most of your reasons are like these examples:

"The reason I know that I have an enormous nose is because my parents always said it was enormous."

"The reason I know that I am too fat is because I weigh 200 pounds and the insurance company charts say a person my height should never weigh more than 185."

"The reason I know my thighs are ugly is because it makes me sick at my stomach to look at them."

"The reason I know my feet are too big is because I wear a size 8B shoe."

"The reason I know I am too short is because all the other guys are taller."

The point of this exercise is to bring to the level of your conscious awareness the reasons you have for your perceptions of your body, so that you can see how illogical and trivial and downright stupid many of them are. Especially those for which you absolutely cannot get past "because I just *know.*" Seeing or hearing them in all their naked absurdity will help you give some of them up or at least weaken your attachment to them. Go over your final list carefully, and think the items over to determine whether some of them can simply be dropped. But be honest. If—no matter how illogical the reason may appear to you—you still are convinced of the negative perception, leave it on the list to be worked with.

If your perception of yourself is that you are unattractive—because you are too short, too tall, too skinny, too fat, have too big a nose or thighs or mouth, whatever—the chances are 99 to 1 that you are transmitting that message all the time to other people. Unless you are a trained actor or actress, you are going through life behaving AS IF you were the person described by that perception.

It may be that your completed analysis will contain no negatives—that you are entirely satisfied with your physical appearance. This is true for a sizable percentage of *men* in America. Suppose you're not that fortunate, however; then what?

1. You can behave AS IF the negatives you perceive do not exist.
2. You can change your internal perception so that you get rid of the negatives.

If you had to try to do either or both of these things by will power alone, by just deliberately deciding to do them and carrying out that decision, you would probably fail. But you don't have to, because both are part of systems that function automatically. Remember that the negative message you transmit about yourself is not a specific one—not "My nose is too big" or "I have lumpy thighs"—but the more general "I'M NOT AN ATTRACTIVE PERSON." You don't have to find a way to transmit a specific *positive* message about your nose or your thighs either. Just the general message, "I'M ATTRACTIVE," and you're home free. Technique #16—simultaneous modeling—is one of the most effective methods for accomplishing this.

TECHNIQUE #16—SIMULTANEOUS MODELING

It's probable that at some period in your life you have spent some time trying to learn a foreign language from records or tapes; if not, you'll nevertheless be familiar with the way that's done. The traditional method is to listen to a stretch of the recorded language and then to repeat that stretch in an empty space provided, speaking *after* the model. This doesn't work very well. When you listen to the modeled speech and then repeat it on your own, you add to your learning burden the task of remembering what you heard. The result is that the more you practice, the more you train yourself in your own distorted recollection of what you're trying to say.

The effective way for people to learn foreign languages (short of the usually unattainable ideal of being totally immersed in that language's culture) is not to *repeat* the modeled speech after listening to it but to SPEAK SIMULTANEOUSLY WITH THE MODEL. When you do that, your brain goes instantly to work trying to match *your* voice to the modeled voice, automatically making the multitude of tiny adjustments to reduce the differences between the two.

You can use this technique, which is solidly based in neurophysiology and neuropsychology, to improve the perceptions you have of yourself and to achieve the confidence in those perceptions that will enable you to convince others to perceive you in the same way. It makes little difference what specific *items* are on your list of perceived negatives. You need to know what they are so that you will have a clear understanding of the *scope* of your negative image of yourself. There's a big difference between perceiving yourself as unattractive for one minor reason—"I know I am five pounds too heavy because my doctor says so"—and perceiving yourself as unattractive for a dozen different reasons. You need to know what they are because after seeing them clearly you can often delete an item or two from your list on the grounds of ridiculousness. But no matter what your final list is like, there is only one area of your "image" that you need to work on: your nonverbal communication. Your *body* language. With particular emphasis on the quality of your voice, which is the most powerful part of body language.

This is true because for English 90 percent of all emotional content and 65 percent of all information whatsoever is carried not by your words but by your body language. It's body language, especially the quality of your voice, that will carry the message "I AM AN ATTRACTIVE PERSON" for you and make it persuasive to others.

TO IMPROVE YOUR VOICE QUALITY

You need a tape recorder (an inexpensive one will do), a few blank tapes, and a tape roughly thirty minutes long by someone of your own gender whose voice you admire. Be careful not to choose someone as a model whose voice is very unusual and distinctive. You don't want people telling you "Goodness, you sound just like X!" because X has the kind of voice that they can't possibly forget. Choose someone with a voice that you and others perceive as strong and full and resonant and pleasant and compelling. You can work with a commercial tape or with a tape made for you by someone you know whose voice meets your needs. You proceed as follows, at your own convenience, at your own speed, in privacy, and at no cost for experts.

1. Make a *baseline* tape of your own speech, at least twenty minutes long, to be used for comparison later on. Don't read aloud—most people's reading voices are very little like their speaking voices. Don't say something memorized. Just talk. Talk about the teacher you disliked the most, or your opinion of Congress ... anything that you can speak about naturally. Date this tape and put it aside.

2. Listen to the model tape all the way through to get a general feeling for its content. DO NOT WRITE IT DOWN. DO NOT TRY TO MEMORIZE IT.

3. Turn on the tape and begin speaking *with* the model, just for one or two sentences. It's important not to *struggle* consciously to match the taped speech—that effort only interferes with the performance of your brain. Relax; there are no time limits on this process. When you come to the end of the sequence you've chosen, rewind the tape and do it again; a dozen times is not too many, or in any way unusual. When you're bored with that sequence, move on to the next sentence or two on the tape and do the same thing. You will work your way through the entire tape eventually, but there's no "required" amount that you must get through in any single session.

4. After every six hours of practice, make a new baseline tape of your own speech and compare it to the first one you made. When you're satisfied with the improvement in your speech, STOP practicing! Your goal is *not* to be able to do a flawless impersonation of your model, and that is what will happen if you continue too long.

If at any time you find yourself so bored with the model tape that you can't face it again, get another tape by the same speaker and work on that one instead.

This works. It works so well that its only hazard is that of going on too long and achieving not an improved voice of your own but an imitation of your model. That's easily avoided; just use your common sense. You may want to get someone else to listen to your baseline tapes with you and provide a second opinion about how much change has occurred and whether it is enough.

How long this will take depends entirely on the individual. It depends on how much free time you have for the process, how motivated you are, how extensive the changes to be made are, how many years you are past the optional age for learning languages (roughly infancy to puberty), how much patience you have, and so on. There's no "perfect" standard that you have to meet or against which you should measure your performance. Do it until it's *done*. A strong beautiful voice is the most powerful instrument available to you for bringing about positive perceptions in other people, and their *reaction* to you when you have such a voice will quickly build your confidence in your own positive self-perceptions. By contrast, an unpleasant voice, in even the most beautiful woman or the most handsome man, will create strong negative perceptions.

As a very rough guide, from which there may be a lot of individual deviation, you should expect substantial improvement after the first twelve hours spent this way. You are working with your native language, after all; you already know most of what must be learned. It will slow you down if your sessions are too short—less than twenty minutes at a time—and if long gaps of time go by between sessions. A reasonable schedule would be a thirty-minute session, roughly ever other day. But if you can't meet that schedule, do whatever is feasible for you, with the knowledge that it may slow you down a bit.

TO IMPROVE THE REST OF YOUR BODY LANGUAGE

When you're satisfied with your voice, you can move on to such things as posture, gestures, facial expression, and so on. And you proceed just as you did for voice quality, except that this time you need a videotape player and a video of someone whose *total* body language will serve you as a model—and you don't need to make baseline videos of yourself for comparison.

Begin by watching the film all the way through to become familiar with its content. Then go on as you did with the audiotape, using simultaneous modeling. Work in three stages: with the sound off; with the brightness turned down so that you have the sound but not the picture; and with both sound and picture, as in ordinary television-watching. If your preferred sensory mode is sight, work with picture only, then sound only, then the two combined. If your preferred mode is hearing, do sound only, then picture only, then the two together. People who prefer touch mode can use either order. When you can move and speak with your model comfortably—but before you are able to do a flawless imitation—STOP.

Finally, almost everyone today has access to a tape recorder, but videotape equipment is less widely available. Don't be concerned if working with videotapes would be a serious inconvenience for you; just concentrate on working with your voice. Improvement in voice quality is by far the most significant change you can make in your language behavior.

THREE DREAD WORDS

Now let's turn our attention to three words that turn up again and again on lists of things people perceive as negative descriptive features, both for themselves and for others. They are the dread words *fat, old,* and *disabled.* Unlike the word *short,* which is primarily a problem for males, these three words carry heavy penalties for both genders, with severe health consequences. People in our society spend billions of dollars every year trying to change the physical characteristics that they believe are causing them to be perceived as fat, or old, or disabled. Of the three, "fat" is unquestionably the worst, because fatness in America today is viewed as being the fat person's *fault.*

THE DREAD WORD FAT

There are three possible reasons for feeling unhappy about weighing more than the American "ideal." You may feel bad about the way you *look.* You may feel distressed because doctors call your weight unhealthy. Or you may feel miserable because you simply aren't *comfortable*—because your weight makes it difficult for you to sit and walk and get around and pursue the activities of daily life. For the majority, only the third reason is legitimate.

We know that the perfect human being has two legs, two eyes, two ears, two arms. These are absolute standards on which all agree and which have never changed in recorded history. No such standard exists for what the perfect human being should weigh, and "desirable" weight targets change the way hemlines do, according to the fashions of each culture and time period. Most people have the standard number of human body parts, which makes it reasonable to expect that standard of everyone. The standard for weight, however, is based on fantasy, even when we restrict it to today's United States. Listen to doctors Jules Hirsch and Rudolph L. Leibel (*The New England Journal of Medicine* for February 25, 1988, pp. 509–10, on page 9):

> Obesity is the result of a metabolic defect; no, it is no more than the unfettered drive for pleasure derived from eating. Obesity is genetically determined; no, it is the consequence of an abundance of foods

and a sedentary life style. Obesity can be reversed by sensible changes in life styles; no, five-year treatment successes are practically nonexistent.

All these claims appear in current medical literature; all are supported by research studies. Contradictory as they are, they agree on one thing: that overweight is a disease, a medical disorder. And this provides us with an astonishing example of the power of *naming*. When they attach the "disease/disorder" label to overweight, they also attach its presuppositions: that overweight people are by definition patients and in need of treatment by doctors.

This is a common medical practice. For example, every woman who lives past fifty will experience menopause, which logically implies that menopause is a *normal* condition for human females. However, when menopause is renamed "estrogen deficiency," half the human race is at once decreed to be in need of medical treatment. With only a little more skill in the production of medical incantations, menopause becomes "hypoestrogenemia," which sounds very serious indeed. "Obesity" sounds far more grave than "overweight" or "fat," and the new terms "hyperadiposity" and "energy expenditure deficiency" escalate that perceived gravity. Take a look at these two quotations:

> As a treatment for obesity, dieting involves adopting the sick role and making a concerted effort to get well...thus diagnosis of obesity requires that we believe both that fatness is unhealthy and that we can know what causes it. [Stein, 1985, page 775]

> Unfortunately, a person is more likely to recover from cancer in both lungs than he is to be cured of obesity. [Govaker 1987, page 25]

Unfortunately, although the doctors agree that if you are overweight you are sick, they do *not* agree on how the words "fat" and "overweight" and "obesity" are to be defined.

At one extreme are the familiar insurance weight tables developed in the 1940s—with no scientific justification—by a man named Louis Dublin. This definition produces statements like the one made by Nancy S. Carpenter, R.D. and Stephen A. Brunton, M.D. in *Family Practice Recertification* for September 1988, on page 59: "Eighty million Americans—one third of the population—are overweight, and 20 million are clinically obese." In *The Journal of Family Practice* (27:3;285–290, 1988), Barcey T. Levy Ph.D. and Paul S. Williamson M.D. note that Dublin's desirable weights remain "below the average weight of the U.S. population"; nevertheless, these authors claim that the most desirable weights are in fact "even lower than those on the Metropolitan tables." At the opposite extreme—and far more in line with what real people weigh in the real world—is the formula for desirable weight developed by Dr. Reubin Andres of the National Institute on Aging. (You'll need your calculator for this one.)

1. Take your height in inches and divide it by 66.
2. Multiply the answer from #1 by *itself.*
3. Multiply the answer from #2 by your age plus 100.

You already know how tightly the "fat" label is tied to unreliable perceptions and cultural fads. Suppose that your weight does not interfere with your physical activities and you recognize that "looking fat" is only a matter of fashion, with perceptions of proper weight ranging from skeletal *Vogue* models to the original Oprah Winfrey. But your doctor assures you solemnly that studies prove your weight to be a danger to your health. Doesn't that mean you must cut the calories and boost the calisthenics? No. It doesn't.

When I was a small child, doctors knew that the way to treat my fever was to wrap me in blankets and drive my temperature up until it "broke." When my first child was small, doctors knew that a child's fever should be treated with aspirin and alcohol rubs. By the time I had a second child, doctors knew that aspirin and alcohol rubs were dangerous to children; the way to treat fever was to strip children to diaper or underwear and take them for a drive in the car—if that failed, they were to be put into a cool bath. Recently doctors have announced that they know you shouldn't try to bring many fevers down at all, because they are a useful part of the healing process. We have gone almost full circle over the course of fifty years. In every case, the doctors were *certain* that they knew, and their pronouncements began with "studies prove."

I'm not telling you this to put down the doctors, who do the best they can, considering what they have to work with in the way of solid information. I'm telling you because it's important to realize that for doctors—even thousands of doctors—to say something does not make it *true.* As two experienced MDs will tell you:

> Five years after you finish medical school, everything you were taught will be wrong, but if you wait an additional five years it will all be right again.
>
> (David Guttman, M.D., "Things They Never Warned Me About in Medical School," in *Medical Economics* for December 23, 1985; on page 69.)

> I was once told, 'Half of what I teach you today will be proven wrong
> within 10 years. The trouble is, I don't know which half it is!'
>
> (Robert Matz, M.D., "Humanism in Medicine," in *Hospital Practice*
> for April 15, 1987; on page 49.)

It's true that the condition for which medicine reserves the cruel term
morbid obesity—in which people weigh hundreds of pounds more than
average and are severely handicapped by those pounds in even the most
ordinary activities—is dangerous to the health. It is also extremely rare.

The doctors are factually wrong when they claim that a third of the
American population is suffering from the early stages of this condition.
And they are ethically wrong when they maintain a public position that
perpetuates the huge diet industry. A recent *Forbes* article ("Living off the
fat of the land," by Matthew Schifrin, pp. 186–196) tells us on page 187 that
"the diet food business has grown to $33 billion a year in retail sales."
(Note that this is only the diet *food* business; the total for the diet industry
is vastly larger!) Schifrin goes on to explain that "what really makes the
diet business so lucrative is that there is no long-term cure for the truly
overweight. Studies show that within five years most dieters are likely to
gain back any weight they lose." This is well known, but it doesn't hold the
industry back; *Newsweek* tells us on page 59 of its issue for March 7, 1983
that *80 percent* of American women have been on a diet by the time they
reach the age of eighteen. The *Forbes* article was profiling the Nutri/System
Corporation, in its "200 Best Small Companies in America" issue for
November 13, 1989.

This situation—referred to with a straight face throughout the
medical literature as "an epidemic" and "a plague"—has been created by
language. It continues despite significant research proving that the highest
death rates relevant to weight are in very *thin* people. It thrives despite
research proving that fractured hips, a major cause of both disability and
death in the elderly (especially elderly women), are far more common in
thin persons. It would be entirely logical to rename thinness as a
dangerous condition called "hypoadiposity"—but it would not be nearly
so lucrative. Gaining weight is infinitely easier than losing it, and the
market would be too small to earn feature articles in *Forbes Magazine*.

No doctor would ever say to a patient, "You go on home and grow a
couple of inches, and then we'll talk about treatment." But doctors *do* tell
patients they won't treat them until they've lost some specified number of
pounds. And one of the cruelest—and unfortunately one of the com-
monest—uses of the verbal attack patterns is the one that goes like this: "If
you REALLY loved me, YOU'D lose WEIGHT!"

Your best defense against the "doctor knows best and therefore I weigh too much" idea is to read the scientific studies and reports on those studies yourself. The popular media give the impression that there is complete agreement about the medical risk for people heavier than the ideal; the diet industry shores that up with a barrage of ads. The impression is false, and reading the sources will quickly make that clear to you. You will find disarray and disagreement. You will find shaky research designs, often based only on men, often based on a dozen persons or less. You will find obvious prejudice against fat people, entirely independent of the medical facts. You can judge the validity of the claims for yourself, using your own critical language skills. I've given you a list of ten articles for this purpose below to get you started; if your library doesn't have them, it can get them for you on interlibrary loan. Their bibliographies will lead you to additional sources.

1. Carpenter, Nancy S., R.D. and Stephen A. Brunton M.D. "Evaluating the Severity and Causes of Adult Obesity." *Family Practice Recertification*, September 1988, pp. 59–70.

2. Raymond, Chris Ann, Ph.D. "Experts Hold Hope for Obesity Treatments Targeted to Specific Regulatory Miscues." *JAMA*, November 7, 1986, pp. 2202–7.

3. Stein, Howard F., Ph.D. "Fat and Skinny: Cultural Metaphor, Diagnosis, and Disease Entities." *Continuing Education*, November 1985, pp. 775–81.

4. Prewitt, Terry, Ph.D. and Mary Rogers, Ph.D. "Giving weight-loss advice that patients will heed." *Contemporary OB/GYN*, October 1987, pp. 81–2 and 87–90.

5. Govaker, David, M.D. "Helping your patient lose weight." *Emergency Medicine*, March 30, 1987, pp. 24–45.

6. Levy, Barcey T., Ph.D., and Paul S. Williamson, M.D. "Patient Perceptions and Weight Loss of Obese Adults." *Journal of Family Practice*, Vol. 27, #3 (1988), pp. 285–290.

7. Tavris, Carol, Ph.D. "Is Thin Still In?" *Woman's Day*, March 3, 1987, pp. 30–38. (An excellent source, although it is in a mass market magazine rather than a professional journal.)

8. Hirsch, Jules, M.D. and Rudolph L. Leibel, M.D. "New Light On Obesity." *New England Journal of Medicine*, February 25, 1988, pp. 509–10.

9. Roberts, S. B., et al. "Energy expenditure and intake in infants born to lean and overweight mothers." *New England Journal of Medicine*, February 25, 1988, pp. 461–6.

10. Bennett, William, and Joel Gurin. "Do Diets Really Work?" *Science 82* March 1982, pp. 42–50.

We have no method for predicting what "studies" will "prove" about the actual dangers of fatness over the next fifty years. But we already know the dangers created by the current medical position. They include at least—

- [ ] an incredible proliferation of bizarre diets
- [ ] anorexia and bulimia
- [ ] terrible stress
- [ ] cosmetic surgery, with all the risks that accompany any other surgery
- [ ] billions of dollars that should go for other purposes, diverted to the diet industry

And one more problem, made painfully clear by Denise Ann Tiffany in her story titled "Cancer patient voices fear, plea" (in *Medical News* for September 12, 1986, on page 47). Tiffany has cancer of the cervix, a cancer which can be detected by Pap tests at such early stages that it is easily cured. She says, "It wasn't that I didn't understand the importance of a Pap smear. ...I did not go in for a Pap smear because I was afraid my doctor would 'yell at me' about losing weight." There are far too many people like Tiffany—I know two in my immediate circle of friends—who are neglecting their health for this reason and this reason alone.

One fact we can be certain of:

WORRYING ABOUT "OBESITY" IS FAR MORE DANGEROUS THAN OBESITY ITSELF.

THE DREAD WORD OLD

Much of what was said about being perceived as fat applies to being perceived as old. As with fatness, most of the problem is manufactured from linguistic raw materials, independent of real world facts. Being old is not considered immoral, as fatness clearly is. Old age is not considered to be a condition you could prevent if you had sufficient will power. But our culture makes a sharp distinction between *being* old—which is not your fault—and *looking* old, which is. And it makes a sharp distinction between the genders, like that for fatness but with a wider gender gap. For a woman, old age begins at forty, and she is expected to continue to *look* forty; if she is in public life, she has to be extraordinarily good at what she does or look no older than thirty-five. For a man, the upper limit for both years and looks is sixty, and that number is firm.

An experienced women's magazine editor says that "When it is simply impossible to avoid photographs of real older women—when celebrities who happen to be 60 or so are featured—a strange thing happens. Retouching begins. Jawlines are reshaped, eye color is brightened, off come lines, wrinkles and signs of fatigue as art directors and retouching artists conspire to 'help' beautiful women look more beautiful—i.e., less their age." (Dalma Heyn, in *50 Plus* for March 1987, "Why Seven Magazines Pretend You Don't Exist," pp. 39–41, on page 41.) And she notes that old women "look in the mirror and think they look too old—because they're comparing themselves to some retouched face smiling back at them from a women's magazine."

The same thing happens to photographs of men, except that it's done only with men in their seventies and beyond, and it's much less drastic. Men are allowed to have lines and wrinkles and thinning hair, or no hair at all. (Consider the case of actor Telly Savalas, who could accurately be described as an aging fat man. Adults do not perceive him that way at all.) It's all right for a man to look sixty, and for an important and powerful man to look sixty-five (especially if he is flanked by a woman who looks barely thirty and is gazing adoringly at him. For either gender, if you are marked [+OLD] you must also be marked [+VIGOROUS], or suffer negative consequences; the young woman provides the aging man with living proof of vigor.

I am a *lucky* old person. I've had the luck to be closely involved with cultures where the old are greatly honored. I am an Ozark mountain woman, and we Ozarkers place high value on our old people. And my professional training in linguistics put me in long and close contact with several Native American cultures for whom being an "elder" was a mark of status and brought many special privileges. I am fiercely proud of being old, and look forward to being older; the result, of course, is that people do not perceive me *as* old. For society as a whole, despite *Lear's Magazine* and Barbara Bush, the perception that someone is old carries penalties. Terms like "senior citizen" and "elderly" and "aged" and "Golden Years" are no more effective against those penalties than "plump" and "portly" are against the penalties for overweight.

As we age, certain changes take place. They are normal, and they come to everyone to one degree or another. Some are changes associated with unattractiveness: we become shorter, our skin becomes wrinkled and spotted, our hair loses its color and becomes thin, and we tend to lose our teeth. The rest are changes that are already defined as disabilities and disorders in any other age group. Blindness and deafness and dizziness, weakness and forgetfulness and confusion, anosmia and agusia (the medical incantations for loss of the senses of smell and taste), impotence and vaginismus and infertility .... all of these, present to some degree in the old, are classified by our society as *medical* problems.

When you look at the array of diseases and disabilities whose symptoms are synonymous with the normal conditions of old age, it is obvious that to be old is semantically synonymous in English with being unhealthy and unfit. IF THAT WERE NOT TRUE, WE WOULD HAVE SEPARATE AND QUITE DIFFERENT COMMON NAMES FOR SUCH CONDITIONS IN OLD AGE. Medicine does have them—"presbyopia" and "presbycusis" are the names given to old sight and old hearing, respectively. But these are not words used by the general public. Furthermore, doctors do not say that a patient is "getting presbyopia" or "presbycusis"; they say the patient is "losing her eyesight" or "losing his hearing." That there should be a prejudice against the old and a dread of joining their ranks is not surprising, under the circumstances.

It's common to hear that prejudice against the old is about to disappear because there are now so *many* of them; we hear much about the power they hold because their votes are so numerous. This is claptrap. Women have always been numerous; they make up more than half the population and hold more than half the votes. Among the old they are an even higher percentage—so much so that it's no longer unusual for old women to constitute bigenerational sets, with an old woman of sixty responsible for the care of her eighty-year-old mother. (The terms for these two generations are not impressive; we call them the "old" and the "*old* old.") This numerousness has in no way protected women against prejudice. For the old, the primary effect of large numbers is only increased resentment of the perceived "burden" they represent to society. To avoid the negative effects of the prejudice known as *ageism*, the old person must be perceived as *not* old. We express that judgment in utterances like the following:

"You'd *never* guess he was an old person!"

"For someone her age, she's tremendous fun to be with!"

"He's not like an old person at all—his mind is just as sharp as a tack!"

"She doesn't look her age at all! She's absolutely lovely!"

And we make our feelings crystal clear in what we perceive as a *complimentary* response to hearing that someone is old. We say, "My goodness, you certainly don't *look* it!"

The health consequences of the negative presuppositions attached to the word "old" are of two kinds. First, things are done that are at least unnecessary and often dangerous as well. Old people trying to look younger have their faces lifted and their tummies tucked and their thighs and abdomens liposuctioned. If they weigh more than the ideal, they subject themselves to the same hazardous miseries as do young people, although they are far less able to tolerate them. In all such situations, people reflect our society's bias toward the eye and our popular misconceptions about what is real: they struggle to change the "physical facts" and make what is *seen* fit the specifications for a youthful appearance.

Second, and equally dangerous, things that are genuinely necessary for the health and well-being of old persons do *not* get done. Sometimes this is because they have no money to pay for them; we are aware of that problem and efforts are being made to find a solution. What we are not aware of is the serious problem of health care that is not provided even when the resources *are* available to pay for it, simply because it's taken for granted that the cause of the symptom is old age. When the sensory systems of elderly people begin to fail, we often do not investigate to find out *why*. The older the person in question is, the more likely we are to just assume that old age is the cause of the problem, as if the elderly were somehow immune to all the other possible causes.

As a young woman I was once given a medication that had depletion of potassium as a side effect. And one day I found myself unable to locate the post office in the small town where I lived. I was outraged because it had been moved without letting me know. While I hunted for it, I kept coming to intersections with four-way stop signs without knowing exactly how I was supposed to drive through them safely, much to the annoyance of other drivers who also had to get through them. I was shocked at how *rude* these people were. I did manage to find the bank, where I tried to deposit a check stub; the tellers, unable to make me understand why that couldn't be done, suggested that I go home and come back with some member of my family. By the time I got home I was not only worn out and frustrated at being unable to get my ordinary daily business accomplished, I was tearful and angry and confused and frightened. And I was firmly convinced that there was some sort of conspiracy against me.

In fact, the only thing wrong with me was a dangerously low level of potassium, and my doctor quickly set that right. But my condition during that brief episode had only one possible name: *senility*. And if I had been eighty-nine instead of twenty-nine, the chances are very good that no one would have bothered to check my potassium. In the December 1987 issue of *Psychology Today*, Robert Sekuler and Randolph Blake tell readers that it's "comforting to realize that diminished senses seldom indicate a dulling of mental faculties." It may be. But it's not comforting to the elderly person whose children or neighbors or caregivers react to an increasing mental deterioration with "Poor thing ... it's awful the way old people go downhill."

In the past ten years I have managed to rescue three elderly people whose apparent "senility" was due to a lack of potassium, a very common consequence of not eating properly—but each time, I had to fight an uphill battle to get the potassium test done. And in just the past few years, large numbers of old people thought to be in various stages of coma have been discovered to be suffering only from overmedication, sending doctors around the country scrambling to make sure that they had not accepted a comatose condition in any of *their* patients without a thorough search for its cause. The consequences of presupposing that OLD is synonymous with UNFIT are not trivial ones. Which brings us to ...

THE DREAD WORD DISABLED

Once again, we see the problems of negative perceptions and prejudice that arise when you attach a linguistic *label* to a human being. Once again, we see people who are not only struggling with their unavoidable problems, but whose burdens are increased by their efforts to avoid being *perceived* as disabled. We see these people, helped very little by the existence of terms like "physically challenged" or "differently abled" undergoing medical treatments that they need not have undergone. I know far too many people who are suffering needless pain because they flatly refuse to wear badly needed orthopedic shoes or a neck or back brace. I know many more whose lives are greatly complicated by their refusals to use canes or walkers or wheelchairs.

In some ways, the term "disabled" summarizes all three of the Dread Words, because both fatness and old age are disabilities of a kind in our society. The only difference is in the degree to which we hold people responsible for their condition, with fatness at the "completely responsible" end of the scale, old age in the middle, and disability at the other extreme. For all three, however, the message our culture sends is the same:

> You are obligated to do everything in your power to *appear* [−FAT], [−OLD], and [−DISABLED].

It's fortunate, therefore, that the remedy in all three cases is also the same. The long-term remedy is of course to cure society of its illogical reactions; nobody knows whether that is possible or not. In the meantime, the remedy is to stop trying to change the so-called *facts*—usually an impossible task, and one that adds both new dangers and additional stresses—and concentrate on changing the *perceptions*. Perhaps a little scientific support would help at this point; look at the following quotation.

Attempts to understand the personal characteristics of others, in interactions with them, are complicated by the fact that one tends to find what one expects. This happens not only because processing of information is selective, but also because expectancies cause one to act in ways that elicit behavior interpretable as confirming those expectancies, even when the expectancies might have been mistaken. Studies provide ample evidence of such self-fulfilling prophecies....

(Edward E. Jones, "Interpreting Interpersonal Behavior: The Effects of Expectancies," in *Science* for October 3, 1986, pp. 41-6; on page 41.)

That is: Suppose that when I approach you I am thinking to myself "Now this is an old person, who therefore won't be very openminded or intelligent, and who is sure to be irritable and petulant and opinionated." I am then almost certain to behave toward you in ways that distress you and cause you to behave as if you were narrowminded and unintelligent and irritable and petulant and opinionated ... which confirms the suspicions I had about you in the first place. And this loop won't end when the two of us come to the end of our interactions. I will come away from it with my negative stereotype of old people strengthened; you will come away from it more convinced than ever that younger people are too rude and too intolerant to be worth treating courteously; and we will both carry these attitudes into our interactions with others. As the loop churns, the negative presuppositions grow ever stronger.

An inevitable result of feedback loops like this one, for the old, the overweight, and the disabled, is the weakening or the total loss of their social support networks. All the evidence tells us that such a network is essential to health. Its destruction adds yet one more hazard to the list of health dangers these people already must deal with.

TECHNIQUE #17—USING TWIRKS TO CONTROL PERCEPTIONS

A twirk is an element of language behavior which attracts so much attention to *itself* that it outweighs both the form and the content of the speech it occurs with. If you gave a speech while stark naked, you would be wasting your time. No matter how good the speech was, no matter how superbly you delivered it, your audience would not hear it. Your nakedness, which in theoretical terms has nothing at all to do with anything, would have the practical effect of cancelling all the rest of your efforts. It would be a *twirk*. (In every sector of our society except a nudist camp, it would be a Supertwirk.)

Little kids know the usefulness of twirks. The middleclass Anglo child who answers his teacher's "How much is six times seven?" with "I ain't got no pencil" is counting on his teacher to be so distracted by the "bad grammar" twirk that the question will be forgotten. Lawyers know, too. The city lawyer who tells the rural jury "I hope we can all get out of here by suppertime" instead of "I hope court will adjourn in time for dinner" is using a twirk—the twirk of dialect. He is choosing words and phrases that say "I am one of you; I perceive the world as you do; I speak your language." The common prescription for "power dressing" is a twirk prescription, based on the idea that when what you say is badly prepared or badly stated your expensive suit will convince listeners you surely must have said something of the same quality as your clothing.

No twirk is in and of itself either positive or negative. The effect of a twirk depends on the context, the situation, and the communication goal. However, some twirks are more likely to create difficulties than others. One of the most potentially troublesome in adults is a "[+NEGATIVE]" voice. That is: a voice which reliably creates negative perceptions about the speaker that have nothing to do with either the words being spoken or the sort of person actually speaking. The set of such voices includes a number of stereotypes—including the Elderly Voice, the Invalid Voice, the Spoiled Child Voice, the Airhead Voice, the Wimp Voice, and the Silly Person Voice.

All of these voices have a great deal in common. They are all high-pitched. They are all nasal. They all deviate drastically from mainstream society's ideal for *dynamics*—that is, they either have too little variety of intonation, which we call "monotonous," or they have too much, a condition that has no name but which could roughly be called "florid" or "melodramatic." They also deviate in pace and volume, and are perceived as too fast or slow, too loud or too soft. And every last one of them will cause listeners to attach to you whichever label in the set of stereotypes seems to fit the rest of the information they have about who and what you are.

To get rid of this twirk, use Technique #15, presented earlier in this chapter. Choose as your model a voice that transmits the message "I AM AN ATTRACTIVE AND INTELLIGENT AND COMPETENT AND VIGOROUS PERSON," and work with it in simultaneous modeling. If you are someone who is perceived as a fat person, an old person, or a disabled person, the one step you can take that is most likely to counteract those perceptions is an improvement in voice quality.

If your poor voice quality is the result of a physical condition that cannot be changed, this is still worth doing. The reason I put the "[+NEGATIVE]" label for the voice in quotation marks is because that feature is an entirely subjective summary label for a whole group of features whose presence or absence can actually be demonstrated by scientific instruments, such as [+HIGH-PITCHED] and [+NASAL]. The negative perceptions are the result of those features in *combination*. Suppose your physical condition makes it literally impossible for your voice to be other than nasal; if you can lower its pitch, the nasal quality will have a less negative effect. And vice versa. The fewer features your voice has from the group that define an unpleasant voice for our culture, the more powerful and positive its effect upon perceptions will be.

Another twirk that can cause problems for you is poor posture. The stereotypical fat person slumps and slouches because of embarrassment and physical discomfort. The stereotypical disabled person has exactly the same problem, although the physical reasons will differ according to the disability. The stereotypical old person is actually bent over, from aging alone or from such disorders of the elderly as Parkinson's Disease. If your goal is to keep people *from* appreciating the importance of your words, slumping and stooping are two of the most effective methods for achieving that goal.

People tend to try to avoid the use of medical "appliances," because they are so drastically in conflict with the Young & Vital target image. But if wearing a brace or using a cane makes it possible for you to sit and stand erect when you couldn't do so without them, that effect outweighs any negative potential. It's not unusual for people to admire the look of a cane held by a confident and attractive person and to wish they had a legitimate excuse to carry a cane too. They may even go buy themselves an elegant cane to be used on occasions when they feel they can get away with such a gesture. But *nobody* looks at someone and thinks, "Gee, I wish *I* had an excuse to be all bent over and stooped like that!"

Other twirks to avoid are the ones on this list:

1. A facial expression that seems pasted on, and that is always present no matter what is being talked about. The dismal expression of misery, the fixed scowl, and the perpetual smile are all bad; the apathetic "nobody home" face is no better.

2. A *rigid* body with a fixed posture and a near absence of gestures—or its opposite, the body equivalent of the florid voice, with gestures that are too abundant and too dramatic.

3. A child's body language (like a child's voice) in an adult body. Wide eyes, a mouth that falls open and stays that way for long periods. Twirling a lock of hair. Chewing on your lips. Letting your tongue protrude from your mouth when

you're trying to concentrate. A seeming inability to sit still or stay in one place for more than a minute or two at a time. Tapping your feet or swinging your legs. Humming. Giggling. Talking to yourself. Sniffling. And the whole set of "grooming" items that are not ordinarily public in adults, like scratching.

4. The Gestures of Doom, when nothing is happening to justify them. Clutching your brow. Wringing your hands. Twisting a handkerchief around and around. Grinding your teeth. Weeping and wailing. Clapping your hands over your mouth or your cheeks or clutching both fists to your heart.

Eliminating these items from your inventory of language behavior elements will give the words you say a better chance of being heard as you intended them to be heard. Without your listeners being constantly distracted by the intrusive and unintended message, "THIS IS A FAT PERSON (or old, or disabled person) TALKING."

Your physical circumstances may not make it possible for you to get rid of all these potentially negative twirks. They may stand between you and the acquisition of other twirks that have strong positive potential, such as the use of symmetrical gestures made with both hands. But just as with the summary "[+NEGATIVE]" voice, getting rid of *any* of the items listed will improve matters.

TWIRKS AND PERCEPTUAL FILTERS

Once a label has been attached to a person by a medical professional of any kind, the label becomes a perceptual filter. Everything the labeled individual does from "diagnosis" on tends to be perceived as evidence for the label.

The most famous example is the experiment in which a group of psychologists got themselves admitted to various mental hospitals in this country with a diagnosis of schizophrenia, simply by claiming that they heard voices. Although they dropped the pretense of mental illness and behaved normally thereafter, it was weeks before they were released. Throughout their hospitalization they were treated for schizophrenia. When they were released they were labeled as "in remission from schizophrenia." The fact that as patients they took notes all day long and told everyone openly that they were researchers made no difference; this behavior was interpreted as evidence of the delusions symptomatic of schizophrenia. The twirk in this case—"Doctor, I keep hearing a voice saying 'empty, hollow, thud'" —would seem to be a trivial chunk of language behavior, but its power to overrule all other evidence is awesome! Clearly, if you would *like* to be judged mentally ill, this is your twirk of choice.

For an elderly person, the label most likely to be attached in error is *dementia*. (This is another cover term. The actual label may be "senility" or "Alzheimer's" or "delirium," or any of a number of others that refer to a decreased mental competence.) Here's a typical list of the symptoms of dementia:

- □ forgetfulness
- □ restlessness
- □ apathy
- □ a tendency to misplace things
- □ a tendency to repeat words or actions
- □ wakefulness at night, drowsiness during the day
- □ fears of being taken advantage of
- □ suspiciousness of other people
- □ irritability
- □ a tendency to complain constantly (to doctors, to government agencies, to managers of stores, etc.)
- □ a tendency to state extreme opinions and argue about them doggedly
- □ confusion about basic facts and anger when the confusion is pointed out
- □ a conviction of being disliked

All of these characteristics are found to some degree in people of all ages; I suspect that we all can name a relatively young person who demonstrates half a dozen of them. When thirty-year-old Marianne stands in front of her refrigerator and says aloud, "Now what on earth did I come *in* here for?" people laugh and think no more about it. When seventy-year-old Martin does the same thing, they are all too ready to think "Alzheimer's!" From the moment this suspicion arises, they will watch Martin for more signs of mental failure—and *they will find them*. In abundance! Treating Martin *as if* he were becoming demented will annoy him and make him self-conscious and nervous around others, which will increase his perfectly normal missteps and misstatements. The more people notice such things, the more oddly they will behave toward Martin—which will convince him that they are mistreating him, adding "paranoia" to his increasingly clumsy social performance. (If Martin, like many old people, does not hear well, that will make matters even worse.) And shortly the family members will be giving the family doctor a description of Martin's behavior that fits all or part of the dementia symptom list.

Unless you live in total isolation, you don't have to worry about the possibility that you might really *be* suffering from dementia, and nobody will notice it or try to help you. That's not a hazard. The hazard is that someone will misinterpret your ordinary forgetfulness and ordinary irritability as symptoms and tack one of those labels to you, after which everything you do—including your justified outrage—will be perceived as confirming the label.

Obviously, all the "symptoms" will be at their worst when you are upset and tense and under stress. You trigger suspicions about your mental capacity when you address your son Bill as Tom, claim that it's Tuesday when it's really Thursday, drop your pencil in the wastebasket as you put the trash in your pocket, accuse your spouse of taking your glasses when they're pushed up on your forehead, call the local police chief a facist ... things like that. And the one context in which you are most likely to do such things is in hostile interactions with other people. Here the *Gentle Art* techniques—especially those for applying Miller's Law, using the Satir Modes, and managing VAPs—are your first line of defense. *Use* them.

Your second line of defense is in many ways absurd. Please look at the following set of questions and instructions, which is a typical "test of mental status" like those used by medical professionals.

1. What is your name?
2. How old are you?
3. What is the date today?
4. Who is the president of the United States now?
5. Where are we?
6. Who am I?
7. What is this called? (Asked while the examiner points to a wristwatch or some other common object.)
8. What does "a stitch in time saves nine" mean?
9. Start at 100 and count backward by sevens, please.
10. Take this piece of paper, fold it twice, and then give it back to me, please.

I always know my name, but I often cannot remember how old I am. I always know my location in general terms, but even after years of experience with particular buildings, I continue to get lost. Because I work a seven-day week, I *rarely* know what the date is, and often have no idea what day of the week it is either. (George Bush has a similar problem ... you will recall his announcement, during a September speech, that it was the anniversary of Pearl Harbor.) I have many times found myself at a loss for the name of a common object, and this phenomenon happens to others around me with equal frequency. I have trouble counting backward by sevens, even at the best of times. When someone is clearly watching me for signs of incompetence, I am very likely to follow instructions incorrectly. And so on.

None of this causes people to accuse me (or George Bush) of dementia—but if I were eighty, that would change. As a *positive* twirk, therefore, to be used systematically, I suggest that before you are interviewed by a medical professional you memorize all the basic facts that you might reasonably be expected to produce. *Be sure* you know the date, the president's name, the name of the building and the floor and the room where you're located, your age and birthdate, and similar items. You might memorize the list of numbers that is the result of counting backwards by sevens from one hundred.

This is silly. I agree with you. But it's silly in the same way that wearing clothes indoors is silly. Whether you have clothes on or not has nothing at all, logically, to do with whether you are intelligent or kind or competent or moral or well-educated; whether you know how old you are has nothing to do with it either. Nevertheless, people's perceptions of you are shaped by such silly things, not by who and what you "really" are. And the consequences of their incorrect perceptions are potentially too serious to be ignored, particularly when they are so easily avoided.

WORKOUT SECTION

1. For a clear and concise brief article summarizing the medical community's position on dementia, read "Differential Diagnosis of Dementing Diseases," a consensus statement issued by the National Institutes of Health, in *JAMA* for December 18, 1987, pp. 3411–16.

2. Do a semantic feature matrix for the three dread words—*fat, old, disabled*—to determine their exact meaning for you personally. Get some of your family or associates to do the same, so that you can compare your meanings with theirs.

3. Investigate the three dread words a little further. Complete the sentences below with *metaphors* that accurately express your personal perceptions.

   a. "Fat is _____."
   b. "Being fat is like _____."
   c. "A disability is _____."
   d. "Being disabled is like _____."

e. "Old age is _____."

f. "Being old is like _____."

4. In "Giving weight-loss advice that patients will heed" (*Contemporary OB/GYN* for October 1987, pp. 81–2 and 87–90, on page 81), Terry Prewitt and Mary Rogers tell us that the "lexicon of helpful, tactful terms to describe the medically overweight is very inadequate. Clearly, the physician walks a linguistic tightrope." This is true, certainly; it is not so clear why it *should* be true, since medical professionals are more highly skilled at naming things than almost any other segment of society. Can you help the doctors out?

There are six common ways to add to a lexicon (a vocabulary): creating new words from foreign word-parts, as with "telephone" and "phonograph"; making a word from the first letters of the words in a phrase, like "laser" and "sonar"; reintroducing an obsolete word with a new meaning, as with "twirk"; adding to or otherwise modifying an existing word, as with "percepting"; making the new word up from scratch. (The last method is of course the hardest; an example would be "scratstrack," a word I coined to name "a night spent getting up over and over again to tend to sick people or animals, while others in the house sleep blissfully on, either not hearing or pretending not to hear.") Using one or more of these methods, construct a word "to describe the medically overweight" that would get doctors off their tightrope.

5. In "Sensory Underload," by Robert Sekuler and Randolph Blake (*Psychology Today* for December 1987, pp. 48–51), there is a description of an experiment in an architecture class at the University of Michigan. The students involved wore glasses "designed to imitate the impaired vision of an elderly person." Environmental psychologist Leon Pastalan developed the glasses as part of a set of simulations of impaired vision, hearing and touch used at the university to make the students more sensitive to the problems of again sensory systems. Try a similar experiment for yourself, in a setting where it's safe for you to do so. Put on a pair of sunglasses that you've carefully smeared with oil or butter; stuff your ears with cotton; put on a pair of thick gloves. Then try to go about your ordinary activities. Pay careful attention not just to the "facts"—that is, to such things as how much longer things take or what errors are made—but also to what happens to your *mental* state. Do you get confused? Irritable? What kinds of things do you say to yourself *about* yourself?

6. Go back to the set of negative self-perception statements in this chapter—"I know my nose is too big because ..."—and convert as many of them into positive statements—"I know my nose is the proper size because ..."—as possible. Then add to the set as many additional positive statements as you can.

7. One of the most common responses a woman hears when she tells another woman that she has to have surgery is "That's horrible! I'm so sorry! But look at the bright side—at least you'll lose weight!" What does this tell you about the meaning of overweight for women in this country? Would a man say that to another man who was facing surgery?

SIGHT BITES

1. Women tend to distort their perceptions of their bodies negatively. Men, just as unrealistically, distort their perceptions, though in a more positive, self-aggrandizing way...."

    (Daniel Goleman, "Dislike of Own Body Found Common Among Women," in the *NY Times* for March 18, 1985.)

2. "Motivating an older woman to exercise is a challenging task."

    (Mona Shangold M.D. and Gabe Mirkin M.D., "Fitness in Postmenopausal Women: How to Motivate the Patient," in *Medical Aspects of Human Sexuality* for February 1987, pp. 23–9; on page 23.)

3. "I have numerous older patients who need hospitalization, and the best diagnosis I can conceive for them is 'the dwindles'."

    (Walter M. Bortz II, M.D., "Geriatrics: Through the Looking Glass," in *Medical Times* for June 1989, pp. 85–92; on page 90.)

4. "The major lesson of the research reviewed here is that each of us constructs a significant part of the social reality that he or she confronts."

    (Edward E. Jones, "Interpreting Interpersonal Behavior: The Effects of Expectancies," in *Science* for October 3, 1986, pp. 41–46; on page 46.)

5. "Like any ritual, dieting has found a myth to give it meaning. The central tenet of the diet mythology is that thin people are *better* than fat ones— more beautiful, healthier, stronger of will."

    (William Bennett and Joel Gurin, "Do Diets Really Work?", in *Science* 82, March 1982, pp. 42–50; on p. 42) NOTE: Of all the sources you could read on dieting and the research about the subject, this one is the most useful.

6. "After 70, if you wake without any pains at all, you're dead."

    (Quoted in Malcolm Cowley's "About Men: Being Old Old," in the *NY Times Magazine* for May 26, 1985; on page 58.)

7. "A poster distributed during an obesity prevention campaign in an African community depicted an obese woman and an overloaded truck with a flat tire. The caption read 'both carry too much weight.' However, community members thought that the woman in the poster was both rich

and happy—not only was she fat, but she was blessed with a truck full of possessions!"

(Chris Anne Raymond Ph.D., "Biology, Culture, Dietary Changes Conspire to Increase Incidence of Obesity," in *JAMA* for October 24/31, 1986, pp. 2157–8; on page 2158.)

8. "Well into the twentieth century, specific bathing procedures and personal cleanliness products were promoted as *medical therapy* in the same manner as other serious medical regimens and drugs, complete with warnings about contraindications."

(JoAnne Brown, "Take me to the river: the water cure in America," in *Medical Humanities Review* for July 1987, pages 29–34; on page 32.)

9. "If practitioners were to attempt to keep up with the literature by reading two articles per day, in one year they would fall fifty-five centuries behind."

(Quoted by R.W. Curry, MD, from ANNALS OF INTERNAL MEDICINE for July 1986; . . .)

10

YOUR HEAD BONE CONNECTED TO YOUR THIGH BONE

INTRODUCTION—WHY "PARTISM" IS DANGEROUS TO YOUR HEALTH

One of the most basic and important concepts in medicine is the principle of balance known as *homeostasis*. Almost every aspect of health and of medical diagnosis and treatment involves this concept. For a human being to stay alive and function normally, a set of absolutely specific conditions must be maintained. There must be enough water in your body, but not too much. Enough salt, but not too much. Enough sugar, but not too much. And so on through a lengthy list. Furthermore, how much is enough and how much is too much depends not on each individual element in isolation, but on all of them acting together. Increasing the amount of any one of them increases or decreases your need for others. When everything is in balance within the narrow range of safe limits (a very complicated situation and one that is constantly changing), you are said to have "achieved homeostasis."

Doctors know this. It's harped on incessantly in medical education and literature, with particularly urgent warnings that homeostasis is fragile in elderly persons and must constantly be kept in mind. But in today's climate of medical specialization it tends to get lost, and patients don't ordinarily know enough about it to be vigilant. The result is rampant *partism*: medicine done part by part, with one doctor treating your bones and another your kidneys and another your skin and another your digestive tract ... and so on ... without *anybody* treating you as a whole person. Even doctors whose specialties would seem more general—family practice specialists, for example, and general practitioners—are so busy and distracted that they treat "the gall bladder in 103" or "the back in 210" or "the tonsils in Examining Room A" instead of treating people.

Doctors squabble over the opposite position, called *wholism* or (more commonly) *holism*. Some have nothing but scorn for holistic medicine, calling it quackery or worse. Here are two typical medical comments to give you a sense of the position.

> This book is dynamite, an absolute smash! It lays bare holistic medicine as constituting not a distinct concept of medicine, but instead a melange of banalities, truisms, exaggerations, and falsehoods, overlaid with disparagement not only of scientific conclusions but of logical reason itself. ... A mixture of the primitive, the unscientific, and the irrational, holistic medicine is disrobed in this book as the ultimate consumer fraud—snake oil medicine.
>
> (Victor Herbert M.D./J.D.), reviewing Douglas Starker and Clark Glymour's *Examining Holistic Medicine*, in *JAMA* for September 5, 1986, pp. 1202–3; on page 1202.)

> Holistic medicine is a pablum of common sense and nonsense offered by cranks and quacks and failed pedants who share an attachment to magic and an animosity toward reason.
>
> (Clark Glymour Ph.D. and Douglas Stalker Ph.D., "Engineers, Cranks, Physicians, Magicians," in *The New England Journal of Medicine* for April 21, 1983, pp. 960–963; on page 963.)

Other doctors claim that holistic medicine is the medicine *they* practice, and have always practiced, even if they specialize in cosmetic surgery for female noses. While the caregivers are thrashing this out in the medical community, patients must learn to fend for themselves. They must learn to recognize partism when it's coming at them. They must learn to remind the offending doctors to stop and consider them (w)holistically.

Let's consider a typical scenario in health care that demands recognition of the connection between headbones and thighbones and all the rest. Suppose you find yourself suffering from *edema*, which most typically means that your ankles and legs are swollen because you are retaining too much water in your body. This distresses you and you go to a doctor for help. The doctor diagnoses the edema, determines its cause, and prescribes a diuretic—a drug that will cause you to excrete more urine and get rid of more water. So far, so good—the doctor has treated your "swollen legs and ankles," and the treatment works. You are the satisfied patient of a competent doctor.

But the welfare of your entire bodymind depends upon your maintaining a specific level of *potassium*. Too much potassium and your heart is in danger; too little potassium and your brain is in danger. Not *just* your heart and not *just* your brain, but they're sufficient for our purposes here. The more urine you excrete, the more potassium you excrete as well, so that giving you the diuretic for your legs and ankles endangers your brain and puts you at risk for all sorts of neurological problems up to and including coma. (See the account of my experience with low potassium on page 182 for an example.) To counter this, a doctor might try to protect your brain by giving you extra potassium—but would have to take great care, because with too much potassium the heart rate goes out of whack. And that's not all. The level of potassium also has to be in balance with your levels of calcium and magnesium. This is *electrolyte* balance (often misheard by mystified patients as "electric light balance"), and when it's not right you face still other dangers.

The doctor who considers only your swollen legs and ankles is guilty of partism. The patient who allows that to happen, and who fails to ask, "What will this do to my electrolyte balance?" before accepting a prescription for a diuretic, is cooperating in a partist medical encounter and is at risk. The same is true for the patient who asks that question and settles for a wave of the hand and a casual "No problem!" You must be *sure* that the doctor (a) knows your present electrolyte levels and (b) has heard and understood your question and (c) is answering that question and not some other question and (d) is aware of the facts. Whether being questioned about this "bothers" the doctor or not is irrelevant.

Another common hazard of partist medicine arises when you are seeing several doctors, each of whom is prescribing medicines for you without considering those prescribed by the others. Tell the doctor who has just handed you a prescription for Potion X that you are already taking Potion Y. Even if just one doctor is doing the prescribing, find out if it's okay to take both medications.

You can't afford the risks associated with being treated as if your body were made up of isolated separate blocks. Whatever your doctor's orientation on holistic medicine may be, the only safe patient in our health care system is a *holistic* patient. And the only tool available to you for getting across to your doctor that that's what you are is language.

TECHNIQUE #18—PRESUPPOSING HOLISM

Let's review, briefly, the concept of presupposition. In the GENTLE ART system, a presupposition is defined as anything that native speakers of a language know is part of the meaning of a sequence of that language, even when it does not appear on the surface of the utterance. At the level of words, that means that "bird" has the feature [+FEATHERED] as part of its meaning. It not only isn't necessary to say "a feathered bird," it would be silly to do so. At the level of the phrase, it means that "managed to walk" presupposes that the walking was not accomplished without difficulty. At the level of the sentence, it means that "EVen JOHN could pass THAT test!" presupposes that the test is easy and John is no great shakes as a scholar. Roughly speaking, what is presupposed by your language is presupposed to be true, relieving you of the necessity to make an open claim for it.

As communication strategy in your language interactions with medical professionals, you can use the power of presupposition to accomplish two important tasks:

1. To communicate messages that, for reasons of your own, you prefer not to state openly.
2. To compress a great deal of information into so few words that they can get past the 18-second medical limit on listening to patients.

We're going to look at three different areas of language you can use for this purpose: factives, nominalizations, and time words.

FACTIVES

When you say "The fact that [X] amazes me," as in "The fact that antibiotics work amazes me," whatever is included in X is presupposed. English has a set of predicates called *factives* that have "X is a fact" as part of their meaning. It's characteristic of factives that sentences embedded immediately after them are presupposed to be true, even when the factives are negative. This sounds a lot more complicated than it is; a few examples will clear it up.

1. "I knew I had a fever." (Or, "I knew that I had a fever.")

The sentence "I had a fever" is embedded here as the grammatical object of "knew"—as what was known. And this presupposes the truth of "I had a fever."

2. "I didn't know I had a fever."

Although "know" has been made negative, it is still presupposed that the speaker had a fever.

Compare these examples with...

3. "I thought I had a fever."
4. "I didn't think I had a fever."

Now "I had a fever" is embedded as the grammatical object of "think" rather than "know." For both the positive and the negative examples, it may or may not be true that the speaker had a fever.

This tells us that "know" is a factive verb, but "think" isn't. You can test any predicate for the feature [+FACTIVE] by embedding the sentence about fever after it in a larger sentence in this same way, both in a positive and a negative version, and observing what happens, like this:

5. "I was aware that I had a fever."
6. "I wasn't aware that I had a fever."
7. "I forgot that I had a fever."
8. "I didn't forget that I had a fever."

9. "I realized that I had a fever."
10. "I didn't realize that I had a fever."

11. "I regretted that I had a fever."
12. "I didn't regret that I had a fever."

13. "It was fortunate that I had a fever."
14. "It was unfortunate that I had a fever."

This tells you that "be aware, forget, realize, regret" and "be fortunate" are all factives.

Asking your doctor "Did you check my electrolyte levels before you decided to prescribe this diuretic?" is confrontational. It is very likely to be interpreted as a challenge, especially in today's environment of malpractice suits and defensive medicine. If the doctor *has* forgotten to check your electrolytes, answering your question truthfully means a loss of face; if the doctor remembered, your having asked is likely to be perceived as insulting. A simple way to find out without putting the doctor up against a linguistic wall is by using "know" to presuppose what you sincerely hope is true, like this:

"I know you checked my electrolyte levels before you prescribed this diuretic, Doctor. I'm glad they're okay."

Now the doctor who remembered to check the levels has been complimented on performance. And the doctor who didn't can avoid a loss of face by saying, "I'm glad you mentioned that, because there is just one more test I really think we ought to run before you start taking the medication."

If you find yourself in the awkward position of needing to tell a medical professional something that professional ought to already know, you can do it easily with factives. You use the expression "as you know" or "as you are aware," which is only another way of saying "I know that you know X" and presupposing "you know X."

Suppose it's obvious to you that your doctor has forgotten about your penicillin allergy. Suppose you've been sent to a specialist in one or more of your parts, and this new doctor hasn't bothered even to *ask* about your allergies. In both cases, you realize that the doctor is getting ready to write you a prescription for penicillin. "You are aware that I'm allergic to penicillin, Doctor" is too abrupt. But "As you are aware, Doctor, I'm allergic to penicillin" is less confrontational. The doctor given this can then say, with no loss of face, "Right! And that's why I've decided to prescribe (Z) for you instead." If this sort of thing happens often, you should change doctors. Absolutely. But doctors, like patients, are human, and are equally likely to make occasional errors. You have both the right and the obligation to use language for self-defense against such errors, but rubbing the doctor's nose in them won't accomplish anything useful.

NOMINALIZATIONS

Whenever you are able to put the words "the" or "this, that, these, those," or a possessive like "my" or "John's" in front of a nominal, its existence is presupposed. For example, if you say "I have a new car," you are making an open claim, the truth of which is not in any way presupposed. But if you say "The new car I bought last week..." or "That new car of mine..." or "My new car..." and add a predicate like "wouldn't start this morning," you have *presupposed* the sentence "I have a new car." The only thing you are openly claiming is that you couldn't get it started this morning. The more you add to your description, the stronger the presupposition; thus, "My new foreign car with the turbowhuffles and magwhippers wouldn't start this morning" makes the presupposition almost overpowering.

In just the same way, "I have a cold" is an open claim, but "My cold is a real nuisance" presupposes the cold and claims only that it's a nuisance. Ideally you will finish your sentence—after the nominalization—with something that no one would want to argue with you about, like the idea that a cold is a nuisance.

As long as the item you want to use this way is a noun, the process is simple. But often you want to presuppose a verb or other predicate, which can't be put into a descriptive sequence the way "car" or "cold" can. In that case, what you do is *nominalize* the predicate—turn it into a noun. Any verb of English can be nominalized by adding "–ing" to it; for other predicates, you can always put "being" or "having been" in front of the word. In addition, many English predicates have special noun alternative forms, like "abandonment" from "abandon" and "resignation" from "resign" and "cruelty" from "cruel."

Let's look at some examples. In each set, the first sentence is an open claim. The other two presuppose what the first one claimed, by nominalization with "–ing" and with a special noun form. Either nominalization is technically correct. The differences between them are matters of style, with one being more formal or more cumbersome or more acceptable than another. Choose the one you feel most comfortable with.

15. a. "I'm allergic to penicillin."

    b. "My being allergic to penicillin is a nuisance."
    c. "My allergy to penicillin is a nuisance."

16. a. "That technician is careless."

    b. "That technician's being careless is strange."
    c. "That technician's carelessness is strange."

19. a. "I can't (am unable to) sleep."

    b. "My being unable to sleep puzzles me."
    c. "My inability to sleep puzzles me."

20. a. "The clerk destroyed my records."

    b. "That clerk's having destroyed my records amazes me."
    c. "That clerk's destruction of my records amazes me."

If you find yourself in a tense linguistic situation, perhaps facing an angry doctor or nurse, or caught in the middle of an argument between two caregivers, you can often defuse it even more. Use the presupposition strategy, and then add a switch to Computer Mode. Remove both yourself and the caregiver(s) from the sentence and restructure it as a depersonalized abstraction. For example:

21. "Being allergic to penicillin is a nuisance."
22. "Being unable to sleep is puzzling."

TIME WORD PRESUPPOSITIONS

The English words used to describe intervals of time—*after, while, before, during, when,* and the like—carry presuppositions with them that you can put to good use in medical encounters. They are particularly helpful as a way to let a doctor know what you want done without giving a direct order or making an open request.

Suppose you want your doctor to prescribe zippostatin instead of the more usual wheeyostatin. Because although wheeyostatin helps with the headaches you're being seen for, it makes the ulcer (that you're seeing someone else for) worse. You can say "Write me a prescription for zippostatin, Doctor" or "Would you please write me a prescription for zippostatin, Doctor?" But doctors are much happier when *they* are the ones telling people what to do. You can avoid the appearance of ordering your doctor around by saying any one of these:

> "After you write my prescription for zippostatin, Doctor, do you want me to get dressed or wait for the nurse?"

> "While you're writing my prescription for zippostatin, Doctor, shall I just go ahead and fill out this insurance form?"

> "I'll go on to the front desk and give the receptionist my check— unless you'd rather I waited until you've written my zippostatin prescription."

> "When I fill my prescription for zippostatin, Doctor, should I tell the pharmacist not to substitute a generic drug?"

> "When I start taking the zippostatin, Doctor, should I take it with food or on an empty stomach?"

These sentences should cause the doctor to say, "Oh, do you want a prescription for zippostatin?"—to which you can say yes. If that doesn't happen, and the doctor says, "I'm not going to give you zippostatin, I'm going to give you wheeyostatin," you will have to deal with that. But it's much better to go into a potential argument with the doctor that way than after "Look, don't try to tell me what to prescribe for you—*I'm* the doctor here, not you!"

It's important to realize that tailoring your language for the medical professional in this way is not toadying or fawning or being a wimp. It's not cowardice. It's linguistic skill for the sake of your health. A doctor who is angry or defensive or frustrated is a doctor who will provide less than optimum care; those emotions not only affect the decisions made, they interfere with competence. It is in your own best interest for your doctor to be relaxed and comfortable with you.

Doctors who think you question their knowledge or their competence are going to order extra tests and procedures for you, because they are very wary creatures these days. They're afraid you'll sue them for malpractice if anything goes wrong. You have every moral right, when talking to doctors, to say whatever you darned please. No question about it. *As long as you know the consequences and are willing to accept them for the sake of the principle.* You should not find yourself facing your fifth barium enema just because you don't know what it is about your language that annoys or alarms your doctor. You should not find yourself paying a four hundred dollar bill for lab tests because—although you know what you're saying that leads to communication breakdown—you don't realize that other linguistic choices are available to you.

Now, please look at the following examples, which demonstrate that you can use the three presuppositional strategies discussed above in various *combinations*, to increase their linguistic power.

> 23. "As you know, Doctor, sleeping badly can cause serious health problems."

The factive "know" plus the nominalized "sleeping badly"—plus a Computer Mode statement in which the speaker talks of generic insomnia rather than his or her own sleep problems.

> 24. "It's fortunate that when you were checking with the other specialist about my medications you didn't find any problems with drug interactions."

The factive "it's fortunate" plus a time word—"when"— presupposing that the doctor has already checked to find out which medications the consultant is prescribing.

> 25. "As you are well aware, Doctor, taking diuretics can cause all kinds of problems with electrolytes."

The factive "be aware" plus the nominalized "taking" plus a Computer Mode statement that refers to "problems" in an abstract rather than a personal way.

Finally, don't overlook the usefulness of these strategies (notice—I have presupposed "these strategies are useful") when you must deal with family members, relatives, friends, and others outside the medical professions who feel free to tell you what *they* think about your health and your health care.

TECHNIQUE #19—TRANSLATING MEDICAL REGALIAN

Every group of human beings has an "insider" language, to some degree—made up of words, phrases, body language, jokes and anecdotes that are part of the group's private culture and have no meaning (or a different meaning) for people outside the group. The technical jargon of computer hackers is a good example, as are the special vocabularies of football and trout fishing and ballet. Every profession has its own private lexicon. So do many families. In each case, the metamessage transmitted by use of the private language is "WE ARE ALL PART OF THIS GROUP AND EVERYBODY ELSE IS AN OUTSIDER."

The private language of medical professionals has as one of its most powerful components a vocabulary that I call *Medical Regalian* (after the "regalia" worn at graduation ceremonies ... the fancy hats and long robes and brightly colored stoles.) In previous chapters I have occasionally referred to the incantations and magic formulas of medicine—all of them are in Medical Regalian. They take advantage of the power of naming to wrap ordinary things, entirely understandable by ordinary people, in an aura of mystery. This is intended to inspire awe and fearful respect, and it works superbly well for that purpose. However, learning this particular private vocabulary isn't difficult, and it's one of the most useful steps you can take to defend yourself in your contacts with the medical system.

Some years ago a friend of mine was hospitalized for what was supposed to be minor surgery and perhaps a day or two of uneventful recovery. But she reacted so badly to the chemicals used for housecleaning purposes in that hospital that she woke up from her minor surgery gasping and wheezing. Her condition got rapidly worse, and it was truly a frightening experience both for her and for her family. When her doctor came in to talk to her about the problem, he spoke to her in his solemnest voice, and he said: "Helen—I'm sorry ... you have *nosocomial dyspnea.*" This sounded so grave to my friend, and shocked her so deeply, that she asked no questions and heard little of what he said about the measures being taken to deal with the matter. After the doctor left, she cried a while, and then she called me to find out whether I knew anything about the disease. She was both embarassed and furious when I explained to her that "nosocomial" means "hospital-related" and "dyspnea" means "difficulty breathing." "Well," she demanded, "why didn't he just say *that*?!!"

I have no idea what her doctor's reasons were. But I do know that if Helen had had a basic understanding of Medical Regalian she would have been spared a lot of unnecessary stress and concern.

Medical Regalian is a partist vocabulary. It divides your body up into

tidy units, gives each one of them a name based on a chunk borrowed from
Latin or Greek, and hooks them together like Tinkertoys. And it does the
same for the various medical processes used to do your repairs. Join me,
please, for a tour of this Human Parts Department. It won't teach you *all* of
Medical Regalian, but it will give you a good solid foundation from which
to work. There are four questions we can use to organize our tour:

1. Which part is being referred to in the incantation?
2. Where is it?
3. What's wrong with it?
4. What are the medpros proposing to do to it?

I'll answer these questions with charts and diagrams and lists.
Whenever possible, I'll provide examples of familiar words from *outside* the
medical vocabulary as learning and memory aids.

WHICH PART IS BEING REFERRED TO?

Figures 10-1 and 10-2 present this information for your convenience,
from the top of your head (Cephalic/Cranial Section) to the tips of your
toes (Pod/Dactyl Section).

WHERE IS IT?

INSIDE   endo
           eso
           intra

Knowledge that is restricted to an inner group is described as *esoteric*.
When a basketball tournament includes only teams from inside a single
area, we call that *intramural* sports.

OUTSIDE   ecto
            exo

An *exodus* is a going out, an *exorcism* is a throwing out, and if we had
alien beings like E.T. around to study we would call that field *exobiology*—
the biology of living beings outside the boundaries of Planet Earth.

ON, ABOVE, OVER   epi
                    supra

FIGURE 10–1
(PARTIST UNISEX HUMAN)

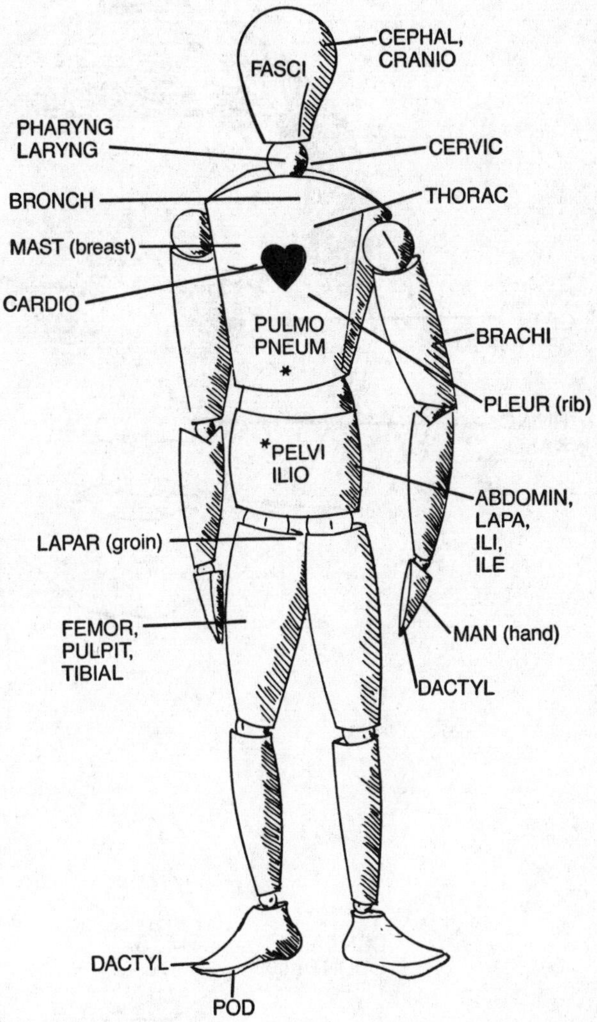

*USEFUL EXTRAS

adip, lip, stear	fat
glyco	sugar
hem	blood
hydr	water
ur	urine
lact	milk
adeno	gland
angio	vessel
cyto	cell
os	bone
myel	marrow
neuro	nerve
phleb, veno	vein
arterio	artery
arthro	joint
myo, tendo	muscle
derm	skin

*AND INSIDE

gastro	stomach
hepato	liver
nephro	kidney
splen	spleen
cholecyst	gallbladder
enter, ili, ile	intestines
hyster	uterus
oophor	ovary
colpo	vagina
orchiio	testicle
cysto, vesic	bladder
procto	rectum/anus
colo	colon

Figure labels: FASCI, CEPHAL, CRANIO, PHARYNG, LARYNG, CERVIC, BRONCH, THORAC, MAST (breast), CARDIO, PULMO PNEUM *, BRACHI, PLEUR (rib), *PELVI ILIO, ABDOMIN, LAPA, ILI, ILE, LAPAR (groin), FEMOR, PULPIT, TIBIAL, MAN (hand), DACTYL, DACTYL, POD

FIGURE 10–2
HUMAN FACE

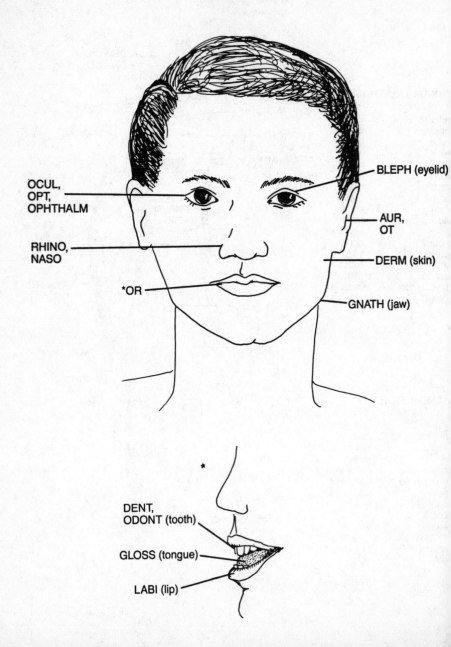

OCUL,
OPT,
OPHTHALM

RHINO,
NASO

*OR

BLEPH (eyelid)

AUR,
OT

DERM (skin)

GNATH (jaw)

DENT,
ODONT (tooth)

GLOSS (tongue)

LABI (lip)

When we write a few words on the stone over someone's grave, we call that their *epigraph*. An organization that has authority of some kind over more than one country is a *supranational* organization ... and of course "supra" is enough like "super" to be easily recognized.

UNDER, BELOW   infra

sub

Ships that operate under the water are called *submarines*. Sounds too low for human ears to hear are called *infrasonic*. We call such things as roads and bridges and sewers *infrastructure* because they are the underpinnings upon which our nation is built.

BETWEEN   inter

The period of time between two acts of a play, or two parts of a concert, is called an *intermission*.

BESIDE, AROUND   para

A *paralegal* is not exactly a lawyer, but works beside and around the work of a lawyer; a *paramedic* has the same relationship to a doctor.

BEHIND   retro

When we regret something that is already behind us in the past, we say that in *retrospect* we wish we had handled it differently. And the *retrojets* will always be at the rear of your craft.

AWAY FROM   ab

Things that are away from the normal are called *abnormal*.

NEAR   ad

When two rooms are side by side, we say that are *adjoining*.

THROUGH, ACROSS   dia

The line that crosses a square, going through it from corner to corner, is a *diagonal* line.

BEYOND   meta

In order to talk about two proposed systems of linguistics, you have to go beyond them to a larger system that can include them both; such a system is called *metalinguistics*.

WITH, TOGETHER   syn (also sym, syl, sys)

The point where two neurons in your brain almost touch one another is called a *synapse*. If I want my watch to keep time with yours exactly, I have to *synchronize* our watches. Two chunks of sound that can be combined with one another to make a word may be called *syllables*.

AGAINST   anti, contra

This one needs no explanation, not in the United States today!

WHAT'S WRONG WITH IT?

IT HURTS.	algia, dynia
IT'S INFLAMED AND/OR INFECTED.	itis
IT'S GOT A TUMOR, OR SWELLING.	oma
IT'S HARDENING.	scler
IT'S BLEEDING, OR POURING OUT.	rhage, rhagia, rhea
IT'S GROWING, MAYBE TOO MUCH.	plasia
IT'S DEVELOPING WRONG.	trophy
IT'S *TOO* (X).	hyper
IT'S NOT (X) *ENOUGH*	hypo
IT'S NOT (X) AT ALL, OR WITHOUT (X).	a, an, in
IT'S BIG.	macro, mega
IT'S SMALL.	micro
IT'S BAD, OR WRONG.	mal
IT'S PHONY.	pseudo
IT'S FAST.	tachy
IT'S SLOW.	brady
THERE'S MORE THAN ONE OF IT, OR A LOT OF IT.	poly, multi
THERE ARE TWO OF IT ... OR IT'S DOUBLE.	ambi, amphi
THERE'S ONLY HALF OF IT, OR ONLY HALF IS RELEVANT.	hemi
IT'S CHANGING.	meta
IT'S RED.	erythr
IT'S WHITE.	alb, leuko, leuco

IT'S BLUE.	cya
IT'S FALLING OR DROOPING.	ptosis
IT'S DIFFICULT.	dys

WHAT ARE THEY PROPOSING TO DO TO IT?

REMOVE IT.	ectomy
LOOK INSIDE IT.	oscopy
MAKE AN OPENING IN IT.	ostomy
FREE IT UP.	lysis
FUSE IT.	desis
FIX IT, OR SEW IT UP.	pexy
MAKE IT, OR RECONSTRUCT IT.	plasty

There you are. Now, if you go to a doctor because your eye aches when you move it, you will be less impressed by a diagnosis of optic myalgia, and you will know that it's the eye *muscle* that's causing the pain, not the nerves that would be involved in optic *neuralgia*.

If you want to add to your store of Medical Regalian, all you need is a medical dictionary. The rules of combination sometimes cause a final "o" to disappear, or a final consonant to change, or an extra letter to be inserted, but you'll have no trouble with the translation now.

WORKOUT SECTION

1. For the sentences below, identify the claims that are being hidden away in the presuppositions. I've done the first one as an example.

a. "My inability to move my right arm interferes with my work."

HIDDEN CLAIM: "I can't move my right arm."

b. "Painful swallowing has kept me from eating properly."

c. "Your callousness about my broken elbow is inexcusable."

d. "My failure to take the capsules was not intentional."

e. "Everyone has noticed your determination to practice medicine holistically."

f. "After you've completed that form, I'll take it to the front desk."

g. "When you were explaining about my dyspnea, did I understand you to say that it's caused by ragweed?"

h. "As Dr. Cleaver will already have told you, the antibiotic gives me hives."

2. Much of Medical Regalian is very hard to pronounce. Often it violates the English rules for combining sounds into words—the word "dyspnea" is one of the best examples of that tendency. However, even the dullest ear can hear the incantational superiority of "You have hyperemesis gravidarum" over "You're throwing up all the time because you're pregnant," or "You're suffering from nephrolithiasis" over "You've got a kidney stone." In order to make the most effective use of your new Medical Regalian skills, you need to know not only how the words look but also how they sound. Get out your dictionary and your tape recorder and make a tape of at least fifty examples—from "ptosis" right on up to the ones with a dozen syllables. (The list in item #3 below will get you started.)

3. Translate the words below into ordinary English.

a. blepharitis	b. blepharoplasty
c. cephalalgia	d. adactylia
e. bradycardia	f. dystrophy
g. enarteritis	h. extrahepatic
i. gastromegaly	j. hydropneumothorax
k. hyperpnea	l. hypoplasia
m. ileocolitis	n. optic neuritis
o. lipoma	p. pleurodynia
q. arthrotomy	r. cardiolysis

4. Fill in the blanks.....

a. If *dipsia* means "thirst," what is polydipsia?

b. If *phagia* means "swallowing," what is dysphagia? Aerophagia?

c. If *lith* means "stone," what would an otolith be?

d. If *eu* means "good," what does it mean when a doctor says, "Mr. Jones, you are euthyroid"? And what is "eupnea?"

e. If *dyspepsia* is indigestion, what is "eupepsia?"

f. If *iatro* means "medical," what kind of illness is an iatrogenic illness?

5. For an overview of the hazards associated with not understanding what your doctor is saying and failing to find out, read Lawrence C. Horowitz' book titled *Taking Charge of Your Medical Fate* (Random House 1988.)

6. Here is a typical example of medical writing, discussing some information about the human immune system. In this example, the writer uses not only Medical Regalian but also *Academic* Regalian, the analogous professional jargon of college professors. What is the writer trying to say, in ordinary English?

"Commensurate with the elucidation of the mechanisms involved in this system is the opportunity to clinically intervene. Rather than assault the body with exogenous synthetic compounds, we are developing an ability to help the body use its own biologically active factors to fight diseases...."

This is from page 60 of "The role of the mononuclear phagocyte system in human immune response," by Richard B. Johnston Jr. M.D., on pp. 60–69 of the June 1989 issue of *Modern Medicine*.

7. As if Medical Regalian were already not impenetrable enough, it contains a constantly changing alphabet soup of initials. I would not be writing science fiction if I put the sentence "Do you think the TBA over at the HMO will get past PPO with that DRG?" into a doctor's mouth. Work up a Computer Mode sentence for instructing your medical caregiver to cough up all the words that go with the strings of letters.

SIGHT BITES

1. "[NORMAN] Cousins indicates that the physician's failure to listen is one prominent cause of the dissatisfaction that led 85 percent of his patient sample to change physicians. ... If we are to address this problem with its clinical and economic implications, it might be useful to have a term for the problem. The term I would suggest is 'anotodynia' (Greek: absence of ears for pain)."

   (Victoria Lewin-Fetter, M.D., in a letter to the *New England Journal of Medicine* for May 15, 1986; on page 1318.)

2. "The patient who complains of 'feeling tired' presents a semantic as well as a diagnostic challenge. ... Begin by asking the tired patient, 'What do you mean by "tired"?'"

   (Stephen G. Reich, M.D., "The Tired Patient: Psychological Versus Organic Causes," in *Hospital Medicine* for July 1986, pages 142–54; on page 142.)

11

HOW TO COMMUNICATE WITH A MEDICAL PROFESSIONAL AND SURVIVE THE EXPERIENCE

INTRODUCTION: MDEITYSPEAK AND MALPRACTICE OF THE MOUTH

Ideally, patients would have conversations—perhaps rather formal ones, but conversations all the same—with their doctors. Patients are *employing* their doctors. They are under no more obligation to be subservient to them than to their plumbers, their lawyers, their auto mechanics, or anyone else for whose services they pay. If the doctors were donating their services for the good of humankind, it would be natural to use a sort of awestruck and profoundly respectful language with them. But they're not.

In the United States today, the average yearly income of a doctor is over one hundred thousand dollars, and that figure is *net*. That is, it's the doctor's take-home pay, after taxes, after malpractice insurance premiums, and after business expense. One of the most telling proofs of the medical profession's extraordinary power appears in the charts comparing doctors' earnings with those of other professions and trades. Never do such charts make it clear that the sum shown for the doctor is *net* income, while all the others show *gross* income. Even the medical journals routinely compare the doctor's "hourly wage" with a lawyer's or a plumber's without so much as a hint that one is an orange and the other is an apple. I have talked to scores of doctors who are totally unaware of these facts and are stunned to learn that their hundred thousand cannot be compared straight across the board with a nurse's twenty-five thousand.

And let us not forget: the first thing you see when you go to consult a doctor is a sign reading "PAYMENT IS EXPECTED AT THE TIME

SERVICES ARE RENDERED." Patients should therefore be able to take it for granted that when they talk with their doctors that talk will be conversation.

Jay Katz, M.D., author of *The Silent World of Doctor and Patient*, agrees. Trust, he tells us, "must be earned through conversation," and "Above all, physicians and patients must learn to converse with one another." (Pages xiv and xxi.) Katz knows this is a goal rather than a current reality. He knows doctors study not "the medical conversation" but "the medical interview." A primary purpose of his book is to help doctors reverse that. However, what happens linguistically between patients and doctors is neither conversation *nor* interview.

In a medical conversation, the turn-taking sequence between doctor and patient would be either Doctor and then Patient, or Patient and then Doctor, repeated for as long as it took. Either one would be free to introduce topics and both would be expected to participate in topic support. The length of each person's turn would be roughly equal, and neither speaker would have control over the other's turn except in terms of *personal* conversational skill, as in any other conversation.

In a medical interview, the turn-taking sequence would be first Doctor and then Patient, for as long as it took. But the doctor would have total control over the length and number of turns, as well as the topics, and that control would be *overt*, as it is in a job or loan interview.

In medical interactions, however, the turn-taking sequence is first Doctor and then Patient and then Doctor again, for as long as it takes. The doctor has total control of turns and topics in every way, but most of the time that control is a *covert* operation—both doctor and patient make an attempt to pretend that it does not exist. Remember elementary school?

ELEMENTARY SCHOOL THREE-STEP:

TEACHER: "How much is two times six?"	(OPENING)
PUPIL: "Twelve."	(RESPONSE)
TEACHER: "Very good."	(CLOSING)

The pattern in the medical interaction is exactly like that. And the patient, as in elementary school, tries hard to please the doctor and stay out of trouble. Alice Stewart Trillin, writing in "Of Dragons and Garden Peas: A Cancer Patient Talks to Doctors," describes this effort very well:

To a patient, it becomes immediately clear that the best way to please a doctor is to be healthy. If you can't manage that, the next best thing is to be well-behaved.

(In the *New England Journal of Medicine* for March 19, 1981, pp. 699–701; on page 700.)

Often doctors choose silence and/or body language—usually writing notes—for the closing sequence in the three-step. For example—

DOCTOR: "Where is this pain?"

PATIENT: "In my chest."

DOCTOR: "Mmhmm." (Writes.)

DOCTOR: "When did it start?"

PATIENT: "Early this morning."

DOCTOR: (Writes, nodding head.)

DOCTOR: "And how long does it go on?"
... and so on ...

This is a checklist process. The situation has triggered a specific list of questions in the mind of the doctor, who is checking them off one by one mentally as the patient inserts the requested data into the interaction, on cue.

Because the medical interaction is a thoroughly rotten excuse for an interactive feedback loop, doctors are ordinarily UNAWARE of their patients' hostility, dissatisfaction, disagreement, secretiveness, fear, and outright lies. Doctors following this pattern are really talking only to themselves, with the patient as data source. The result is hazardous to your health. Because after such interactions doctors think information has been transmitted that in fact has not. They believe, incorrectly, that mutual agreement and understanding has been negotiated with the patient. They believe, incorrectly, that patient commitment to specific acts like taking medication three times a day until instructed to stop has been obtained. The doctors are then genuinely bewildered when malpractice suits are filed against them, because they actually believe everything *was* explained in full and all questions *were* answered and everyone involved *was* satisfied.

You will recognize the Medical Three-Step as an action chain, of course, and you will realize that you can break that chain and force doctors to behave otherwise. (By taking notes during the medical interaction yourself, for example, and asking them "How many 'N's' are there in 'dyspnea'?") You are free to do that, and this book will equip you for the task. But you should be aware of the consequences: The doctors will be upset, frustrated, and defensive. The wider the gap they perceive between your status and theirs, the worse that effect will be. If you are a woman (especially a middle-aged or elderly woman), or a minority person, or a blue-collar or pink-collar worker, or a person on welfare, it will be extreme.

With most doctors, your refusal to join them in the Three-Step wreaks havoc and interferes with the care they give you. But it's not, as is so often alleged, because you have made them feel threatened. Good doctors know they don't know everything, they know you may know lots, and they don't mind either one. As Joseph E. Hardison M.D. tells us in "The House Officer's Changing World": "It is impossible to keep up with medicine today. Knowledge is accumulating and changing so fast that you can't be sure that what is fact today will be true tomorrow." (*New England Journal of Medicine* for June 26, 1986, pp. 1713–15, on page 1714.) Rotten doctors, on the other hand, are convinced that they *do* know everything, and the thought that you doubt that (or know anything useful yourself) never enters their heads.

In both cases, the problem is the same. They know no way to do their doctoring except in Mdeityspeak, and when you won't let them use it they suddenly don't know what to do. It's as if you were asking them to shake hands with their feet. This association of language behavior with a specific role is called a *register*; Mdeityspeak is the medical register. Misuse of the medical register is Malpractice Of The Mouth.

Consider the doctors' dilemma when you disrupt their linguistic environment. They know that they're not supposed to *converse* with you, but they don't know what to do instead. They can't explain the problem without being offensive, even if they understand it (which is unlikely). And they come UNGLUED. They may stay unglued for the rest of the day, with serious consequences not only for you but for the other patients and for the staff. They will do their best to find ways to avoid seeing you again, with important-sounding explanations—called *intellectualizations*—attached. I once was careless about this, and found myself involved in an adversary relationship with a young internist. It was so awful that out of simple compassion I suggested that he transfer me to some other doctor. His reply was, "I don't know any doctor I dislike that much." This is unusual; doctors do not use Leveler Mode with patients except in extremis. Usually the message will be a lot more subtle.

It's safer to know what happens linguistically in the medical interaction, to understand why, and to work within that system. I know only two exceptions. First: when your medical problem is a chronic one that makes a long-term effort to establish *normal* communication between you and the doctor worth all the awkwardness and bumbling and unpleasantness. Second: if you view it as your contribution to the future of American health care and you welcome the challenge. In this chapter I will assume that neither of these applies and that you're going to follow the more conservative course. The techniques presented below are based on that assumption.

TECHNIQUE #20—USING THE GENTLE ART TECHNIQUES IN RESPONSE TO THE MEDICAL REGISTER

Refusing to accommodate your language behavior to your doctor's is like joining someone for a game of tennis and insisting on your right to play without a racket. You will lose; you will probably get hurt; you will create chaos all around you; and whether you are morally right or not isn't even relevant. Given that unpleasant fact, let's look at what we know about Mdeityspeak and what can be done to combine that knowledge with your skill in using the *Gentle Art* techniques, for your health's sake. We'll begin with Technique #5: Following the Language Traffic Rules, for turns and topics.

1. As outlined above, doctors will maintain a three-step sequence in their turntaking. They will say something to open the sequence, you will respond, and they will say something to close it. Then they will start a new sequence, you will respond, and they will say something to close it. Then they will start a new sequence, and this will continue for the rest of the interaction.

Be aware that this will happen, and keep track of the turns. Never waste yours. Make a list—in advance, if possible—of the things you strongly want the doctor to hear. Insert one of them in each of the response slots you are offered. Even if the doctor has a different agenda. Even if it means you must use the dogged repetition device called "Broken Record."

Suppose the topic on your list that matters most to you is the pain in your right eye, but the doctor is determined to discuss your smoking. To the question, "Do you smoke more than a pack of cigarettes a day?" you will respond, "Yes, I do, and I have a pain in my right eye." If the doctor says "Mmhmmm ... and how long have you smoked that much?" you will respond with "Seven years, but the pain in my right eye has only been around for a week." Eventually, the doctor will say, "Tell me about this pain in your right eye."

2. Doctors only allow patients to talk for roughly eighteen seconds before they interrupt—and almost no patients, once interrupted, are ever able to finish what they were trying to say.

Since you know this, make sure that every item on your list of things the doctor must hear can be expressed in eighteen seconds or less. If you're not sure how long it will take you to present the urgent items, say each one aloud and check it against a second hand to be sure it fits. Use nominalizations to condense your predicates into single words and to place them early in your sentences. You want the most important information in the sentence at the beginning, so that it will have been said before you are cut off. That is, instead of "Recently I've noticed that I'm having kind of a hard time seeing, and that worries me," say "My recent poor vision worries me."

This is especially hard for people whose personal language style is a storyteller style. I'm not referring here to people who ramble on endlessly or cannot stay on their subject; those are separate problems. But many people are accustomed to embedding requested information in a narrative frame. Asked "How much do you weigh?" they will answer with "Well, I always used to be pretty thin. But then after I turned thirty I started gaining, and I've had trouble with my weight ever since. It's worse than usual right now, because we've had a lot of company lately and I've eaten more than I should. I'm sorry to have to admit it, but I'm up to 170 pounds." By the time this patient gets to "But then after I turned thirty" the doctor will be fuming, and the interruption will follow swiftly thereafter.

If this is the sort of talk that is more comfortable for you, memorize— *literally* memorize—the things you want the doctor to hear, and don't deviate from your memorized speech. If the doctor comments that it sounds like you've memorized what you're saying, go to Leveler Mode. Say, "You're right. I have. I want to be sure I get it all said."

Never mind whether you sound "natural" or not. You can't sound natural in medical interactions, as they are structured today, no matter what you do. If you try to provide plenty of information and details, your language will be perceived as "overly dramatic and florid," which is a twirk associated with hypochondria and hysteria. If you try to speak absolutely calmly, you will be perceived as "suffering from bland affect," and that's abnormal too. You risk being given the label "alexithymic," or worse. As for "just being yourself" ... please look at the following quotation:

> The primary and ultimate reason for consulting a physician is fear: Even the simplest blood-pressure check is a cautious inquiry into a patient's mortality. *The calm and relaxed patient is uncommon enough to make the physician suspect abnormal behavior.*
>
> (Jack D. McCue M.D., "The Effects of Stress on Physicians and Their Medical Practice," in *New England Journal of Medicine* for February 25, 1982, pp. 458–63; on page 459. Emphasis supplied.)

3. Doctors ordinarily choose the *first* problem or symptom you bring up and proceed to investigate that. They rarely select a later one or take up more than one.

Rank your list of topics in order of their importance to you, so that nothing important gets introduced by "Oh, there's just one more thing!" as the doctor is going out the door. Be sure you don't waste your first response slot. If the doctor starts with, "Well, do you still have that rash?" respond with "Yes, I do, but the pain in my right eye bothers me more than the rash does." If you have two separate problems, both of which you feel must be attended to in a single medical interaction, make that absolutely clear during your first opportunity to talk. Say, "Two things are bothering me today: a pain in my right eye, and a mole on my hip. I want to be sure we get to both of those." (I've timed that—it won't take eighteen seconds.) And stick with it. If the doctor deals with your right eye, says, "Well, that about takes care of it for today!", and appears to be leaving, say, "I'm sure you haven't forgotten my concern about the mole on my hip, Doctor."

4. Doctors tend to hear patients' words under only three circumstances: (a) when they fill an empty slot in the list of information they are after; (b) when they're on a list of sequences doctors are taught to notice because they signal serious situations; and (c) when they're on a list of sequences doctors associate with somatization, under labels like "hysteria," "hypochondria," "malingering" and the like.

With regard to (a), continue to attach what you want to say firmly to the item requested. When the doctor asks you what you weigh, say, "I'm sure you will want to know that I have a pain in my right eye, doctor, and I weigh 170 pounds." There's nothing much you can do—or should do—about (b); it may even be useful to you. With regard to (c), do your best to eliminate all sequences of this kind from your language behavior. If you really *are* suffering from hysteria, hypochondria, etc., you won't be able to do this successfully; you needn't worry about that. But it's important to do everything possible to avoid giving that impression accidentally.

The best way to become familiar with the list of language behaviors that serve as Somatization Twirks is by reading their descriptions in the medical literature. There are six articles on my suggested list (and their bibliographies will lead you to others).

1. "A Clinical Approach to the Somatizing Patient," by Robert C. Smith M.D., in *Journal of Family Practice* for April 1985, pp. 294–301.

2. "Somatization Disorder: One of Medicine's Blind Spots," by Timothy E. Quill M.D., in *JAMA* for December 6, 1985, pp. 3075–9.

3. "The Physician and the Hypochondriacal Patient," by Gerald Adler M.D., in *New England Journal of Medicine* for June 4, 1981, pp. 1394–6.

4. "A Positive Approach to Somatization Disorders," by Cayne Lerman Ph.D. and Davis S. Brody M.D., in *The Female Patient* for March 1988, pp. 33–46.

5. "Hypochondriasis and Somatization," by Robert Kellner M.D., in *JAMA* for November 20, 1987, pp. 2718–22.

6. "Somatization Disorder in a Family Practice," by Frank deGruy M.D., in *Journal of Family Practice* for January 1987, pp. 45–51.

A few examples from these sources will make my meaning more clear.

Here's an item from page 37 of #4: "Elaborate, bizarre, or personified descriptions (e.g., 'It feels like someone is stabbing me with a knife') tend to reflect a psychological element in the presenting problem." This means that a patient trying to present a full and honest description of a symptom risks having the content of that description outweighed by this "elaborate, bizarre, or personified" twirk—in spite of the enormous variation in what any two people might regard as elaborate or bizarre. Article #5, page 2719, tells us that "hypochondriacal patients tend to get symptoms of a disease that they have heard or read about." This means that the unwary patient who approaches the doctor with "I was reading this story in *Newsweek* about Lyme Disease, and I got to wondering...." is likely to trigger the "Uh-oh, another hypochondriac!" reaction in the doctor. Almost every article on this phenomenon will say that somatizing patients come to the doctor with more than one symptom and—very important—symptoms from more than one organ system. This makes a report to your doctor that you have a chest problem *and* a stomach problem *and* an earache, at a single visit, bad strategy. Despite the fact that there are many diseases in adults that do involve multiple organ systems and do have multiple symptoms.

As is always true with twirks, the more of them you have from a set that defines a stereotype, the more likely they are to distract doctors from your message. Doctors read lists of these Somatization Twirks and are told that patients showing more than some arbitrary number are almost certainly "somatizers." Figure 11-1 is a summary list compiled from several typical ones, for your reference. If some of your own characteristics are on the list, be aware of the possible perceptions they will trigger in doctors— and keep their number *low*.

It's very important to be aware that the accepted *treatment* for the "somatizing patient" is a regular schedule of appointments with the doctor. Almost every article on the subject tells the doctor "Never let the patient leave your office without another appointment" and explains that such patients use symptoms as "a ticket into the medical system." A regular monthly appointment, doctors are told, will keep patients from working up new symptoms to explain their presence in the doctor's office.

FIGURE 11–1
THE SOMATIZATION TWIRKS

1. Elaborate and flamboyant descriptions of symptoms.
2. Recital of a long, detailed medical history, with symptoms usually beginning before age 30.
3. Extensive use of terms from the medical vocabulary.
4. Dependency and clinging, especially toward caregivers.
5. Total preoccupation with health and the body.
6. Misinterpretation of normal body sensations as pain, or as evidence of illness.
7. Multiple vague symptoms.
8. Symptoms from more than one organ system.
9. Complaints that symptoms are hopeless and constant—"Nothing ever helps."
10. Negative reaction to hearing that the doctor finds no evidence of anything physically wrong.
11. Claim to have "been in poor health for most of my life."
12. Insistent and demanding, often hostile, behavior.
13. Lengthy tales of unpleasant experiences with doctors and the medical system at large.
14. Symptom-shifting . . . "Yes, my headaches have gone away, but now my chest has started hurting."
15. Obsessive preoccupation with a "chosen" illness, with every minor complaint presented as evidence for it.

Nothing is more likely to lock you into a close and extended relationship with doctors than their perception that you are somatizing. This is not just a poor use of your time and money and energy, it also has two built-in dangers. First: After a while the doctor may feel obligated to *do* something, leading to tests and trials you might prefer to avoid. Second: Doctors who have you labeled as a somatizer are not likely to notice when you really *do* need active medical attention from them unless something catastrophic happens.

     5. In Mdeityspeak, it's ungrammatical for doctors to talk about other doctors in anything but positive terms. They cannot introduce or support a topic negative toward other doctors.

It's important never to say things like "I've seen three doctors about this already, and none of them have been any help." Or "I saw Dr. Cleaver about this and he gave me some medicine for it that only made it worse." Such sentences put doctors in a terrible linguistic position. They can't respond to your statement about the other doctors' alleged errors or weaknesses, because then they'd have to talk about them, and that's not allowed. They can't *tell* you that, however; that's not allowed, either. And they've never been taught how to get out of this bind gracefully.

They may ignore what you said completely, as if you had not said it at all; this will make you feel put down and irritated and will get things off to a bad start. They may say, "I doubt that. Now how much do you weigh?", which forces you either to abandon your topic and answer the question or initiate an argument by asking why they doubt your word. Or they may argue with you very forcefully, telling you how little you know about anything and how lucky you are to have had a doctor or doctors you're complaining about. No matter what happens, you have goofed. Your time is too limited to waste on something that you know will irritate your doctor and be a distraction from your real problem.

6. Doctors will use Medical Regalian instead of the ordinary vocabulary as much as possible. Those who don't use it may resort to terms and expressions of their own, often for reasons that you would not be happy about.

Whenever you hear a word or phrase you don't understand, get it cleared up. Use the factive predicate "be sure" and say "I'm sure you won't mind translating that into English for me, doctor." And if you run into one of those doctors who says things like "I'm going to examine you *down there*," because you are assumed to be too ignorant to know the names of your "down there" body parts, change doctors immediately. Preferably at that instant, before the examination. You're not *safe* with a Neanderthal Medpro like that.

7. All ordinary rules of conversation are suspended for the duration of the interaction.

You can't do anything useful to change this, but you certainly can take advantage of it. Patients worry about responding appropriately, about supporting the doctor's topics, about being courteous, about not "boring" or "bothering" the doctor, about not interrupting, about not asking too many questions, and so forth—because those are concerns in ordinary conversation. Then they come out of the medical encounter furious and go home and complain that "the doctor never gave me a chance to talk about what *I* wanted to talk about!" The single most important thing to remember is this:

> **CONSECUTIVE UTTERANCES IN MEDICAL INTERAC-
> TIONS DO NOT HAVE TO HAVE ANY CONNECTION
> WITH EACH OTHER.**

Doctors feel free to answer your "Am I having a heart attack?" with "When did the pain start?" or "How many packs of cigarettes do you smoke?" or "I noticed your blood pressure is up this morning," or even "Lie down and unbutton your shirt." You are equally free to answer the doctor's "How much do you weigh?" with "I'm sure you want to know that I have a pain in my right eye." A doctor determined to know your weight, with a good reason for doing so, will ask you again before the visit ends.

MDEITYSPEAK LIVES, NO QUESTION ABOUT IT—BUT WHY?

If the medical language patterns described in this book were used only by hateful, incompetent, callous doctors, life would be simpler. We could just say that bad doctors use Mdeityspeak and patients unfortunate enough to be stuck with bad doctors must learn to defend themselves. That may well have been accurate in the days of Good Old Doc, but today physicians who speak in any other way are as rare as green swans. I've spent a great deal of time with doctors in the course of bearing and raising a large family, as well as in my work as a professor and seminar leader, and in half a century I have met only two such doctors. I have treasured both, but they were an astonishment to everyone who knew them.

Very competent, very caring, very compassionate doctors use Mdeityspeak, differing from other doctors only because they so rarely commit Malpractice Of The Mouth. And they tell me with genuine distress that they are baffled by people's reactions to their language. "What on earth," they ask me despairingly after major breakdowns in communication, "did I *say*?" We must forget the connotations of BAD DOCTOR versus GOOD DOCTOR that are commonly attached to our perceptions of doctors' language. The question is, of course, why don't things change—at a time when doctors *know* that 70 percent of all malpractice suits are communications problems and that 75 percent of all people who change doctors do so because they don't like their doctor's "attitude"? When the language behavior they're using so obviously doesn't work, and they know it doesn't work, why do they keep on with it? There at least three reasons.

First, people usually learn language registers for their roles in life not by reading books or taking courses but by observing the language behavior of others already filling those roles. When they make mistakes, "native speakers" of the register correct them. Medical students learn Mdeityspeak during their training, modeling their own language behavior on that of their professors, more senior students, and doctors already in practice. The fact that what they learn by example is often in radical conflict with what is written down in books on "the medical interview" (and with the idea of a doctor as altruistic healer) doesn't bother them. By the time students (in any field) get to college they are accustomed to such conflicts. And by the time they have been practicing doctors themselves for a few years the medical register has become absolutely automatic. They are no longer aware that they're using it.

Second, when registers are used competently and fluently, they carry with them all their presuppositions. The fact that speakers may not be consciously aware of them, or may even consciously *disagree* with them, is not information available to listeners. Suppose I'm a young doctor who does not consciously realize that part of the message transmitted by "You have nephrolithiasis" is "The words I say are much more significant and elegant than the words *you* say." Suppose my firm conviction is that I am in no way inherently superior to my patients just because I am a doctor. Nevertheless, when I use that Medical Regalian instead of saying "You have a kidney stone," I transmit the other message. I can only use "nephrolithiasis" safely if I am consciously aware of the Mdeity presupposition and am making a deliberate effort to cancel it with my tone of voice or other body language. My situation is much like that of the man who is unaware that calling adult women "girls" is insulting to them and who is convinced that he is in no way sexist—the women who hear him say, "Good morning, girls!" will still be insulted. THE ONLY PRACTICAL MEANING ANY UTTERANCE HAS IN THE REAL WORLD IS THE MEANING THE LISTENER UNDERSTANDS IT TO HAVE.

I have had good friends who were medical students and who openly expressed their fear of turning from "laypeople" into Mdeities—that didn't keep it from happening. You cannot follow the rules laid down for the medical register without sounding *as if* you think you are a god or goddess, because that's built into the grammar of the register. As medical professor Robert Matz says, writing of medical training in America: "We have not yet come to grips with the process by which we convert an intelligent, caring student into a human physician." (Page 52, "Humanism in Medicine," *Hospital Practice* for April 15, 1987, on pp. 37–8 and 42–52.)

The doctor in training who uses the medical register *sounds* like an Mdeity, regardless of his or her personal feelings. The doctor in training who refuses to use it rarely survives, and that rare survivor will always have trouble communicating with other medical professionals. Under the circumstances, Mdeityspeak is as much a part of the equipment physicians are trained to use as their stethoscopes are. The saddest case is the doctor who loses all fluency in any other register and uses Mdeityspeak everywhere. Such doctors will eventually spend almost all of their time in medical facilities—complaining bitterly about it all the while—because they're can't communicate anywhere else without being rejected. They get very lonely.

The third factor that perpetuates Mdeityspeak is the problem of *responsibility* for language. Medical students could be taught about Mdeityspeak, so that they could make deliberate decisions about when to use it and when not to. The excuse medical educators give me—"The medical curriculum is so full that it's impossible to add a linguistics course"—is an unconscious intellectualization. All medical professionals quite naturally prefer to believe that as long as they give the correct medication, use the correct surgical procedure, etc., *Patients Will Get Well*, regardless of the language used. (Or, if they cannot get well, their lives will be of the best quality consistent with their incurable disorder.) This is the Magic Bullet metaphor. Caregivers who admit the critical role language plays in healing or harming would be obligated to take responsibility for their language behavior, including their nonverbal communication. Of *course* they don't want to do that, or even accept the idea that they have that choice; it would be a terrible burden. Therefore, nothing changes.

Using the medical register *with* doctors, which is not all that difficult, won't help you communicate with them. If your cat or dog suddenly began talking to you in English, you'd be speechless. Doctors are just as stunned when a patient begins using Mdeityspeak. They can't use it with you because it doesn't fit the situation—you're not a doctor. (You can imagine what this means for the unfortunate doctor who becomes a patient of other doctors!) If you insist on doing it they will consider you an insolent smartalec and do everything possible to get you out of their lives—it's not wise. Use the techniques outlined in this book instead, and try to maintain some compassion. I know it would be easier to do if the doctors' income didn't contaminate the semantic environment. It's hard to feel sorry for someone netting a hundred thousand a year and holding the power of life and death over you. But do try, for your own sake and for the sake of health care in the American future.

LANGUAGE BEHAVIOR MODES, THREE-PART MESSAGES, AND VERBAL ATTACK PATTERNS

You don't need a detailed explanation of how to use the techniques for Sensory Modes, Satir Modes, Three-Part Messages and Verbal Attack Patterns in medical interactions. I don't intend to waste your time with one. The rules are exactly the same as they are in any other situation, but they must always be applied with a clear recognition of the language handicap—fluent Mdeityspeaker status—from which the medical professional suffers. In addition, you must keep in mind the unfortunate fact that the medical professional has all of the power, most of the time.

Match the medpro's Sensory Modes whenever you can, and be careful not to clash with them when you can't. In situations of crisis you may become locked into your own preferred Sensory Mode and be unable to do this. That can't be helped. But you can be *aware* of the possibility, so you won't automatically assume that communication problems are due to someone's personal dislike for you, indifference to your problem, or incompetence. (This is critically important if you are a touch-dominant person.)

Use only Computer Mode or Leveler Mode in medical interactions, and make your choice between the two in the usual way. When Leveling is appropriate and safe, it's always best; with a hostile caregiver, it may be dangerous. If you don't know what to do, use Computer Mode. And if you find yourself locked in Blamer or Placater or Distracter Mode by severe stress, do everything you can to remain aware that that is what's happening.

When you must complain to a doctor, construct a Three-Part Message, carefully. Say "When you don't return my calls, I feel distressed, because I don't have clear instructions for taking my medications."

Never use a Verbal Attack Pattern with a medical professional. Never say to a doctor, "If you REALLY knew anything about surgery, YOU wouldn't THINK of scheduling me as an outpatient!" or "If you REALLY cared anything about your patients, you'd LISTEN when they try to talk to you!" Never say to a nurse, "EVen a NURSE should be able to see that I'm in PAIN here!" or "WHY do you ALways igNORE me when I ask for help?" If such things must be said, say them. But get rid of the emphatic stresses, so that they aren't VAPs. And think carefully about whether they should be converted to Computer Mode.

When the language coming at you *from* a medical professional is a VAP, that constitutes Malpractice Of The Mouth. Deal with it just as you would with anyone else's VAP. Ignore the bait. Respond to one of the presuppositions. And be sure that your response is made with neutral body language so that it doesn't sound like a counterattack.

WHY SHOULD YOU CARE?

This brings us to another point at which you may say "So what?" Why can't you just accept it as a fact of life that even very good doctors are trained to be rotten communicators, and put up with it like any other nuisance? As long as you're careful to go only to doctors who are competent in traditional medical skills, why should you go to the trouble of adjusting your language to the medical encounter?

Let's set aside the question of whether it's possible for you to be sure of that traditional competence without good doctor/patient communication. Let's assume that you can verify it by the doctor's reputation in the community, by the diplomas and certificates on the doctor's wall, and so on. Even so, when you leave your medical communication to chance you face at minimum the following health hazards.

1. The doctor recommends surgery for you, and you do in fact *need* that surgery—but you refuse it because you don't trust him or her.

2. The doctor suggests that you undergo a hazardous surgery or treatment and means it *only* as a suggestion—but you assume it's an order and go ahead with it in spite of the danger.

3. The doctor prescribes a medicine that you do in fact need—but you don't fill it, because it wasn't made clear to you that it was really necessary.

4. The doctor gives you a prescription that you *do* fill, and that should not be taken in combination with some other drug you're already taking—but the doctor's not aware of your other medications.

5. The doctor orders a treatment for you that is dangerous because of another medical problem you have—but is never made aware of that other problem.

6. The doctor gives you a medication and instructions for its use, and assumes you understand—but you don't, and you proceed to take it incorrectly.

7. Because you keep encountering doctors who frighten you, or offend you, or confuse you beyond your tolerance, you keep *changing* doctors. As a result, no doctor ever has time to gain an understanding of your problems. Meanwhile, you acquire a "doctor-shopper" reputation that gives doctors a negative perception of you in advance, and that causes payment difficulties with your medical insurance carriers.

8. For the reasons stated in #7, you simply stop going to doctors at all, even when you need help. As a result, you see them only on an emergency basis, perhaps long after anything useful can be done.

9. You're seeing two doctors, and they are giving you contradictory instructions—but neither one will discuss those contradictions with you.

10. Your inability to communicate skillfully with your doctor causes him or her to diagnose you, incorrectly, as having one of the "all in your head" problems.

11. You are unaware that certain symptoms you have—trouble swallowing food, for example—indicate potentially grave emergencies, so you don't mention them and the doctor doesn't ask you about them.

12. The negative message you constantly get from your doctors and other medical professionals make you so miserable (or so frightened, or so discouraged) that you stop even trying to get well.

I hope this Dirty Dozen convinces you that as long as you must deal with organized medicine it is to *your* advantage to learn how to improve communication in medical encounters. The doctors are not going to do it; they would tell you that they're far too busy. If anyone is going to do it, it will have to be patients. It's not fair, because it's the doctors who are supposed to be the skilled experts and who are getting paid for the interactions. But in the current situation, refusing to do this work for them is like refusing to stop your car at red lights. It has nothing at all to recommend it, and it can kill you.

THE PERIL OF THE SUBJECTIVE SIGN: WHAT YOUR DOCTOR IS READING

There is something very important to the medpros called "the objective sign." It includes your blood pressure, your temperature, your white blood count, etc. Anything that can be measured "scientifically" (independent of your caregiver's personal feelings) is an objective sign. Recently doctors have learned that these signs may only be objective in one direction. For example, much has been written about the "White Coat" or "Lab Coat" phenomenon, in which blood pressure readings are higher in doctors' offices than when they are taken at home, and are higher yet if a doctor is taking the reading. But they continue to be a mainstay of diagnosis, and are openly part of the medical curriculum.

In addition—but not openly identified—there is a set of *subjective* signs. They have to be sort of tucked away among the odds and ends of medical literature because they are (a) totally unscientific and (b) completely dependent on the medical professionals' feelings. Here's an example from *Harrison's Principles*, one of the most widely used medical textbooks, from page 1947:

> "The extent of a patient's inner sense of helplessness may be measured by the physician's impulse to protect or rescue the patient."

And here are a few more, from various sources.

> "If you're sitting with a patient and you start to feel frightened, that's probably the best indicator that the patient is potentially violent."
>
>> ("Being Alert for Clues Can Head Off Patient Violence," *Medical World News* for December 9, 1985, page 100; no byline.)

> "If you feel annoyed, irritated with a patient, you might be suspicious that he is hypochondriacal."
>
>> (Dr. Charles Ford, quoted in "Managing Hypochondriac Can Seem Like Walking a Tightrope," by Phyllis M. Schaeffer, in *Internal Medicine News* for October 1–14, 1985; on page 21.)

> "If you feel the patient is going to be trouble, don't try to help. Give the patient a referral to avoid trouble. Doctors don't have to take patients."
>
>> (Attorney Dick Wiles, quoted in "Referrals: What Are Your Malpractice Risks?", by Ted Schwartz, in *Physician's Management* for February 1987, pp. 260–6 and 275; on page 265.)

These statements, and the many others like them, may or may not be accurate. But we can be sure of one thing: the medical professional who spends only five minutes with a patient, who spends most of that five minutes looking at a single body part and writing notes, and who uses none of that five minutes *listening* to the patient, does not have enough information to make subjective judgments. You need to be aware that doctors are reading this sort of thing and are likely to try to make use of it as they do of the objective signs. If you find yourself mysteriously rejected by a doctor and shuffled off abruptly to someone else, this may be the explanation. If it is, you are better off without the doctor in question—and you should be careful before accepting his or her recommended alternatives. Only if you have good reason to believe that working with this particular doctor is critical to your health should you use your language skills in an attempt to get past the "subjective sign" barrier.

TECHNIQUE #21—SETTING UP TRAUMA MINDFILES

It may be that in spite of your best efforts you occasionally will find yourself obliged to go through a traumatic medical experience. In the medical literature this would mean surgery, perhaps, or major dental work, or a painful and invasive medical test. But I want to emphasize that this is another instance in which you should define the word ("traumatic") for *yourself.* There are people who can sail right through open heart surgery and people who will tell you that having six wisdom teeth pulled was nothing at all for them. There are women who deliver ten-pound babies with scarcely a twinge. We can all admire such stalwart souls. But one person's "nothing at all" is another person's nightmare. You can't undergo medical experiences successfully and recover from them uneventfully if your bodymind is completely occupied by *terror.*

Suppose you are a person for whom getting an injection is terrifying. For you, that injection is trauma. It makes absolutely no difference how routine the process is for everyone else, including the medical professionals carrying it out. If it terrifies you, it counts as trauma. If you add a grim determination to keep a stiff upper lip to the burden your fear already imposes on you, and then top it off with a substantial layer of shame, you can make yourself very sick. However, you must deal with this problem yourself. You are the only one who can truly know what you need, and you are the only one who has the time and the patience required.

In Chapter 7, you learned the technique of establishing mindfiles and indexing them to be instantly available to you. When you know you are facing a medical experience that fits your personal definition for trauma, your best defense is to set up a Trauma Mindfile that will enable you to *relax.* Because here the limitations of your bodymind are all on your side: it is not possible to be terrified and relaxed at the same time.

I don't recommend using a mindfile that you rely on regularly, like the Small Pool Of Water example in Chapter 7. You don't want to set up a link in your mind between that file and something unpleasant. Instead, construct a new mindfile specifically for use in situations you find traumatic, using the following three steps:

1. Choose a perception of yourself as something that is *by definition* relaxed.
2. Construct a mindfile in the usual way, and index it.
3. Give the file a cue that will be available to you in the trauma situation you are facing.

For example, construct a vivid perception of yourself as a very soft, very smooth, very supple ribbon of velvet. Use your favorite color for the ribbon; drape your supple ribbon-self limply over something you consider both sturdy and beautiful. A branch of your favorite tree. A step on a ladder you value and know to be reliable. Anything that means security and comfort for you. Use all your senses, and especially the sensory system that is most important to you, and fill the file with information until it is sufficiently vivid to be "real" for you. Give it an appropriate index, just as you would for any other constructed perception.

Now, carefully choose the cue that will call this mindfile for you. If you are going to be in traction for two weeks, a cue that requires you to touch your left wrist with your right hand will be useless to you. If you're going to be surrounded by people, all observing you, a cue that would make you feel conspicuous won't be useful. If you have reason to expect that you will be extremely weak for a while, a cue requiring physical effort may be impossible for you. Choose something that you will be able to do, for yourself and by yourself, with as little effort as possible. For example—

- □ tracing a tiny circle in the air with one fingertip (or with your toes, if you're having surgery on your hands)
- □ counting backward silently from fourteen to zero by twos
- □ saying one particular word or phrase to yourself, silently, three times (being sure it's not something negative—that is, say "I am relaxed" rather than "I'm not afraid")
- □ taking three deep breaths, from your abdomen, with a pause after each one for a silent count of three
- □ blinking your eyes, very slowly, four times

Practice with this mindfile, using the cue you have chosen, until you're at ease with it and can call it up effortlessly. And then, when you are in the traumatic situation, remember to use it!

Much evidence exists that listening to music can bring about significant relaxation, and that smelling certain odors—spiced apple is the best known example—can do so as well. By all means, arrange to have spiced apple in your hospital room or the pocket of the shirt you'll be wearing to the dentist's office. Arrange to have a music tape played during your surgery or in your sickroom. I strongly recommend that you add these additional relaxation aids if you can, even if you're going to be unconscious. People who are unconscious can still hear sounds around them, although the memory of those sounds will not be readily available to them afterward. But you don't want your Trauma Mindfile cued by Beethoven's Seventh Symphony unless hearing it with your mind's ear is *enough*. You may need the cue at a time when you can't play the tape yourself and when it would be embarassing or impossible to have someone else play it for you.

If you suddenly find yourself involved in medical unpleasantness without any warning, constructing a Trauma Mindfile on the spot is better than sitting or lying there in helpless panic. It will pass the time and distract you from the crisis. But it's terribly difficult to give the technique your full attention when you are already in pain and frightened. It's much better to construct the file in advance and put it away for later use, checking once in a while to be sure it's still there and in good condition, in the same way that you stock and maintain a first-aid kit. Then, whether you have advance warning or not, it will be available in an emergency.

It would be best, unquestionably, if you never had to interact with the medical system at all. (The fact that 70 percent of all health problems are handled by self-care demonstrates that people are making a sincere effort to interact with it as little as possible.) But with life in this world being what it is, you probably can't avoid medical professionals completely. Even if you and all your family members are magnificently healthy and fit, the medpros are the only source for such essential items as smallpox vaccinations and insurance physicals. You *can*, however, use your language skills, both verbal and nonverbal, to make sure that the time you share with them is as safe for you and as pleasant for you as is possible under the circumstances.

WORKOUT SECTION

1. I rarely read a medical journal that does not contain at least one reference to "The Problem Patient" or "The Difficult Patient." Several times a year I see entire articles on the subject. Recently the country was blanketed with versions of a Daniel Goleman article listing "What Physicians Most Dislike About Their Patients' Behavior"—including "the patient is disrespectful, critical or demeaning of me." What I *never* see is an article on "The Problem Doctor." Look at the following quotation (from Robert Smith's article on "the somatizing patient," on page 386) written to explain why doctors so frequently *dislike* problem patients.

> One approach is to examine what physicians appreciate in a 'good patient,' typically described as one who presents with a clear-cut and treatable organic disease, follows directions, makes no demands upon the physician, gets well, and expresses appreciation to his successful physician. It is clear that the common somatizing patient has few or none of these qualities.

Using that as a pattern, explain why patients so frequently dislike "Problem Doctors." How do you describe a *good* medical professional?

2. *The Journal of Family Practice* for June 1987, pp. 607–10, carried an article by Chandy John et al. titled "Medical Care and Demographic Characteristics of 'Difficult' Patients." The study had compared the medical charts of 92 patients— identified by their doctors as difficult—with 166 randomly selected charts. It

concludes on page 607 that such patients are "more often divorced or widowed, and had a higher percentage of women than the random patient group." In addition, it claims to confirm the existence of what doctors refer to as "thick-chart syndrome." What do you think would be the probable demographic characteristics of difficult doctors? You might want to do a small pilot study based on your own experiences and those of your family and friends.

3. Several research studies have established that doctors are very poor judges of time. The eighteen seconds a doctor allows to go by before interrupting apparently seems much longer than that. The time patients spend talking apparently seems *interminable*. Check your own time perception. Have someone watch a second hand while you allow eighteen seconds .... thirty seconds .... one minute ... to go by. Tell your timekeeper when you think each of these intervals is up. How accurate would you be in judging how long a doctor had allowed you to talk?

4. In "The Medical Interview: Problems in Communication," Roger W. Shuy reports that at the head of a list of questions patients most frequently ask doctors, compiled by the National Hospital Association, was this one: "Why don't doctors explain a medical problem in simple language that a patient can understand?" Shuy then quotes heart surgeon Michael E. DeBakey's response: that doctors don't want patients to understand them, and prefer to keep what they do sufficiently mysterious that patients won't be able to bother them with questions. (*Primary Care* for September 1976, pages 365–86, on page 367.) This idea is not unique to DeBakey; it proposes that doctors are deliberately maintaining a metaphor something like "A doctor is a high priest." Do you think this is accurate? Apply Miller's Law: if it's true, what is it true of? What else must be true for this to be true?

5. For a complete account of the landmark research on doctor/patient communication—especially with regard to the language traffic rules—read "The Effect of Physician Behavior on the Collection of Data," by Howard B. Beckman M.D. and Richard M. Frankel Ph.D. in *Annals of Internal Medicine* for May 1984, pages 692–6. This is the article that first reported physicians' eighteen second limit on listening before interrupting patients.

6. It is well known that in male/female conversations men do most of the interrupting and men control the topics and turns; it is well known that in doctor/patient conversations, it is doctors who do the interrupting and controlling. However, researcher Candace West (*Routine Complications: Trouble with Talk Between Doctors and Patients*, Indiana University Press 1984), found that when the doctor is female and the patient is male the *patient* takes the dominant role. What does this tell us about communication training in female physicians?

7. The *New England Journal of Medicine* for June 3, 1982, carried an article with the title, "Prevention of Recurrent Sudden Death." You will recognize this as a phrase full of nominalizations ... what do they presuppose?

8. Much literature now exists describing the medical register, demonstrating that across the entire population of doctors there is a sufficient amount of shared language behavior to make discovery of patterns possible, despite individual

variation. So far as I know, the only medical literature on a *patient* register is the descriptions of language behavior in "difficult" patients. This is not because people of all kinds don't have shared language characteristics when they take the role of patient. Based on the information in this chapter, and your own experience as a patient and a family member accompanying patients, list some of those characteristics. For example: Patients allow themselves to be interrupted by the doctor in less than thirty seconds, often repeatedly, in spite of the anger they feel about that.

9. Medicine makes a careful distinction between *acute* health problems—hemorrhage, convulsion, heart attack, severe burns or other massive injury, red-hot appendix, and the like—and *chronic* ones like arthritis. What predictions can you make about changes in the medical register when the patient's problem is acute? What about changes in the patient register you constructed for #8?

10. If you are involved in a long-term relationship with a doctor and want to establish something approaching normal communication between the two of you, begin keeping a diary record of the language interactions you share. Keep track of each modification that you introduce into the medical encounters and the effects it has over time.

11. In *Annals of Internal Medicine* for February 1978 ("Culture, Illness, and Care: Clinical Lessons from Anthropologic and Cross-Culture Research," by Arthur Kleinman M.D., Leon Eisenberg M.D., and Byron Good, pages 251–8, on page 256), the authors propose that an interviewing doctor needs answers from the patient for the following eight questions:

a. What do you think has caused your problem?

b. Why do you think it started when it did?

c. What do you think your sickness does to you?

d. How does it work?

e. How severe is your sickness?

f. Will it have a short or long course?

g. What kind of treatment do you think you should receive?

h. What are the most important results you hope to receive from this treatment?

i. What are the chief problems your sickness has caused for you?

j. What do you fear most about your sickness?

You can use this list in two ways. First, as a basis for comparison of your own doctors' medical encounters with you. (Do they ask you these things? Do they know them without asking? Does it matter?) And second, before going into any medical encounter, ask *yourself* these questions and write or tape the answers. Whether the doctor feels obligated to have those answers or not, *you* certainly should have them.

SIGHT BITES

1. "The patient who irritates any physician the most is the one who continually complains of all sorts of ills, but has no apparent physical problem. An early sign of trouble ahead is often that this type of person will come in for the initial visit and say, 'I've already been to Doctor X and Doctor Y and they were useless, but I hear you're good.'"

    (Donald L. DeMuth, "The Toughest Patients: How to Defuse Tense Situations," in *Physician's Management* for May 1988, pp. 88–94; on page 88.)

2. "By itself, a rapid gait, abrupt movements, a forced smile, or even a provocative question, might not mean a patient is hostile. A cluster of such signs, though, probably means your patient is challenging you."

    (Garrett Oppenheim, "How To Defuse A Hostile Patient," in *Medical Economics* for September 5, 1988, pp. 125–34; on pages 125–6.)

3. "We professionals have the power to channel the information in such a way that if we really want to, we can predetermine the outcome. It's important to be aware of this and to avoid 'persuading' patients to make the choices we think are best for them."

    (Ethicist Johnny Cox, Ph.D., quoted in "Conversation With a Hospital Ethicist," by Mitch Finley, in *Physician's Management* for February 1988, pp. 193–203; on pages 194–5.)

4. "According to previous reports, the quality of the physician-patient relationship plays an important role in medical outcome."

    (Samuel LeBaron Ph.D., Joseph Reyher, Ph.D., and Jack M. Stack M.D., "Paternalistic vs Egalitarian Physician Styles: The Treatment of Patients in Crisis," in *Journal of Family Practice* for January 1985, pp. 56–62, on page 56. NOTE: I include this quotation, from a stack of others equally fatuous, because it is so amazing that it has to be said. Notice that it begins with "according to reports," rather than with "as everybody knows and common sense would dictate.")

12

CONCLUSION
YOU'RE IN CHARGE HERE

══

INTRODUCTION—WHY A FEELING OF HELPLESSNESS IS DANGEROUS TO YOUR HEALTH

Common sense says, "Stress is bad for you and must be avoided." But common sense is forever being proved to be common nonsense, and the human dedication to such activities as climbing sheer cliffs and riding on roller coasters proves that we need a definition of terms and some clarification.

Hans Selye (who first proposed the concept of stress as we understand it today, in the 1930s) pointed out that there is both good stress and bad stress, with a certain minimum level of stress being necessary to human survival. In the 1960s, researchers Richard Rahe and Thomas Holmes did a landmark investigation in which people assigned personal values for stress (in "Life Change Units," or LCUs) to major life events both positive and negative—such as marriage, being fired from a job, retiring, pregnancy, being jailed, etc. Ranking scales based on the responses were then developed for use in further research.

With the death of a spouse ranked at 100 LCUs, personal injury or illness at 53, a jail term at 63, and so on, Rahe and Holmes proposed that stress over the course of one year is mild if a person's LCU score is 150–199, moderate at 200–299, and high if it's over 300. Studies showed that people with higher LCU scores had more accidents and illnesses than those with low scores. Next, Richard Lazarus and his colleagues took a good look at the minor life events called "hassles" and discovered that they were an even better predictor of illness and trauma than the major events. In combination, the research seemed to bear out common sense. That is: the more stresses there are in your life beyond the necessary minimum, the more you will pay in sickness and trauma. It looked very straightforward—but it wasn't good enough. The problem was the *exceptions*.

One or two exceptions prove the rule, certainly. But when you have thousands of exceptions, the rule itself is suspect. As Maya Pines put it in *Psychology Today* for December 1980 ("Psychological Hardiness: The Role of Challenge in Health," pp. 34–44 and p. 98; on page 34), "Some people survive even the horrors of a concentration camp, while others cannot cope with everyday problems without falling apart, mentally or physically." The critical question is: What's the difference between those two sets of people? Why do some people come out of violent homes and abused childhoods without a hitch, while others are severely damaged, perhaps for life? Why do some people have a heart attack after being fired from their job, while others move cheerfully on to new and better things? Why do some people go into a decline when a spouse dies, while others, equally devoted, mourn awhile and then begin again? If we knew what the difference was, perhaps we could *all* learn to be good copers.

Researchers have devoted much energy to the investigation of this problem. And they have identified four crucial elements that go together and interact to create what they call "hardiness." Hardy people not only can encounter stress without being harmed by it, they are often able to *benefit* from it. Here are the Four Cs that define hardiness.[1]

COMMITMENT.   The willingness to involve yourself in what you do. Being interested in events and eager to take part in them. Being interested in *doing* rather than in just passively observing life as it goes by.

CONTROL.   The feeling that even when things are not going well, you still are not a helpless victim. The conviction that there are things you can do, choices you can make, steps you can take on your own behalf.

CHALLENGE.   The ability to perceive a stressful event as an opportunity. The ability to look upon change as something potentially good and valuable, and the willingness to seek out that side of change instead of the down side. The ability to reinterpret events instead of being locked into just one perception of them.

COHERENCE.   The ability to perceive the world, and the demands the world makes upon you, as making *sense*—as a rational whole rather than unrelated pieces "in loose formation."

People who score high in tests for these four items are good copers . . .

---

[1]The first three C's are from the work of Suzanne Koubasa, and—more recently—Salvatore Maddi. The fourth is from the work of Aaron Antonovsky.

survivors ... for whom a high score in LCUs does not lead automatically to illnesses and accidents. And the differences are not trivial. In some studies, people with low hardiness scores have proved *twice* as likely to have health problems in reaction to a stressful event as those with high scores. The rule has been revised to read: for people who lack *hardiness*, stress means illness or accident.

We can be sure now, based on overwhelming evidence, that stress itself is not the crucial factor in health. It is the *reaction* to the stress that truly matters. Remember how we tend to base our judgments of people on *perceived* height and weight, rather than on the numbers shown by yardsticks and scales? In just the same way, we tend to base our judgments of how much danger we are in not on the actual facts but on our *personal perceptions* of the threat, which are as completely real to us as any number on a scientific measuring instrument.

The bodymind threatened by an event that everyone agrees is a catastrophe—fire, earthquake, tornado, bombing, military combat, airplane crash—immediately sets up reactions to the danger. If this happens often or lasts more than a short time, it leads to a weakened immune system, a soaring heart rate and blood pressure, disturbed homeostasis, tension that causes stomach upsets and pain, and harmful negative emotions. The bodymind threatened by a *perception* of catastrophe does exactly the same thing even if the average person would not consider the event a threat. So does the bodymind that perceives threat in an event ordinarily considered positive, such as a marriage or a promotion. There are even people for whom the *absence* of danger constitutes a catastrophe; for them, the real stress is peace and quiet. These stress reactions were badly needed when our ancestors had to be ready to fight or flee savage bears and tigers half a dozen times a week, but they are not suitable for modern human beings. Their end result is illness or accident or both.

You can't fix your life so that you'll never be exposed to either positive or negative stresses. You are unlikely to find a bear in your bedroom, but you have to deal with drunken drivers and urban crime and taxes and the inevitable crises of families. You can't avoid the hassles ... traffic jams, phone calls not returned, letters demanding that you pay bills you've already paid, computers that suddenly stop working ... either. They are part of life and you can't change that. BUT YOU AREN'T HELPLESS. You can't create a stressless paradise for yourself (and it wouldn't be good for you if you could), but you *can* change your *response* to stress so that it won't be so destructive.

The only thing that all four hardiness characteristics have in common is quite simply *information*. You can't be committed to the unknown. You can't feel in control if you have no idea what's going to happen, or when or why. You can't perceive a stressful event as a challenge if you don't know what it is or what it means. And you can't make sense of your world in an informational void.

In a famous experiment by Schlomo Bresnitz, soldiers facing a long march were divided into four groups. One group was told that the march would be forty kilometers long and was frequently advised about how much of that distance had already been covered. The second group was given no information at all, at any time. The other two groups were given misleading information. In one case the men were told that the march would be thirty kilometers, and then—just as that distance was almost completed—that they had to go on for ten more. In the other they were told that it would be sixty kilometers, an impossible distance for a single day's march, and then were stopped at forty and told that it was over. All the men marched the same distance under the same external conditions, but their *internal* marches were radically different. Based on measurements of actual performance, morale, and hormone levels in the blood, the group with full information and frequent updates did very well. The other groups had serious problems, with the group that was given no information at all having the most difficulty.

You are now in roughly the position of the first group of soldiers. By completing this book and putting to use what you have learned from it, you have given yourself the priceless gift of information that is the key to hardiness. You may not know exactly how long your personal march will be or what its conditions are. But you know how to find *out*, and you know how to stay fully informed as you go along. And unlike the soldiers, you are not dependent on anyone else for that information. You are personally in charge.

SAILING THE FOUR C'S

COMMITMENT

You have already *proved* your commitment to your health and well-being and to improving the quality of your life.

- ☐ Reading this book, just reading it, was taking an active step. You could have been watching television or taking a nap instead, but you chose to read *Staying Well*.

- ☐ Using any *one* of the *Gentle Art* techniques is evidence that you are a person with commitment. Even the very first one—applying Miller's Law—is evidence. When you respond positively to language that would have been nothing but hassle before, by assuming that it's true and trying to find out what it could be true *of*, you are involving yourself positively in life instead of observing it passively or negatively.

☐ Each additional technique that you put into practice is more proof that you are personally and enthusiastically involved in taking charge of your own well-being.

CONTROL

Your inventory of control skills is sizable. It includes at least all of those listed below.

☐ You are no longer a person who could be convinced that either bad things or good things just *happen* to you randomly or at the whim of fate. You know better.

☐ You know how to distinguish between real threats and false ones, so that you can decide what you will ignore and what you will defend yourself against.

☐ You know the value of a strong social support network, and you know exactly what to do to build one and maintain it at maximum strength.

☐ You know the peril of hostile interaction, and you know a set of expert techniques for clearing all such linguistic toxic waste out of your life.

☐ You know the danger of tension and panic and negative thinking, and you are equipped with techniques for getting rid of all three and replacing them with healthful alternatives.

☐ You know the falseness of treating body and mind as separate, and you know how to establish yourself as a whole person and—when a doctor is necessary—as a holistic patient.

☐ You know what to do when you must manage pain, and when you are navigating the deep and stormy waters of our health-care system.

☐ You know a set of methods for gaining conscious access to the wealth of information in your subconscious mind, information that is not available to you anywhere else; and you know how to translate that information into a form that your conscious mind can use.

☐ You know the power of perceptions, both external and internal, and you know how to work to construct the ones you need, both in yourself and in others.

□ You are now equipped to explore the subject of maintaining your health and fitness further, in as much or as little detail as you choose. You know what additional resources are available to you, and you know how to use them.

Remember—these skills are yours *because you are a fluent speaker of your language*. They cannot be taken away from you the way physical objects can, and you are not dependent on anyone to prescribe them or regulate them for you. As long as you have your language, they are all yours, free of charge, no matter what your circumstances are. Nobody can tax your language mastery or set up preconditions for it or demand payment for it or make changes in it or subject it to search or seizure. It is magnificent equipment that is yours by right of birth alone, and it is under *your* control.

CHALLENGE

The *Gentle Art* techniques make it easy for you to analyze your first (and subsequent) perceptions of your world, to determine their true significance for your life. They make it possible for you to use your language to analyze potentially negative situations and transform them into opportunities. You are able to face the world with the serene confidence that you will benefit from every change, large or small, in the long term, even when the initial impact is severe.

For you, there will be no more need for Victimspeak, the language register of the perpetual victim. You can eliminate all of the following utterances from your personal language behavior for good.

□ "I don't know what's wrong with me, and I don't know how to find out."

□ "I know what's wrong with me, and it's *hopeless*."

□ "I know what's wrong, but I don't know what to do, and I don't know how to find out."

□ "I know what to do, but there's no way I could ever do it. It's too painful ... it's too expensive ... it takes too long ... I'm too scared."

□ "I'm a born loser. Nothing good ever happens to me and nothing good ever will."

□ "It's not my fault. I don't have any choices, and I never did, and I never will."

—and the grim metamessage that goes with every other utterance of Victimspeak—

☐ "I give up."

COHERENCE

Reading this book has introduced you to (or extended your previous acquaintance with) the concept of your native language—and your use of that language—as a coherent *system*.

☐ You know that communication is not random, and that it is always an interactive feedback loop over which you have substantial control.

☐ You know the basic principles that allow you to anticipate, analyze, and react to the language behavior of others.

☐ You know that those same principles apply to your *internal* communication, including the constant interactions going on within your bodymind.

☐ You know where to look in a situation of language crisis, what to do when you find the source of the difficulty, and how to find help when the problem is beyond your personal competence.

☐ You know how everything *works*.

On page 246 of this book you will find a section titled "RXtras." It lists other books you can read, other media you can turn to, other activities you can try, other steps you can take, to expand your knowledge of subjects and skills I have discussed here or have only briefly mentioned. They are called RXtras because they are extra resources—you don't have to have them. If you decide that you want one or more of them, however, the information you need to follow up on your decision is provided.

If you have questions that I've overlooked, or comments you would like to make, feel free to write to me. I would always be pleased to hear from you.

I wish you the very best.

Suzette Haden Elgin, Ph.D.
Ozark Center for Language Studies
PO Box 1137
Huntsville AR 72740

WORKOUT SECTION

1. In Chapter 8 I mentioned the use of affirmations—brief concise expressions of positive thoughts like "I am completely relaxed." You can reinforce your perception that you are in charge by constructing affirmations of control and substituting them for typical "I'm a victim" utterances. For example:

"I can put up with this discomfort for fifteen minutes."
"I can sit down and work at this for fifteen minutes."
"I can wait fifteen minutes before I eat/drink anything."

instead of

"I can't stand this pain."
"I can't make myself start this job."
"I can't keep from eating/drinking."

Construct some of these for your own use, tailoring the time to your own needs; if fifteen minutes is too long, use a shorter period. As always, be sure not to include any negative words or phrases. Every time you use an affirmation of control successfully you are demonstrating to yourself that you're not helpless and that there is something you can actively do in stressful situations. WARNING: Pain research shows that more painkillers are required to deal with pain that has been ignored too long than would have been needed if it had been attended to promptly. Don't put off taking medication so long that you fall into this trap.

2. There are many people writing about and working with the concept of challenge in hardiness, often using the terms "reframing" or "transformational reframing." When the optimist looks at the glass his pessimistic friend has said was half-empty and says, "No, it's not half empty, it's half *full!*", that's reframing. When the Pony-Finders perceive the job of cleaning out a roomful of manure as an opportunity to find a pony, that's transformational reframing. Begin paying close attention to your language, watching for negative statements, no matter how trivial. When you spot one, write it down or tape it, and then redo it as a *positive* statement. For example, if you hear yourself saying or thinking, "I only have twenty-five minutes," change that to "I have almost half an hour." Your goal is to acquire the habit of using positive language in the first place, except when it's literally not possible.

3. One of the best ways to deal with stresses in your life without letting them get to you is putting them down on paper or taping them (or turning them into music or dance or art or craft, if that's more useful for you.) They're less likely to

fester, you're less likely to make little perpetual-loop tapes about them and play them in your head all day long, and you're far less likely to express your discomfort about them through *symptoms*. Make good use of whatever diary medium is best for you. If you're facing hospitalization, or dealing with a long-term illness or disability, buy the handsomest journal you can afford, to write and draw in. It's just as important to your health as the doctor bill is.

4. Where *are* the stresses in your life? Do you know? Make a stress map for yourself and locate them. Use the system of different-sized dots that ordinary mapmakers use to indicate how big towns are—a very small dot for a stress you consider minor, a small dot for an average stress, and a big dot for the ones you feel really put you under strain. You may be surprised at which items get the biggest dots—much research shows that people feel more strain from a lot of repetitions of relatively minor stresses than they do from a much more serious problem that happens only once or twice.

5. In an interview in *New Age Journal* for May/June 1989 ("The High Priest of Healing," by Florence Graves, pp. 34–90 and 90–96, on page 36) surgeon Bernie Siegel is quoted as follows: "Whenever I say to an audience, 'You cut your finger—how do you get it to heal?' Nobody ever says anything. They just sit there looking dumb." This is a classic example of something so obvious that you don't realize it's there ... the fact that reliably, all your life, you've been growing your body parts and replacing your cells—doing a *total* replacement every five or six years—and healing your cuts and burns and bruises and keeping yourself in good repair. *Think* about it.

SIGHT BITE

1. "Training can be provided doing visualization exercise using colorful photos, say of impressionist art or pictures from *National Geographic*. One looks at the photo ... examining it in detail ... then closes one's eyes. What does one see? Then reexamining the photo one sees what one missed; the process is repeated; and the attempt is to see more detail each time."

   (Jerome A. Yesavage M.D., "Age-Associated Memory Impairment," in *Psychogeriatrics* for December 1987, pp. 70–71; on page 71.)

Appendixes

GOALS DIRECTORY

Because the *Gentle Art of Verbal Self-Defense* is a system, all the techniques in *Staying Well* interact to help with all problems. The list below will direct you to the techniques that I think are *most* effective for particular goals, especially if your time is very limited.

For Goals One and Four—Reducing Hostility and Building Strong Social Support Networks

1. Applying Miller's Law; page 7.
2. Using the Satir Modes; page 19 and page 44.
3. Using three-part messages; page 29.
4. Following language traffic rules; page 63.
5. Dealing with verbal attack patterns; page 72 and 101.
6. Matching Sensory Modes; page 124.

For Goal Two—Reducing Tension

1. Setting up mindfiles; page 137 and page 228.
2. Syntonic listening; page 68.
3. Dream-mapping; page 157.

For Goal Three—Replacing Negative Thinking with Positive Thinking

1. Applying Miller's Law; page 7.
2. Finding your real-symptom filter; page 53.

3. Setting up mindfiles; page 137 and page 228.
4. Semantic modulation; page 152.

For Goal Five—Building a Perception of Yourself as Someone in Control

1. Applying Miller's Law; page 7.
2. Finding your real-symptom filter; page 53.
3. Dealing with verbal attack patterns; page 72 and page 101.
4. Defining pain with semantic features; page 86.
5. Finding your personal metaphor for pain; page 90.
6. Setting up mindfiles; page 137 and page 228.
7. Simultaneous modeling; page 171.
8. Using *Gentle Art* techniques in response to medical language; page 216.

PROBLEMS DIRECTORY

For help in coping with the health problems listed below, I recommend the pages cited. It goes without saying that none of this information is intended to replace the care of a physician or other practitioner.

ALLERGY: Pages 53–55; 128–133; 133–137; 152–157

ANXIETY: Pages 53–55; 68–70; all of Chapter 7

ARTHRITIS: Pages 228–231; all of Chapters 3, 5, 7 and 12

ASTHMA: (See **ANXIETY**)

CANCER: All of Chapters 3, 5, 7, 8, 11, and 12

CHRONIC ILLNESS: All of Chapters 3, 5, 7, 8, 11 and 12

COMMON COLD: Pages 47–55

CRAMPS: All of Chapter 5

DENTAL WORK: Pages 228–231; all of Chapters 5, 7, 8 and 12

DEPRESSION: All of Chapters 3, 4, 5, 7, 8 and 9

FATIGUE: All of Chapters 7 and 12

FLU: Pages 47–55; all of Chapter 5

HEADACHE: All of Chapters 5, 7 and 8

HEART DISEASE: Pages 9–10; all of Chapters 2, 3, 4, 6, 7, 8, 10, 11 and 12

HIGH BLOOD PRESSURE: Pages 9–10; all of Chapters 2, 4, 6, 7 and 11

HOT FLASHES: Page 228–231; all of Chapter 7

INFECTION: All of Chapters 7 and 8

INJURY: All of Chapters 5, 7, 8 and 12

INSOMNIA: Pages 228–231; all of Chapters 7 and 8

MEMORY GLITCHES: All of Chapters 7, 8 and 9

MENOPAUSE: (See ANXIETY; see HOT FLASHES)

NAUSEA: All of Chapter 7

PAIN: All of Chapters 5, 7, and 8.

PANIC: (See ANXIETY)

RHEUMATISM: (See ARTHRITIS.)

SKIN TROUBLES: All of Chapters 7 and 8

SURGERY: All of Chapters 5, 7, 10, 11 and 12

ULCERS: Pages 9–10; all of Chapters 2, 3, 4, 5, 6, 7 and 8

WEIGHT PROBLEMS: All of Chapters 9, 11 and 12

RXTRAS: A SET OF ALTERNATIVES TO PRESCRIPTIONS

For More "Mental Muscles" Exercise...

1. Read *Newthink*, by Edward de Bono (Avon Books)—or any of his more recent books on thinking; listen to his tapes.

2. Subscribe to *Games Magazine* (PSC Games Limited Partnership, 1350 Avenue of the Americas, New York, NY 10019), and use every issue.

3. Do four or more crossword puzzles every week, and keep moving to more difficult ones as the others become easy for you.

4. Ready *They Have a Word for It*, by Howard Rheingold (J. Tarcher) to stretch your mental dictionary with wonderful words that English doesn't yet have—and then check out the wonderful words English *used* to have, by reading *Lost Beauties of the English Language*, by Charles Mackay (Bibliophile Books, available in this country through Barnes & Noble or B. Dalton Bookstores.)

For More Practice with the Gentle Art Techniques

1. Read the other books in the *Gentle Art* series, including:

> *The Gentle Art of Verbal Self-Defense*
> *More on the Gentle Art of Verbal Self-Defense*

The Last Word on the Gentle Art of Verbal Self-Defense
Success with the Gentle Art of Verbal Self-Defense

The first book is available through Barnes & Noble or B. Dalton Bookstores; the others are from Prentice Hall.

2. Listen to *Mastering the Gentle Art of Verbal Self-Defense*, a six-cassette tape set with an accompanying workbook; from Prentice Hall.

3. Write to Suzette Haden Elgin, Ph.D., Box 1137, Huntsville, AR 72740 for a complete list of *Gentle Art* products and services available directly from OCLS, including: newsletters, cassette tapes and videotapes; handbooks for special interests such as parents, medical professionals, and *Gentle Art* trainers; seminars, workshops, and consulting.

For More Information on Percepting...

1. Read *Mind Power*, by Gini Graham Scott (Prentice Hall); although this book has a business focus, it's one of the finest manuals on "visualization" techniques, and all its materials are readily adaptable for nonbusiness use.

2. Read *Total Runner*, by Dr. Jerry Lynch (Prentice Hall). This is the ideal book on "visualization" if you're interested in *any* sport or exercise. Not just for runners!

3. Read *Creative Visualization*, by Shakti Gawain (Bantam Books). This is an inexpensive brief introductory book with a slightly "New Age" slant. Listen to the tape with the same title (Whatever Publishing), available through most bookstores.

For More Practice Getting in Touch with—and Translating—the Language of Your Subconscious Mind...

1. Read—and use—Betty Edwards's two wonderful books, *Drawing on the Right Side of the Brain* (J. Tarcher) and *Drawing on the Artist Within* (Simon and Schuster). Even in you think you can't draw and wouldn't care to, these books are valuable to you.

2. Read *Writing the Natural Way: Using Right-Brain Techniques to Release Your Expressive Powers*, by Gabriele Lusser Rico. Lots of good techniques for getting past your left brain's hidebound convictions about using written language.

3. Read and use Lucia Capacchione's *The Well-Being Journal* (Newcastle Publishing). This book is *very* "New Age"; however, it offers such a wide and varied assortment of techniques and activities that there's something here for even the most conservative person.

For More Information About (and Practice with) Relaxation...

1. Listen to any of the following tapes or records: "Winter Solstice" (Wyndham Hill); "Alleluia" (Spring Hill Music); Brahms Violin Concerto in D (many sources); any Gregorian chant that you find pleasant; any of the many "environment" tapes widely availble ... of running brooks, woodland noises, rainstorms, etc.

2. WALK for twenty minutes. This is not only relaxing, it also is good for you and for weight control.

3. Spend five minutes every day doing abdominal breathing—with your palm on your abdomen as a feedback monitor until you can be sure it's your abdomen that's moving instead of your chest.

4. Take up a handicraft that appeals to you. Woodcarving, knitting, embroidery, basketry, crocheting ... whatever you would enjoy and can afford. Half an hour spent with your craft as often as you can find the time is half an hour spent relaxing. (NOTE: If the craft you choose seems to make you frantic rather than serene, switch to something else—but make allowances for the natural tension that goes with doing anything unfamiliar. Give yourself time to get past the rank beginner stage.)

5. Get yourself an aquarium and stock it with at least three tropical fish. Then sit and watch the fish ...

6. Read *Minding the Body, Mending the Mind*, by Joan Borysenko (Addison-Wesley.) One of the very best sources.

7. Read *The Three Minute Meditator*, by David Harp, with Nina Feldman, Ph.D. (Mind's I Press). This brief book delivers what it promises, and actually *will* get you started in meditation in three minutes.

8. Choose a word, or a very short phrase, or a symbol that is meaningful to you—a cross, a rose, a bird, etc. Write the word (or draw or paste in the symbol) in the empty circle in the center of Figure A-1. Now, spend a few minutes looking at the word or symbol, without letting your eyes stray away to the moire pattern all around it.

For More About Diaries...

1. Read *The New Diary*, by Tristine Rainer (Tarcher); I don't think there is any better book on this subject.

2. Read and use the Betty Edwards books mentioned on pages 127 and 247.

Figure A-1

For Living with a Chronic—and Perhaps Life-Threatening—Illness or Disability...

1. Read and use *Cancer & Hope: Charting a Survival Course*, by Judith Garrett Garrison (CompCare). This entire book is an extended metaphor. It takes you from The Harbor of Denial, through the Rapids of Helplessness, to the Sea of Serenity. It shows you how to construct and maintain this

metaphor: "My illness is a journey." Through troubled waters, certainly, but still a journey. It includes a very fine journal section (called "Captain's Log"), and offers every kind of needed resource. The title specifies a Cancer Journey, but *Cancer & Hope* is entirely suitable from beginning to end for *any* long-term illness or disability. And I would unhesitatingly give it to someone who was facing even a brief serious illness, or had months in bed ahead due to surgery or trauma.

2. Read Bernie S. Siegel's two fine books from Harper & Row: *Love, Medicine & Miracles*; and *Peace, Love & Healing*. These two books also have cancer patients as their focus, but their contents are adaptable for any chronic health problem. The author, who refers to his hospital visits as his "clerical rounds," is a surgeon writing of his own practice, his own patients, and his own problems getting past the Mdeityspeak barrier.

For More Information on Psychoneuroimmunology (PNI)...

1. Read *Who Gets Sick: Thinking and Health*, by Blair Justice (Peak Press). This is a straightforward and thorough review of current studies and research findings on PNI.

2. Read *The Healer Within: The New Medicine of Mind and Body*, by Steven Locke and Douglas Colligan (New American Library). This is my first choice. It's an inexpensive paperback, written in nontechnical language, extremely well done and complete. I find it indispensable.

3. Read *The Healing Brain: Breakthrough Discoveries About How the Brain Keeps Us Healthy*, by Robert Ornstein and David Sobel (Simon & Schuster). My second choice; a bit more technical than *The Healer Within*.

4. Read *Advances*, a quarterly journal devoted to PNI research; not overly technical. From The Institute for the Advancement of Health, 16 East 53rd St., New York, NY 10022. For less thorough but more easily read articles on PNI, check the tables of contents in *Psychology Today*. (From APA, 1200 17th Street NW, Washington DC 20036.)

For More Information on Being Your Own Doctor Much of the Time...

1. Subscribe to *Medical Self-Care*, the magazine specializing in the subject. (From P.O. Box 1000, Point Reyes, CA 94956.) I liked this magazine a lot better in the early years when it didn't look like a glossy clone of every other magazine, but it remains the best and most useful self-care resource.

2. Subscribe to *In Health* (formerly *Hippocrates*), a magazine that is a kind of "People's Journal of American Medicine." It has all the latest news on

what you need to know both for self-care and medical self-defense. (From P.O. Box 56863, Boulder, CO 80322-6863.)

3. Rely on Rodale Books, in Emmaus, Pennsylvania 18098, unquestionably the most reliable publisher of medical self-care books. Rodale's books are not inexpensive; however, they are well-made hardcover volumes that will still be around for your grandchildren to read, and you can always be sure of getting your money's worth in information.

4. Read *The Food Pharmacy*, by Jean Carper (Bantam) for the best presentation for general readers of research on the healing effects of the food you eat.

5. If you want a technical reference book, don't buy a medical text written for doctors. They all cost a fortune, they're written exclusively in Medical Regalian, and the only advice they offer you will be for things only licensed physicians have access to. Get a good *nursing* textbook instead, plus a copy of *The American Medical Association Family Medical Guide*, edited by Kunz and Finkel (Random House). If you must have a medical text, buy a current edition of the Merck Manual at your nearest college bookstore.

For More Information About Music and Health ...

1. Write to the National Association for Music Therapy, 1001 Connecticut Avenue NW, Suite 800, Washington DC 20036.

2. Write to the Institute for Consciousness and Music, ICM West, Box 173, Port Townsend, WA 98368.

3. Write to Professor Arthur Harvey, Music Department, Eastern Kentucky University, Richmond, KY 40475. EKU is a good source of videotapes on this subject, and also sponsors an annual conference on music and health.

For More Information About Surviving the Health Care System ...

1. Read *Talking with Patients*, *Volumes One* and *Two*, by Eric Cassell (MIT Press). This is your best source on how doctors communicate with patients, written by a doctor who is obviously working exceedingly hard to do it right.

2. Read and use *Take This Book to the Hospital With You: A Consumer Guide to Surviving Your Hospital Stay*, by Charles B. Inlander and Ed Weiner (Rodale). I would not, ever, go to a hospital *without* this book, not if I had a choice. Like *Cancer & Hope*, this book is an extended metaphor; this time the hospital patient is traveling through exotic and dangerous foreign lands, with *Take This Book* as a travel guide. Indispensable.

REFERENCES & BIBLIOGRAPHY

ARTICLES

Adelmann, P. "Mind Openers: Possibly Yours." *Psychology Today*, April 1988, pp. 8–10.

Adler, G., M.D. "The Physician and the Hypochondrial Patient." *New England Journal of Medicine*, June 4, 1981, pp. 1394–96.

American Medical Association Council on Scientific Affairs. "Dementia." *JAMA*, October 24–31, pp. 2234–38.

Anderson, A. "How the Mind Heals." *Psychology Today*, December 1981, pp. 51–56.

Anderson, E.G., M.D. "How to Improve Rapport with Your Geriatric Patients." *Physician's Management*, September 1988, pp. 84–89.

Angell, M., M.D. "Disease as a Reflection of the Psyche." *New England Journal of Medicine*, June 13, 1985, pp. 1570–71.

Astrachan, A. "Five Ways to Blow a Patient Interview." *Medical Economics*, June 20, 1988, pp. 113–125.

Bagne, P. "Dark Heart." *Omni*, October 1988, pp. 34 and 214.

Banks, J.T. "Suffering and sentimentality: a thematic essay on literature and medicine." *Medical Humanities Review*, July 1987, pp. 16–24.

Baron, R.J., M.D. "Finding New Models for Medicine." *JAMA*, June 27, 1986, pp. 3404–5.

Baskin, Y. "The Way We Act." *Science 85*, November 1985, pp. 94–99.

Bass, M.J., M.D. et al. "The Physician's Actions and the Outcome of Illness in Family Practice." *Journal of Family Practice*, January 1986, pp. 43–47.

Bates, R.C., M.D. "What an Old Doctor Can Tell You About Elderly Patients." *Medical Economics*, December 7, 1987, pp. 30–35.

Beckman, H.B. and R.M. Frankel. "The Effect of Physician Behavior on the Collection of Data." *Annals of Internal Medicine*, November 1984, pp. 692–96.

Begley, S. "The Stuff That Dreams Are Made Of." *Newsweek*, August 14, 1989, pp. 41–44.

Bell, C. "Family Violence." *JAMA*, September 19, 1986, pp. 1501–2.

Bennett, W. and J. Gurin. "Do Diets Really Work?" *Science* 82, March 1982, pp. 42–50.

———. "A Matter of Fat." *New York Times*, March 16, 1985.

Berman, H.S., et al. "The Fine Art of Getting What You Want (and Need) from a Doctor." *Woman's Day*, November 15, 1983, pp. 41–48 and 51–53.

Berman, R., M.D., et al. "Physiology of aging. Part 1: Normal changes." *Patient Care*, 1/15/88, pp. 20–35. And "Physiology of aging. Part 2: Clinical implications." Same issue, pp. 39–66.

Beuttler, B. "Music's Charms: Tuned In for Surgery." *American Health*, November 1986, p. 10.

Birosik, P.J. and J.S. Goldman. "Healing With Sound." *Body, Mind and Spirit*, May–June 1989, pp. 32–34 and 67–68.

Blaiss, M.S., M.D. and C.F. Springgate, M.D. "Human immune system response to allergens and anti-allergenic agents." *Modern Medicine*, March 1988, pp. 52-55.

Blakeslee, S. "Cynicism and Mistrust Tied to Early Death." *New York Times*, January 17, 1989.

Blendon, R.J., Sc.D. et al. "Uncompensated Care by Hospitals or Public Insurance for the Poor: Does It Make a Difference?" *New England Journal of Medicine*, May 1, 1986, pp. 1160–63.

Bloom, P. "Soul Music." *New Age Journal*, March–April 1987, pp. 58–63.

Brooten, K.E. Jr., J.D. and S. Chapman. "Establishing Effective Patient Relationships." *Physician's Management*, May 1987, pp. 233–37.

Brown, J. "'Take me to the river': the water cure in America." *Medical Humanities Review*, July 1987, pp. 29–34.

Burnum, J.F. "Medical Practice A La Mode: How Medical Fashions Determine Medical Care." *New England Journal of Medicine*, November 5, 1987, pp. 1220–22.

Carey, B. "Sport: Playing Under Pressure." *Hippocrates*, November–December 1988, pp. 110–112.

Carpenter, N.S., R.D. and S.A. Brunton, M.D. "Evaluating the Severity and Causes of Adult Obesity. *Family Practice Recertification*, September 1988, pp. 59–70.

Cassell, E.J., M.D. "The Nature of Suffering and the Goals of Medicine." *New England Journal of Medicine*, March 18, 1982, pp. 639–45.

Cassell, E.J., M.D. et al. "Making good interview skills better." *Patient Care*, March 30, 1989, pp. 145–166.

Cassem, E.H., M.D. "When Symptoms Seem Groundless." *Emergency Medicine*, June 30, 1987, pp. 62–87.

Cassileth, B.R. et al. "Psychosocial Correlates of Survival in Advanced Malignant Disease." *New England Journal of Medicine*, June 13, 1985, pp. 1551–55.

Chassin, M.R. "Does Inappropriate Use Explain Geographic Variations in the Use of Health Care Services?" *JAMA*, November 13, 1987, pp. 2533–42.

Check, W.E. "Homicide, suicide, other violence gain increasing medical attention." *JAMA*, August 9, 1985, pp. 721–30.

Clark, M. et al. "Allergy: New Insights." *Newsweek*, August 23, 1982, pp. 40–45.

Clynes, M. "Sentography: Dynamic forms of communication of emotion and qualities." *Computer in Biology and Medicine* 3 (1987), pp. 119–130.

Clynes, M. and N. Nettheim. "The Living Quality of Music: Neurobiological Patterns of Communicating Feeling." In M. Clynes, ed., *Music, Mind, and Brain: The Neurophysiology of Music*. New York: Plenum 1982, pp. 47–82.

Cosmides, L. "Invariance in the acoustic expression of emotion during speech." *Journal of Experimental Psychology*, December 1983, pp. 864–81.

Cousins, N. "The Mysterious Placebo: How Mind Helps Medicine Work." *Saturday Review*, October 1, 1977, pp. 9–16.

———. "Proving the Power of Laughter." *Psychology Today*, October 1989, pp. 22–26.

Cowley, M. "Being Old Old." *New York Times Magazine*, May 26, 1985, page 58.

Davis, L. "The Height Report." *Hippocrates*, January–February 1988, pp. 90–91.

deGruy, Frank M.D. et al. "Somatization Disorder in a Family Practice." *Journal of Family Practice*, January 1987, pp. 45–51.

DeMuth, D.L. "The Toughest Patients: How to Defuse Tense Situations." *Physician's Management*, May 1988, pp. 88–94.

Dimsdale, J.E., M.D. "A Perspective on Type A Behavior and Coronary Disease." *New England Journal of Medicine*, January 14, 1988, pp. 110–12.

Easterbrook, G. "The Revolution in Modern Medicine." *Newsweek*, January 16, 1987, pp. 40–74.

Eddy, D.M. "Variations In Physician Practice: The Role of Uncertainty." *Health Affairs*, Summer 1984, pp. 74–89.

Elgin, S.H. "Verbal Self-Defense in Emergency Medicine." *Emergency Medical Services*, September 1987, pp. 49–52.

Eliot, R.S., M.D. and H.M. Morales-Ballejo, M.D. "Stress and the heart: Measuring and evaluating reactivity." *Illustrated Medicine*, June 1987, pp. 2–16. (Whole Issue.)

Enthoven, A. and R. Kronick. "A Consumer Choice Health Plan for the 1990s." *New England Journal of Medicine*, January 5, 1989, pp. 29–37.

Epstein, S.E., M.D. et al. "Myocardial Ischemia—Silent or Symptomatic." *New England Journal of Medicine*, April 21, 1988, pp. 1038–43.

Feiner, B. (Interview with Candace West.) "Communication Breakdowns: Are Your Patients Turned Off?" *Options*, August 1986, pp. 33–6.

Fellman, B. "Talk: the not-so-silent killer." *Science 85*, December 1985, pp. 70–71.

Ferguson, T., M.D. "Laypeople as Providers of Health Care." *Medical Self-Care*, July–August 1987, page 72.

———. "A Conversation with Ira Progoff." *Medical Self-Care*, July–August 1978, pp. 11–12.

Fincher, J. "Inside an Intensive Journal Workshop." *Medical Self-Care*, July–August 1978, pp. 6–10.

Finkbeiner, A. "The Puzzle of Child Abuse." *Science Illustrated*, June–July 1987, pp. 14–19.

Finley, M. "Conversation With A Hospital Ethicist." *Physician's Management*, February 1988, pp. 193–203.

Foege, W.H., M.D. "Highway Violence and Public Policy." *New England Journal of Medicine*, May 28, 1987, pp. 14:7–8.

Ford, C.V., M.D. "Caring for the Paranoid Elderly." *Medical Aspects of Human Sexuality*, August 1989, pp. 97–103.

Fox, B.H., Ph.D. "Depression symptoms and Cancer." *JAMA*, September 1, 1989, page 1231.

Friedman, M., M.D. "Type A Behavior and Mortality From Coronary Heart Disease." *New England Journal of Medicine*, July 14, 1988, page 114. (See also other letters under same title, through page 117.)

Frohlich, E.D., M.D. "A portrait of the immune system." *Modern Medicine*, December 1987, pp. 36–40.

———. "The role of the mononuclear phagocyte system in human immune response." *Modern Medicine*, June 1989, pp. 60–74.

Gary, F. et al. "Little Brother Is Changing You." *Psychology Today*, March 1974, pp. 42–46.

Gevitz, N., PhD.D. "Sectarian Medicine." *JAMA*, 3/27/87, pp. 1636–40.

Gibbs, R.R., M.D. et al. "Patient Understanding of Commonly Used Medical Vocabulary." *Journal of Family Practice*, February 1987, pp. 176–78.

Glymour, C., Ph.D. and D. Stalker, Ph.D. "Engineers, cranks, Physicians, Magicians." *New England Journal of Medicine*, April 21, 1983, pp. 960–63.

Gold, P.W., M.D. et al. "Clinical and Biochemical Manifestations of Depression: Relation to Neurobiology of Stress." (In two parts.) *New England Journal of Medicine*, August 11, 1988, pp. 348–51: *New England Journal of Medicine*, August 18, 1988, pp. 413–20.

Goldberg, J. "Anatomy of Scientific Discovery." *Science Illustrated*, January–February 1989, pp. 5–12.

Goleman, D. "Research Affirms Power of Positive Thinking." *New York Times*, February 3, 1987.

———. "The Mind Over the Body." *New York Times Magazine*, September 27, 1987, pp. 36–39 and 59–60.

———. "Probing the Enigma of Multiple Personality." *New York Times*, June 28, 1988.

———. "What Physicians Most Dislike About Their Patients." *New York Times*, October 17, 1988.

———. "Researchers Find That Optimism Helps the Body's Defense System." *New York Times*, April 20, 1989.

———. "A Feel-Good Theory: A Smile Affects Mood." *New York Times*, July 18, 1989.

Gorman, C. "Can't Afford to Get Sick." *Time Magazine*, August 21, 1989, page 43.

Govaker, D., M.D. "Helping your patient lose weight." *Emergency Medicine*, March 30, 1987, pp. 24–45.

Graves, F. (Interview with Bernie Siegel, M.D.) "The High Priest of Healing." *New Age Journal*, May–June 1986, pp. 34–39 and 90–92.

Groden, J., Ph.D. "Children with Asthma Breathing Easier." *Mind–Body–Health Digest* 3:1 (1988), pp. 3–4.

Growald, E.R. and A. Luks. "The Immunity of Samaritans: Beyond Self." *American Health*, March 1988, pp. 51–53.

Grumbach, M.M., M.D. "Growth Hormone Therapy and the Short End of the Stick." *New England Journal of Medicine*, July 28, 1988, pp. 238–41.

Guralnik, J.M., M.D., Ph.D. "Assessment of Health Status in Older Patients." *Quality of Life and Cardiovascular Care*, Winter 1988, pp. 151–5.

Gurney, A.R. "Conversation Piece." *Newsweek* for June 1989, pp. 7–8.

Hall, E. "Giving Away Psychology in the 80's: George Miller Interviewed by Elizabeth Hall." *Psychology Today*, January 1980, pp. 38–50 and 97–98.

Hall, S.S. "A molecular code links emotions, mind and health." *Smithsonian Magazine*, June 1989, pp. 62–71.

Hardyson, J.E., M.D. "The House Officer's Changing World." *New England Journal of Medicine*, June 26, 1986, pp. 1713–15.

Harris, T.G. "Heart and Soul." *Psychology Today*, January–February 1989, pp. 50–52.

Hellerstein, D. "Cures That Kill." *Harper's*, December 1980, pp. 20–24.

Herbert, V., M.D., J.D. "Review of *Examining Holistic Medicine* (Stalker and Glymour, eds., Buffalo NY: Prometheus 1985). *JAMA*, September 5, 1986, pp. 1202–3.

Herbert, W. "The Sources of Cooperation." *Psychology Today*, January 2, 1989, page 72.

Heyn, D. "Why Seven Magazines Pretend You Don't Exist." *50 Plus*, March 1987, pp. 39–41.

Higgins, L.C. "Hostility Theory Rekindles Debate Over Type A Behavior." *Medical World News*, February 27, 1989, page 21.

Hirsch, J., M.D. and R.L. Leibel, M.D. "New Light on Obesity." *New England Journal of Medicine*, February 25, 1988, pp. 509–510.

Hollien, M. "Vocal Indicators of Psychological Stress." *Annals of the New York Academy of Science* 347 (1980), pp. 47–72.

Holmes, M.D., M.D. et al. "An Analytic Review of Current Therapies for Obesity." *Journal of Family Practice*, May 1989, pp. 610–16.

Holoweiko, M. "This Program Takes Doctors Off the Pedestal." *Medical Economics*, February 16, 1987, page 55.

Hopson, J.L. "A Pleasurable Chemistry." *Psychology Today*, July–August 1988, pp. 29–33.

Horn, J. and J. Meer. "The pleasure of their company." *Psychology Today*, August 1984, pp. 52–57.

House, J.S. et al. "Social Relationships and Health." *Science*, July 29, 1988, pp. 540–44.

Ignatieff, M. "The soul returns to the sickbed: Modern Dying." *The New Republic*, December 26, 1988, pp. 28–33.

Jaroff, L. "Stop That Germ!" *Time Magazine*, May 23, 1988, pp. 41–6.

John, C. et al. "Medical Care and Demographic Characteristics of 'Difficult' Patients." *Journal of Family Practice*, June 1987, pp. 607–10.

Jones, E.E. "Interpreting Interpersonal Behavior: The Effects of Expectancies." *Science,* October 3, 1986, pp. 41–6.

Kahn, J.P. (Interview with Robert Keidel.) "What Game Are You Playing?" *INC.,* November 1985, pp. 35–58.

Kamiya, G. "The Cancer Personality." *Hippocrates,* November–December 1989, pp. 92–93.

Kellner, R., M.D. "Hypochondria and Somatization." *JAMA,* November 20, 1987, pp. 2718–22.

King, J.H. "Medicine a La Mode." M.D., January 1988, pp. 25–27.

Kiparsky, C. and P. Kiparsky. "Fact." In M. Bierwisch and K.E. Heidolph, eds. *Progress in Linguistics* (The Hague: Mouton 1970), pp. 143–73.

Kleinman, A., M.D. et al. "Culture, Illness and Care: Clinical Lessons from Anthropologic and Cross-Cultural Research." *Annals of Internal Medicine,* February 1987, pp. 251–7.

Kobasa, S.O. "Test for hardiness: How much stress can you survive?" *American Health,* September 1984, page 64.

Kohn, A. "Beyond Selfishness." *Psychology Today,* October 1988, pp. 34–38.

Korn, E. "Remainders." *Times Literary Supplement,* August 14, 1987, page 874.

Kosslyn, S.M. "Aspects of a Cognitive Neuroscience of Mental Imagery." *Science,* June 19, 1988, pp. 1621–26.

Kurfees, J.F. and R.L. Dotson. "Drug Interactions in the Elderly." *Journal of Family Practice,* May 1987, pp. 477–88.

Lambers, L. "Dreams: Now you can make them work for you." *American Health,* July 1987, pp. 50–55.

Langer, E.J. "The Mindset of Health." *Psychology Today,* April 1989, pp. 48–51.

Langs, R. "Understanding Your Dreams." *New Age Journal,* July–August 1988, pp. 50–55, 74–77, and 83.

Larson, E.B., M.D. et al. "Memory loss: Is it reversible?" *Patient Care,* April 30, 1987, pp. 54–66.

Lasagna, L. "Pain and Its Management." *Hospital Practice,* October 15, 1986, pp. 92C–92X.

Lazarus, R.S. "Little Hassles Can Be Hazardous To Health." *Psychology Today,* July 1981, pp. 58–62.

Lebaron, S., Ph.D. et al. "Paternalistic vs Egalitarian Physician Styles: The Treatment of Patients in Crisis." *Journal of Family Practice,* January 1985, pp. 56–62.

Lerman, C., Ph.D. and D.S. Brady, M.D. "A Positive Approach to the Somatization Disorders." *The Female Patient,* March 13, 1988, pp. 33–46.

Lesser, I.M., M.D. "Alexithymia." *New England Journal of Medicine*, March 14, 1985, pp. 690–92.

Levy, B.T., Ph.D. and P.S. Williamson, M.D. "Patient Perceptions and Weight Loss of Obese Adults." *Journal of Family Practice*, March 1988, pp. 285–290.

Lewin-Fetter, V., M.D. (Letter, untitled.) *New England Journal of Medicine*, May 15, 1986, page 1318.

Lewis, S. "Overcoming Fear: An Interview with Norman Cousins." *Advances*, Summer 1989, pp. 33–35.

Lynch, J.J. Ph.D. "Listen and Live." *American Health*, April 1985, pp. 39–43.

Malesky, G. "Music That Strikes a Healing Chord." *Prevention*, October 1983, pp. 57–63.

Marx, J.L. "The Immune System 'Belongs in the Body'." *Science*, March 8, 1985, pp. 1190–92.

Matz, R. "Humanism in Medicine." *Hospital Practice*, April 15, 1987, pp. 37–52.

May, J.R. "Sporting Life: Using Psychological Tools to Improve Your Game." *Psychology Today*, May 1989, pp. 23–25.

McCue, J.D., M.D. "The effects of stress on physicians and their medical practice." *New England Journal of Medicine*, February 25, 1982, pp. 485–63.

Miller, S.M. "Why having control reduces stress: If I can stop the roller coaster I don't have to get off." In J. Garber and M.E.P. Seligman, eds. *Human Helplessness: Theory and Applications* (New York: Academic Press 1980.)

Miller-McLemore, B.J. "Doing Wrong, Getting Sick, and Dying." *The Christian Century*, February 24, 1988, pp. 186–190.

Monson, R.A., M.D. and G.R. Smith Jr., M.D. "Somatization Disorder in Primary Care." *New England Journal of Medicine*, June 16, 1983, pp. 1464–45.

Mossey, J.A. and E. Shapiro. "Self-rated health: A prediction of mortality among the elderly." *American Journal of Public Health* 72 (1982), pp. 800–808.

Olsen, E. et al. "Beyond Positive Thinking." *Success*, December 1988, pp. 31–38.

Oppenheim, G. "How to Defuse a Hostile Patient." *Medical Economics*, September 5, 1988, pp. 125–34.

Pankratz, L., Ph.D. and Lial Kofoed, M.D. "The Assessment and Treatment of Geezers." *JAMA*, February 26, 1988, pp. 1228–9.

Pelletier, K.R. and R. Lutz. "Mindbody Goes to Work: A Critical Review of Stress Management Programs in the Workplace." *Advances*, Spring 1989, pp. 28–34.

Perry, P. "Minding Your Health: The Pretended Self." *Psychology Today*, May 1989, pp. 60–62.

Pickering, T.G., M.D. et al. "How Common Is White Coat Hypertension?" *JAMA*, January 8, 1988, pp. 225–28.

Pines, M. "Psychological Hardiness: The Role of Challenge in Health." *Psychology Today*, December 1980, pp. 34–45.

Prewitt, T., Ph.D. and M. Rogers, Ph.D. "Giving weight-loss advice that patients will heed." *Contemporary OB/GYN*, October 1987, pp. 81–82 and 87–90.

Price, J.H. et al. "Perceptions of Family Practice Residents Regarding Health Care and Poor Patients." *Journal of Family Practice*, June 1988, pp. 615–621.

Quill, T.E. "Somatization Disorder: One of Medicine's Blind Spots." *JAMA*, December 6, 1986, pp. 3075–79.

Quinn, Janet F., Ph.D., R.N. "Building a Body of Knowledge: Research on Therapeutic Touch 1974–1986." *Journal of Holistic Nursing*, January 1988, pp. 37–45.

Raymond, C.A., Ph.D. "Biology, Culture Dietary Changes Conspire to Increase Incidence of Obesity." *JAMA*, October 24–31, 1986, pp. 2157–8.

———. "Experts Hold Hope for Obesity Treatments Targeted to Specific Regulatory Miscues." *JAMA*, November 7, 1986, pp. 2202–7.

Reade, J.M., M.D. and R.M. Ratzan, M.D. "Yellow Professionalism: Advertising by Physicians in the Yellow Pages." *New England Journal of Medicine*, May 21, 1987, pp. 1315–19.

Riesenberg, D.E., M.D. "Some medical maxims do not age well: Andres." *JAMA*, February 21, 1986, page 867.

Ritter, Louise, "Words To Grow On." *Guideposts*, July 1989, pp. 32–33.

Robbins, A.S., M.D. and L.Z. Rubenstein, M.D. "Communicating With the Elderly Patient." *Medical Times*, October 1987, pp. 81–101.

Rosen, R. "Healthy People, Healthy Companies: Striking the Critical Balance." *Advances*, Spring 1989, pp. 8–11.

Rosenbaum, R. "The Body's Inner Voices." *New Times* 6/26/78, pp. 45–59.

Rosenblatt, M. "Neuropeptides: Future Implications for Medicine." *Medical Times*, November 1983, pp. 31–37.

Ross, I.E. "The Paradox of Health." *New England Journal of Medicine*, August 11, 1988, page 378. (See also other letters under this title through page 379.)

Rossman, M.L., M.D. "The Healing Power of Imagery." *New Age Journal*, March–April 1988, pp. 46–56.

Rozanski, A., M.D. et al. "Mental Stress and the Induction of Silent Myocardial Ischemia In Patients with Coronary Artery Disease. *New England Journal of Medicine*, April 21, 1986, pp. 1005–12.

Sacks, H. et al. "A Simplest Systematics for the Organization of Turn-taking for Conversation." *Language 50*, (1974), pp. 696–735.

Scarf, M. "Images That Heal." *Psychology Today*, September 1980, pp. 32–45.

Scherwitz, L. et al. "Self-involvement and the risk factors for coronary heart disease." *Advances*, Winter 1985, pp. 6–18.

Schifrin, M. "Living off the fat of the land." *Forbes Magazine*, November 13, 1989, pp. 186–96.

Schwarz, T. "Referrals: What Are Your Malpractice Risks?" *Physician's Management*, February 1987, pp. 260–66 and page 275.

Schwenk, T.L., M.D. et al. "Physician and Patient Determinants of Difficult Physician-Patient Relationships." *Journal of Family Practice*, January 1989, pp. 59–63.

Scott, J. "Cancer survival time, group therapy linked." *Los Angeles Times*, May 11, 1989.

Sekuler, R. and R. Blake. "Sensory Underload." *Psychology Today*, December 1987, pp. 48–51.

Selzer R. "The Art of Surgery." *Harper's*, January 1976, pp. 75–77.

Shangold, M., M.D. and G. Mirkin, M.D. "Fitness in Postmenopausal Women: How to Motivate the Patient." *Medical Aspects of Human Sexuality*, February 1987, pp. 23–29.

Shea, M.J., M.D. "Mental Stress and the Heart." *CVR&R*, April 1988, pp. 51–58.

Sherman, B. "The High Cost of Mecical Care: Who's To Blame?" *Private Practice*, November 1988, pp. 18–24.

Shuy, R.W., Ph.D. "The Medical Interview: Problems in Communication." *Primary Care*, September 1976, pp. 365–86.

Smilkstein G., M.D. "Health Benefits of Helping Patients Cope." *Consultant*, January 1988, pp. 56–67.

Smith, J.A., M.D. "Interview Strategies for Difficult Patients." *Diagnosis*, February 1986, pp. 123–28.

Smith, R.C. "A Clinical Approach to the Somatizing Patient." *Journal of Family Practice*, April 1985, pp. 294–301.

Squires, S. "The Power of Positive Imagery: Visions to Boost Immunity." *American Health*, July 1987, pp. 56–61.

Stapp, W. "Imagine Yourself Well." *Medical Self-Care*, January–February 1988, pp. 27–30.

Stein, H.F., Ph.D. "What the Patient Wants—What the Patient Needs: A Dilemma in Clinical Communication." *Continuing Education*, February 1985, pp. 126–35.

———. "Fat and Skinny: Cultural Metaphor, Diagnosis, and Disease Entities." *Continuing Education*, November 1985, pp. 775–81.

Sutherland, J.E., M.D. and R.M. Gebhart M.D. "A Protocol for Periodic Health Examinations." *The Female Patient*. February 1986, pp. 81–84 and 89–95.

Tavris, C. "Anger Defused." *Psychology Today*, November 1982, pp. 25–35.

Tiffany, D.A. "Cancer patient voices fear, plea." *American Medical News*, September 12, 1986, page 47.

Tivnan, E. "Healing Time Sickness." *American Health*, March 1989, pp. 76–80.

Trillin, A.S. "Of Dragons and Garden Peas: A Cancer Patient Talks to Doctors." *New England Journal of Medicine*, March 19, 1981, pp. 699–701.

Ulrich, R.S. "View through a window may influence recovery from surgery." *Science* 224 (1984); 420–21.

Warga, C. "You Are What You Think." *Psychology Today*, September 1988, pp. 56–58.

Weintraub, M. "The Law of Confounding by Sensible Behavior." *Hospital Practice*, July 15, 1988, pp. 223–27.

———. "Hypochondriasis and Somatization." *JAMA*, March 25, 1988, pp. 1809–10.

Weissman, G. "Inflammation: Khartoum to Casablanca." *Hospital Practice*, April 15, 1987, pp. 61–74.

Whorton, J.C. "Traditions of Folk Medicine in America." *JAMA*, March 27, 1987, pp. 1632–35.

Williams, R., M.D. "The Trusting Heart." *New Age Journal*, May–June 1989, pp. 26–30.

———. "Curing Type A: The Trusting Heart." *Psychology Today*, January–February 1989, pp. 36–42.

Wise, P.H., M.D. and L. Eisenberg M.D. "What Do Regional Variations in the Rates of Hospitalization of Children Really Mean?" *New England Journal of Medicine*, May 4, 1989, pp. 1209–11.

Yankelovich, D. and J. Gurin. "The New American Dream." *American Health*, March 1989, pp. 63–67.

Zajonc, R.B. "Emotion and Facial Efference: A Theory Reclaimed." *Science*, April 5, 1985, pp. 15–20.

Zal, H.M., D.O. "The Psychiatric Aspects of Myocardial Infarction." *Cardiovascular Reviews & Reports*, February 1987, pp. 33–37.

Zimmerman, J. "Does Emotional State Affect Disease?" M.D., April 1986, page 30 and pp. 41–43.

Zonderman, A.B. et al. "Depression as a Risk for Cancer Morbidity and Mortality in a Nationally Representative Sample." *JAMA*, September 1, 1989, pp. 1191–95.

Items Without Byline

"Swiftness of spouse's death affects mate's mortality risk." *Medical World News*, September 11, 1989, page 27.

"Chronic headache: Predict the outcome at the first visit." *Modern Medicine*, December 1986, pp. 96 and 101.

"What Ails Type A Research?" *Medical World News*, October 14, 1985, page 57.

"Laughter and Immunity." *Advances*, Summer 1989, page 5.

"What Your Patients Are Reading." *Drug Therapy*, January 1987, pp. 20 and 25.

"Communication Breakdowns." *Options*, August 1986, pp. 33–37. (Interview with Candace West.)

"Consensus Conference: Differential Diagnosis of Dementing Disease." *JAMA*, December 18, 1987, pp. 3411–16.

"Group therapy support increases cancer survival." *Brain/Mind Bulletin*, August 1989, page 1.

"Review of Ira Progoff, *At a Journal Workshop*" (New York: Dialogue House Library 1975.) *Medical Self-Care*, July–August 1978, pp. 4–5.

"Comic Relief." (In "Risus.") *Medical World News*, February 27, 1989, page 60.

"Acute drug reactions in the elderly." *Emergency Medicine*, August 15, 1987, pp. 79–87.

"Trimming the Dangers from Obesity." *Emergency Medicine*, May 15, 1988, pp. 49–50 and page 55.

"Education About Adult Domestic Violence in U.S. and Canadian Medical Schools 1987–88." *JAMA*, February 17, 1989, pp. 972 and 978.

"The High Cost of Health." *The Washington Spectator*, April 15, 1988, pp. 1–4. (Whole issue.)

Books

Achterberg, J., 1985. *Imagery in Healing: Shamanism and Modern Medicine.* Boston: New Science Library.

Ader, R. ed., 1981. *Psychoneuroimmunology.* New York: Academic Press.

Antonovsky, A., 1979. *Health, Stress, and Coping.* San Francisco: Jossey-Bass.

Barsy, A.J., M.D. 1988. *Worried Sick: Our Troubled Quest for Wellness.* Boston: Little, Brown.

Beattie, G., 1983. *Talk: An Analysis of Speech and Non-Verbal Behaviour in Conversation.* Milton Keynes, England: Open University Press.

Beck, A. and A. Katcher. 1983. *Between Pets and People: The Importance of Animal Companionship.* New York: G.P. Putnam.

Benson, H., M.D. (with M.Z. Klipper), 1975. *The Relaxation Response.* New York: Avon Books.

Benson, H., M.D., 1979. *The Mind/Body Effect.* New York: Simon & Schuster.

Benson, H., M.D. and W. Proctor, 1984. *Beyond the Relaxation Response.* New York: Times Books.

Berkow, R., ed., 1982. *The Merck Manual: 14th Edition.* Rahway NJ: Merck & Company.

Biffle, C., 1989. *A Journey Through Your Childhood.* Los Angeles: Jeremy Tarcher.

Bolton, R., 1979. *People Skills: How to Assert Yourself, Listen to Others and Resolve Conflicts.* Englewood Cliffs NJ: Prentice Hall.

Borysenko, J. (with L. Rothstein), 1987. *Minding the Body, Mending The Mind.* Reading, MA: Addison–Wesley.

Bosnak, R., 1988. *A Little Course in Dreams.* Boston: Shambhala.

Bricklin, M. et al., eds., 1990. *Positive Living and Health: The Complete Guide to Brain/Body Healing and Mental Empowerment.* Emmaus PA: Rodale Books.

Capacchione, L., 1989. *The Well-Being Journal: Drawing on Your Inner Power to Heal Yourself.* Newcastle Publishing.

Carper, J., 1988. *The Food Pharmacy.* New York: Bantam.

Cassell, E.J., 1985. *Talking with Patients, Volume 1: Theory of Doctor-Patient Communication.* And *Talking with Patients, Volume 2: Clinical Technique.* Cambridge: MIT Press.

Chaesney, M. and R.H. Rosenman, eds., 1985. *Anger and Hostility in Cardiovascular and Behavioral Disorders.* Washington DC: Hemisphere Corporation.

Charlesworth, E.A., Ph.D. and R.G. Nathan, Ph.D., 1982. *Stress Management: A Comprehensive Guide to Wellness.* New York: Ballantine.

Cousins, N., 1981. *Anatomy of an Illness as Perceived by the Patient*. New York: Bantam.

————, 1983. *The Healing Heart*. New York: Norton.

deBono, E., 1968. *Newthink*. New York: Avon.

Edwards, B., 1979. *Drawing on the Right Side of the Brain*. Los Angeles: Jeremy Tarcher.

————, 1986. *Drawing on the Artist Within*. New York: Simon & Schuster.

Ekman, P. et al., 1972. *Emotion in the Human Face*. New York: Pergamon.

Elgin, S.H., 1979. *What is Linguistics? 2nd Edition*. Englewood Cliffs NJ: Prentice Hall.

————, 1985. *The Gentle Art of Verbal Self-Defense*. New York: Dorset. (Originally published by Prentice Hall, 1980.)

————, 1983. *More on the Gentle Art of Verbal Self-Defense*. New York: Prentice Hall Press.

————, 1986. *Manual for Gentle Art Syntonics Trainers: Level One*. Huntsville AR: Ozark Center for Language Studies.

————, 1987. *The Gentle Art of Verbal Self-Defense Workbook*. New York: Dorset.

————, 1987a. *Language in Emergency Medicine: A Verbal Self-Defence/Syntonics Handbook*. Huntsville AR: Ozark Center for Language Studies.

————, 1987b. *The Last Word on the Gentle Art of Verbal Self-Defense*. New York: Prentice Hall Press.

————, 1987c. *Medicine Talk: Volume One*. Huntsville AR: Ozark Center for Language Studies.

————, 1989. *Success With the Gentle Art of Verbal Self-Defense*. Englewood Cliffs NJ: Prentice Hall.

————, 1989a. *Mastering the Gentle Art of Verbal Self-Defense*. Englewood Cliffs NJ: Prentice Hall/ (Audio program.)

Elgin, S.H., Ph.D. and R. Haden, 1989. *Raising Civilized Kids in a Savage World*. Huntsville AR: Ozark Center for Laguage Studies.

Ekman, P. et al., 1972. *Emotion in the Human Face*. New York: Pergamon.

Fisher, S., 1986. *In the Patient's Best Interest: Women and the Politics of Medical Decisions*. New Brunswick NJ: Rutgers University Press.

Fisher, S. and A.D. Todd, 1983. *The Social Organization of Doctor-Patient Communication*. Washington DC: Center for Applied Linguistics.

Frank, J., 1973. *Persuasion and Healing*. Baltimore: Johns Hopkins.

Friedman, M. and R.H. Rosenman, 1974. *Type A Behavior and Your Heart*. New York: Alfred A. Knopf.

Friedman, M. and D. Ulmer, 1984. *Treating Type A Behavior and Your Heart*. New York: Alfred A. Knopf.

Garrison, J.G., M.Ed. and S. Sheperd Ph.D., 1989. *Cancer & Hope: Charting a Survival Course.* Minneapolis: CompCare Publishers.

Gawain, S., 1978. *Creative Visualization.* New York: Bantam.

Goleman, D., 1985. *Vital Lies, Simple Truths: The Psychology of Self-Deception.* New York: Simon & Schuster.

————, 1988. *The Meditative Mind.* Los Angeles: Jermy Tarcher.

Gordon, T. *Leader Effectiveness Training: L.E.T.* Wyden Books.

Harp, D. (with Nina Feldman, Ph.D.), 1989. *The Three Minute Meditator.* Mind's I Press.

Inlander, C.B. and E. Weiner, 1985. *Take This Book to the Hospital with You: A Consumer Guide to Surviving Your Hospital Stay.* Emmaus Pa: Rodale Books.

Justice, B., 1987. *Who Gets Sick? Thinking and Health.* Houston: Peak Press.

Katz, J., 1984. *The Silent World of Doctor and Patient.* New York: The Free Press (Macmillan).

Keshan, L., 1974. *How to Meditate.* Boston: Little, Brown.

Klein, A., 1989. *The Healing Power of Humor.* Los Angeles: Jeremy Tarcher.

Kunz, J., M.D. and A.J. Finkel, M.D., 1987. *The American Medical Association Medical Guide.* New York: Random House.

Langer, E.J., 1989. *Mindfulness.* New York: Addison-Wesley.

Lazarus, R.S. and S. Folkman, 1984. *Stress, Appraisal, and Coping.* New York: Syringer.

Levy, S.M., 1985. *Behavior and Cancer.* San Francisco: Jossey-Bass.

Locke, S., et al., eds., 1985. *Foundations of Psychoneuroimmunology.* New York: Aldine Publishing.

Locke, S. M.D. and D. Colligan, 1987. *The Healer Within: The New Medicine of Mind and Body.* New York: New American Library/Mentor.

Lynch, J.J., 1977. *The Broken Heart: The Medical Consequences of Loneliness.* New York: Basic Books.

————, 1985. *The Language of the Heart: The Body's Response to Human Dialogue.* New York: Basic Books.

Mackey, C., 1987. *Lost Beauties of the English Language.* New York: Bibliophile Books (through Barnes & Noble.)

Maltz, M. M.D., 1960. *Psychocybernetics.* Englewood Cliffs NJ: Prentice Hall.

McKeown, T. 1979. *The Role of Medicine: Dream, Mirage or Nemesis?* Princeton NJ: Princeton University Press.

Mullin, R.E. Ph.D., 1986. *Handbook of Cognitive Therapy Techniques.* New York: W. W. Norton.

Oates, W.E., 1973. *The Psychology of Religion*. Waco TX: Word Books.

Ornstein, R. and D. Sobel, 1987. *The Healing Brain: Breakthrough Discoveries About How the Brain Keeps Us Healthy*. New York: Simon & Schuster.

Peale, N.V., 1961. *The Power of Positive Thinking*. Englewood Cliffs NJ: Prentice Hall.

Postman, N., 1961. *Crazy Talk, Stupid Talk: How We Defeat Ourselves by the Way We Talk—and What to Do About It*. New York: Dell.

Progoff, I., 1985. *At a Journal Workshop*. New York: Dialogue House.

Satir, V., 1964. *Conjoint Family Therapy*. Palo Alto: Science & Behavior Books.

———, 1972. *Peoplemaking*. Palo Alto: Science & Behavior Books.

Scott, G.G., 1987. *Mind Power: Picture Your Way to Success in Business*. Englewood Cliffs NJ: Prentice Hall.

Selye, H. *The Stress of Life*. New York: McGray-Hill. (Revised edition.)

Sheikh, A.A., 1983. *Imagery: Current Theory, Research and Application*. New York: Wiley & Sons.

———, 1984. *Imagination and Healing*. Famingdale NY: Baywood.

Sheikh, A.A. and K. S. Sheikh, 1989. *Eastern and Western Approaches to Healing*. New York: Wiley & Sons.

Siegel, B.S., 1986. *Love, Medicine & Miracles*. New York: Harper & Row.

———, 1989. *Peace, Love & Healing*. New York: Harper & Row.

Sontag, S., 1979. *Illness as Metaphor*. New York: Vintage Books.

Starr, P., 1983. *The Social Transformation of American Medicine*. New York: Basic Books.

Todd, A.D., 1989. *Intimate Adversaries: Cultural Conflict Between Doctors and Woman Patients*. Philadelphia: University of Pennsylvania Press.

West, C., 1984. *Routine Complications: Troubles With Talk Between Doctors and Patients*. Bloomington: Indiana University Press.

White, L., B. Tursky, and G.E. Schwartz, eds., 1985. *Placebo: Theory, Research and Mechanisms*. New York: Guilford Press.

Index

A

Andres, R., 176

B

Barsky, A., 81
Berry, C., 104
Blake, R., 182
Blamer mode, 19–20 (*See also* Satir modes)
    typical features of, 20
    typical utterances of, 20
Blaming the victim, 41–42 (*See also* Sick role)
Body language, 19, 21, 22, 72, 173–74
Bonuso, C., 166
"Boring Baroque Response," 75–77, 108, 109
Bresnitz, S., 238
Brunton, S.A., 175
Bush, G., 167, 189, 190

C

Carpenter, N.S., 175
Communicating with medical professionals, 212–34
    Computer/Leveler Modes, preferred use of, 225
    doctors' earnings, 212–13
    health hazards, in poor communication, 226–27
    Malpractice of the Mouth, 215, 222, 225
    Mdeityspeak, as medical register, 215, 216
    medical conversation, 213
    medical interaction, 213–14
    medical interview, 213
    Medical Regalian, dealing with, 221
    medical register, responding to, 216–28
    Medical Three-Step, 214–15
    Sensory Modes, matching, 225
    Somatization Twirks, 218–20
    subjective signs, dangers of, 227–28
    trauma mindfiles, setting up, 228–31
    turns and topics, 216–22
    Verbal Attack Pattern, avoidance of, 225
Complaints, 29–32 (*See also* Three-part messages)
Computer mode, 21 (*See also* Satir modes)
    as neutral response, 23
    typical features, 21
    typical utterances, 21
Conversational traffic rules, 63–68
    turns, 64–66
        achieving optimum sequence of, 64–65
        and eye contact, 65
        and ceasing to talk, 65
    topics, 66–68
        all-one-topic list of, 66–67
        all-taboo list of, 67
        making new list of, 68
        no-topic list of, 66
        reactions of others to, 67
Coué, E., 2
Cousins, N., 54

D

Davis, L., 166–67
Distracter mode, 22–23 (*See also* Satir modes)

Doctor's earnings, 212–213
Dream-mapping, 157–63
   demonstration of, 160-61
   for ear person, 163
   for eye person, 163
   for touch person, 163
Dublin, L., 127

E

Edwards, B., 127
Entrainment, 71 (*See also* Syntonic listening)
Eye contact, and taking turns, 65

F

Factives, 197–99
Feedback loops
   language encounters and, 18, 23
   negative, 17–18
   and self-fulfilling prophecies, 61–63
Frieze, I., 167
Frost, R., 99

G

Galen, 42-43
Garfield, C., 130
Gelles, R., 99
Goleman, D., 80
Gordon, T., 29
Gurin, J., 60
Guttman, D., 176

H

Hall, S.S., 91
Hardiness, and coping with stress, 236–41
   elements of, 236
   and information, 237–38
Hardison, J.E., 215
Helplessness, as danger to health, 235–38
Heyn, D., 180
Hirsch, J., 174
Holism, 195–97 (*See also* Presupposing holism)
Holmes, T., 235
Homeostasis, 194–95

Hostility
   as danger to health, 15–39
   as harmful behavior, 17
   and Type A behavior, 15–16
   types of, 16–19
      active, from you toward others, 16, 18–19
      coming at you from others, 16–17
      coming at you from yourself, 16, 17–18
      passive, from you toward others, 16, 19
Hostility diary, 35–37
   model for, 36
   value of, 35–36
Hostility modes (*See* Satir modes)

I

Illness-prone behavior, avoiding, 44–77
Illness, physical and emotional
   mind/body link and, 1–13
   risk factors for, 1–2
   self-blame for, 6
   traditional theory of, 3
   what we now know about, 3–5

J

Jones, E.E., 184

K

Katz, J., 213

L

Language use, for building and maintaining social networks, 60–79
   feedback loops and self-fulfilling prophecies, 61–63
   rules for, 63–68
   verbal attack patterns, 72–77
Language wellness goals, 9–10
Lazarus, R., 235
Leibel, R.L., 174
LeShan, L., 43
Leveler mode, 21–22, 215 (*See also* Satir modes)
   and "diagnosis of exclusion," 22

Levy, S., 80
Levy, B.T., 175
Life Change Units, 235, 237
Listening, syntonic, 68–72
    to music, 70–72
    to others, 68–70
Loneliness, dangers of, 60–61

M

Malpractice of the Mouth, 215, 222, 225 (*See also* Communicating with medical professionals)
Maltz, M., 124
Martinez, M., 129
Matz, R., 177, 223–24
May, J.R., 130
Mdeityspeak, as medical language pattern, 212–28 (*See also* Communicating with medical professionals)
Medical conversation, 213
Medical interaction, 213–14
Medical interview, 213
Medical Regalian
    defined, 203
    partist vocabulary, 203–4
    responding to, 221
    translating, 203–209
Medical register (*See* Mdeityspeak; Communicating with medical professionals)
Medical Three-Step, as action chain, 214–15
Metaphor math, 148–51
Metaphors
    as dangers to health, 145–48
    dream-mapping, 157–62
    metaphor math, 148–52
    semantic modulation, 152–57
Miller, G., 7
Miller's Law, 7–9, 10, 27, 31, 34, 49–50, 53, 90, 92
Mindfiles, 13–40
    definition of, 137
    index for, 138
    setting up, 138–40

N

National Council for Prevention of Child Abuse, 99

Negative explanations, dealing with, 33–35 (*See also* Three-part messages)
North, O., 156

P

Pain
    bodymind concept, 80–83
    defining, with semantic features, 86–90
        reality statements for, 88–90
    endorphins and, 85, 94
    and language, interaction with, 83–86
    management of, through language, 80–98
    medicine, as last resort for, 94–95
    as object, 93–94
    as perceived sensation, 85–86
    personal metaphors for, 90–93
    threshold for, 86
    tolerance of, 86
    worsening of through language, 83–84
"Partism," as dangerous to health, 194–96
Peale, N.V., 2
    and power of positive thinking, 2–3
Pennebaker, J., 36
Percepting ("Visualization"), 124–44
    actual and imagined experience, nervous system response to, 125–26
    benefits of, 130
    case study of, 133–37
    constructing vivid perceptions, 128–33
        by ear persons, 129
        by eye persons, 128
        by touch persons, 129
    exercise, 142–43
    goals and subgoals in, 132
    military metaphor, danger of, 136–37
    mindfiles, setting up, 137–38
        demonstration of, 138–140
    negative results from, 125
    positive results from, 125–26
    sightism, 126–28
    strategies for, 130–31
Perceptions
    assumptions about, 121–22
    external evidence for, distrust of, 121
    inaccuracy of, 166–168
    internal evidence for, distrust of, 121–22

matching sensory modes, 123
sensory modes and, 122–24
Pines, M., 236
Placater mode, 20–21, (*See also* Satir modes)
typical features of, 20
typical utterances of, 21
Pollyanna mode, 35
Praise, 32–33 (*See also* Three-part messages)
Presupposing holism, as wellness technique, 196–202
Presuppositions
and communicating with medical professionals, 196–209
definition of, 101, 196–97
factives and, 197–99
nominalizations and, 199–200
time words and, 200–202
and verbal violence, 101–13
Progoff, I., 36

R

Rahe, R., 235
Rainer, T., 56
Reagan, R., 157, 167
Real-symptom filter, 53–55
ready access to, 54
record-keeping and, 54
Risk factors, for illnesses
establishing baseline for, 10–11
misconceptions about, 1–2

S

Satir. V., 19, 20
Satir modes, 19–29, 44–47, 123
and avoiding illness-prone behavior, 44–47
blamer mode, 19–20
case study of, 27–29
computer mode, 21–22
distracter mode, 22–23
leveler mode, 21–22
placater mode, 20–21
Schifrin, M., 177
Schmale, A., 44
Sekuler, R., 182

Self-fulfilling prophecies, and feedback loops, 61–63
Self-perceptions (*See also* Perceptions)
as disabled, 183–84
as fat, 174–79
identifying, 168–70
as old, 179–83
simultaneous modeling and, 171–74
twirks and, 184–90
Selye, H., 235
Semantic features, defining pain with, 86–90
matrix for, 87–88
reality statements and, 88–90
Semantic modulation, 152–57
demonstration of, 153–56
Sensory modes, 122–24
matching of, 123
Sick role, 41–59
assumption of, 47–48
and avoiding illness-prone behavior, 44–47
and blaming the victim, 41–42, 47
finding hidden goal of, 48–50
and finding real-symptom filter, 53–55
and keeping a diary, 56, 58
and lexicalization, 50–51
and list-making, 56
as part of family structure, 50–53
positive aspects of, 47–48
and proneness to illness, 42–44
unconscious factors in, 52–53
Siegel, B., 133
Sightism, 126–28
Simonton, O.C., 43, 133
Simultaneous modeling, 171–74
and body language, 171, 173–74
to improve voice quality, 172–73
Smilkstein, G., 61
Somatization, 49
Somatization Twirks, 218–20
Sontag, S., 91
Squires, S., 126
Staying well techniques
applying Miller's law, 7–9
avoiding hostility modes, 19–29
avoiding illness-prone behavior, 44–47

Staying well techniques (*cont'd.*)
 defining pain with semantic features, 86–90
 dream-mapping, 157–63
 finding personal pain metaphors, 90–93
 finding real-symptom filter, 53–55
 following language traffic rules, 63–68
 managing verbal attack patterns, 101–13
 metaphor math, 148–51
 percepting: "visualization" and sensory modes, 124–33
 presupposing holism, 196–202
 recognizing verbal attack pattern, 72–75
 responding to medical register, 216–28
 semantic modulation, 152–56
 setting up mindfiles, 137–40
 setting up trauma mindfiles, 228–31
 simultaneous modeling, 171–74
 translating medical regalian, 203–9
 using three-part messages, 29–37
  syntonic listening, 68–72
 using twirks to control perceptions, 184–90
Stress
 and hardiness, Four C's of, 236–41
  challenge, 236, 240–41
  coherence, 236, 241
  commitment, 236, 238–39
  control, 236, 239–40
 and information, 237–38
 and Life Change Units (LCUs), 235, 237
 and perceived threat, 237–38
Syntonic listening, 68–72
 achieving, 69–70
 definition of, 69
 entrainment and, 71
 music and, 71–72

T

Temoshok, L., 43, 44
Three Rs of personal health
 recognition, 7
 resistance, 7
 reaction, 7
Three-part messages, 29–39
 for complaining, 29–32
 for dealing with negative explanations, 33–35
 for praising and evaluating, 32–33
Tiffany, D.A., 179
Topics, conversational, 66–68, 216–22 (*See also* Conversational traffic rules)
Trauma mindfiles, 228–31
 music and, 230
 odors and, 230
 setting up, 229–30
 and terror, 229
Trillin, A.S., 213
Turns, conversational, 64–66, 216–22 (*See also* Conversational traffic rules)
Twirks
 to control perceptions, 184–90
 definition of, 184
 and perceptual filters, 187–90
Type A behavior, 5–16, 35, 43, 44–46
Type B persons, 15, 43, 44
Type C persons, 43, 44–46
Type D persons, 45

V

Verbal violence, 99–120
 bait in, 101
 codependency and, 113–14
 computing response to, 106
 and indifference to other's pain, 117
 leveling response to, 106
 managing verbal attack patterns, 101–17
 and physical violence, 100, 115–17
 presuppositions and, 101–13
 rules for responding to, 103–4
 self-inflicted VAPs, 112–13
 teaching children, 115–16
 vacuous VAPs, 111–12
 verbal abusers and victims, training of, 114
 verbal attack patterns (VAPs), examples of, 101–12
Verbal attack patterns (VAPs), 72–77 (*See also* Language use; Verbal violence)
 all-purpose response to ("Boring Baroque Response"), 75–77
 contrastive stress and, 73

emphatic stress and, 73
examples of, 74
performance of, 74–75
recognizing, 72–74
Vivid perceptions, constructing, 128–29

W

Williams, R., 15, 16, 35, 36
Williamson, P.S., 175

Y

Yankelovich, D., 60